CIVIC FUSION

Mediating Polarized Public Disputes

Susan L. Podziba

Cover design by ABA Publishing.

Page layout by Quadrum Solutions.

Library of Congress Cataloging-in-Publication Data

Podziba, Susan L. (Susan Lisa), 1960-

Civic fusion: mediating polarized public disputes / by Susan Podziba, ABA Section of Dispute Resolution, American Bar Association.

pages cm.

Includes index.

ISBN 978-1-61438-710-7 (alk. paper)

1. Dispute resolution (Law—United States. 2. Mediation—United States. I. American Bar Association. Section of Dispute Resolution. II. Title.

KF9084.P63 2012

303.6’9—dc23

2012031072

www.ShopABA.org

24 23 7 6 5

For my father,
Benjamin L. Podziba, z"l

CONTENTS

ABOUT THE AUTHOR

Susan L. Podziba has been a Public Policy Mediator for twenty-five years. Her clients have included the U.S. Departments of Commerce, Defense, Education, Energy, Health and Human Services, Housing and Urban Development, Interior, Labor, and Transportation, U.S. Environmental Protection Agency, and U.S. Institute of Peace.

She is listed on the United Nations Mediation Roster and has provided mediation training for the U.N. Department of Political Affairs. Ms. Podziba served as Fulbright Senior Specialist in Peace and Conflict Resolution at the Amsterdam Center for Conflict Studies at the University of Amsterdam, Netherlands, and has taught graduate seminars at the Massachusetts Institute of Technology and the Program on Negotiation at Harvard Law School. She currently lectures and consults internationally.

INTRODUCTION

As I scanned the room, the beauty of the pro-life and pro-choice leaders was striking. Six women, tragically unified by shooting deaths at two women's health clinics, were talking about partial-birth abortions, also referred to as bans on certain abortion procedures.[1] As their absolute and unbridgeable chasm came into clear focus so too did the depth of their relational bonds. It was mysterious. Some called it sacred. As a facilitator of the talks, I called it paradoxical unity. I've since renamed it *civic fusion.*

For years after this experience, I walked around with little red bar magnets in my pocket. In spare moments, I'd take them out and turn their positive ends toward each other to feel the combined power of their mutually insistent forces. It reminded me of the gap that existed among the pro-life and pro-choice leaders. But it also left me continuously puzzled over the binding force that had held the two groups together, even as the gap remained intact. I thought there must be a natural, physical force that would help explain the paradoxical unity of the

1. During the talks, we used this dual nomenclature. Since neither side accepted the way the other framed the issue, we used both to enable the conversation to proceed.

abortion talks. With the benefit of an MIT email address (I was teaching there at the time), I wrote to magnetics professors to ask their indulgence for a brief conversation.

Dr. Alan Lightman, a physicist, novelist, and director of MIT's writing program, generously agreed to meet with me. I explained the puzzle I was trying to solve, and he quickly suggested I was looking for the nuclear force, which holds together protons and neutrons in an atom's nucleus.

Having studied basic chemistry, I found myself shocked that I had never questioned how protons—with positive magnetic charges—stay together in the nucleus of an atom. The answer, Dr. Lightman explained, is that when brought close enough together, a different type of force, a nuclear force, overcomes the magnetic forces that would pull it apart. Importantly, the protons retain their positive magnetic charges while bound by the nuclear force and, therefore, the potential to forcefully repel and break apart.

This seemed to be a workable metaphor for understanding not only what happened during the abortion talks but for explaining what happens during public policy mediation processes. After a few more years of thought, I named this metaphor civic fusion.

This book is my effort to describe the civic fusion theory of public policy mediation. I'll look at what mediators aspire to do, and what we actually do, to bring together disparate groups of people to reach agreements on complicated public policy questions.

Professional mediators bring to the table negotiation and mediation skills and passion for public policy and its dynamics. But how do we guide a group that represents hundreds, thousands, and sometimes millions of people, who have deep disagreements about what should be done, who can't solve the problem without working together, and are frustratingly stuck in place?

The field of public policy mediation began as an offshoot of urban planning in the 1970s when the Kettering Foundation funded an experiment called the Negotiated Investment Strategy (NIS). As part of the NIS project, federal, state, and local officials, with assistance from mediators, developed plans to increase the impact of community development blocks grants.[2] Since then, the use of public policy mediation has expanded at both the federal and state levels and has since been applied in almost every policy area.[3] State and federal agencies and institutions currently exist to educate and support government officials on its use. Practitioners are organized in nonprofit and for-profit organizations, and as solo practitioners. In courses around the world, public policy mediation cases are used to teach complex negotiations and mediation. In books and articles, academics and practitioners theorize, describe, debate, and analyze past and potential applications of public policy mediation.

Over the course of twenty-five years of mediation practice, I've seen unlikely partners solve complex, public problems together. I've sat with pro-life and pro-choice leaders, who were unified against violence committed in the name of one and meted out against the other, act together to protect born life. I've seen leaders of the construction crane industry demand federal regulations to protect their workers, after they worked with labor and government to build technically feasible, cost-effective rules. And I've seen citizens from diverse sectors of a failed city draw up a new charter for effective self-governance.

I wrote this book to share these experiences with future and current public policy mediators and to improve our methods. I want future mediators to understand just how powerful the tool of mediation can be and to strive to achieve its potential. For those of us who have already experienced the extraordinary unifying power of policy mediation, I hope to provide a way of reflecting back on those processes so that we can reproduce the best of what we do with greater frequency.

A complementary purpose of this book is to make people aware that there are alternative ways to face our political conflicts. Political disagreements are fundamental to representative democracies. Democratic governing systems provide mechanisms to contain policy conflict through debate and deliberation as citizens and leaders strive to reflect the

2. Carl M. Moore, "Negotiated Investment Strategy," *National Civic Review*, vol. 77, no. 4, pp. 298–314 (July 1988).
3. Lawrence E. Susskind and Sarah McKearnan, "The Evolution of Public Policy Resolution," *Journal of Architecture and Planning Research*, vol. 16, no. 2 (Summer 1999).

interests and values of ever-changing societies. Today many U.S. citizens are concerned about the polarization and political gridlock that allow for festering disputes and stagnation. Bumper sticker sloganeering may simplify issues and express support for particular political positions, but it may also contribute to the polarization that makes it harder to solve complex problems.

It turns out you don't find the devil in the details of policy conflict, you find constraints and difficult choices that require civic responsibility. If people are willing to fuse their ideas while maintaining their beliefs and values, you may also find consensus strategies for addressing complicated issues.

The Contents of the Book

The book is divided into four parts: Part I, "Civic Fusion Defined and Described"; Part II, "Civic Fusion Illustrated"; Part III, "Building the Foundation for Civic Fusion"; and Part IV, "Initiating and Sustaining Civic Fusion."

In Part I, I construct the metaphor of civic fusion and describe how passion, power, and conflict provide the energy for it. I describe civic fusion and suggest how to increase the likelihood of helping disputants initiate, achieve, and sustain civic fusion to secure its tangible results.

In Part II, I provide background on three projects: the Chelsea charter consensus process, in which culturally diverse citizens restored effective self-governance to their morally and financially bankrupt city; the construction cranes and derricks negotiated rulemaking, a process that enabled government, labor, industry, and manufacturing interests to build cost-effective and enforceable federal regulations to protect workers on, in, and near cranes; and the abortion talks, during which pro-life and pro-choice leaders sought to expunge violent rhetoric from their debate after fatal shootings of clinic workers in Massachusetts. Later in the text, I add greater detail to the stories to illustrate abstract concepts of policy mediation and complex negotiations with concrete examples. I draw on examples from a few other past cases as well.

In Part III, I describe what it takes to build a foundation for civic fusion. Specifically, I explain how to conduct a mediator's assessments and what we need to learn about the status quo to construct process designs that promote productive negotiations and overcome perceived obstacles to success.

In the six chapters of Part IV, I bring you to the negotiation table to see civic fusion triggered and sustained to reach actionable agreements. It includes strategies for tracking and managing negotiation dynamics of outcome-based multiparty, multi-issue negotiations and preliminary activities for facing polarization, such as developing a shared goal and procedural ground rules to clarify expectations and prevent process conflict. The additional chapters describe and illustrate how to manage human emotional and intellectual dynamics to make progress on the substantive issues to be resolved. In Chapter 9, I explain how to keep scores of substantive issues in motion among a roomful of stakeholders as they work to build agreements. Next, I describe how people shift from their hardened positions to an exploratory openness. By shedding light on assumptions that limit people's understandings, they pass from certainty through not knowing to curiosity. In Chapter 11, we'll consider how mutual respect and making unpleasant realities explicit contribute to fostering the civil discourse of deliberative negotiations. Chapter 12 focuses on how to institutionalize the bonds created through civic fusion during the "march to closure" as negotiators tackle their most difficult issues. In the last chapter, we'll explore how civic fusion supports ongoing participant ownership of agreements and commitment to action.

Part I

Civic Fusion Described and Defined

CHAPTER 1

CIVIC FUSION DESCRIBED

Introduction

The conflicts seem intractable and yet the disagreements must be resolved. Leaders and the public have a determined will to move beyond a recognizably unstable status quo. But how do tense and frustrated people, with conflicting values and interests and a history of failed efforts, reach consensus on a way forward? The answer may be civic fusion. Civic fusion is when people bond, even as they sustain deep value differences, to solve a common public problem.

As a public policy mediator, my work is to help disparate, passionate parties negotiate actionable agreements. To do so, they must draw close enough together to overcome their polarization, or in other words, achieve civic fusion. To achieve and sustain civic fusion, interested parties engage in assumption-shifting discussions that contribute to unexpected bonding. They connect across common goals all the parties share, and find mutual understanding and respect for their interests and those of others. In addition, they come to understand and accept the constraints of their complex situations. A steady stream of new understandings moves people beyond their long-held perspectives to create opportunities for productive negotiations and innovative ideas. Ultimately, the parties generate pragmatic consensus agreements even as they retain their deeply held and often opposing values and beliefs.

Public policy mediators design processes to foster productive negotiations in high-pressure situations to build uniquely crafted solutions. Seemingly intractable and potentially chaotic situations require process adaptations beyond the mere application of mediation and facilitation techniques to attempt resolution. These adaptations may include a means for moving beyond habitual patterns of communication to surface and acknowledge actual passionate differences in order to create solutions that encompass those differences rather than paper over them.

Civic fusion peaks in the moments of simultaneous connection and recognition of unbridgeable value differences. It is sustained throughout negotiations by a mutual recognition of parties' interdependence and reciprocated understandings during discussions of difference. Many initial mediation tasks, for example, identifying a shared public goal and developing procedural ground rules, are undertaken in support of attaining civic fusion. Memory of having experienced civic fusion results in a fused group that aspires to attain it again.

Civic Fusion Defined

In the term *civic fusion, civic* identifies the citizens or citizen-representatives who have intimate knowledge and wisdom of the public policy conflict as a result of living it, as well as sufficient interests in play to motivate their participation and commitment to action.[1] Thus, in an example we will be studying in the chapters to come, the Chelsea

1. For more information on identifying the parties that compose the civic universe for a process, see Chapter 6, "Conducting the Mediator's Assessment."

city charter consensus process, *civic* refers to the city's re of whom participated as members of a charter negotiatir as facilitators, attendees of public forums and commu callers to a hotline, and viewers of cable television.

For a second example we will be examining—the negotia developing safety rules for construction cranes—members of the civic universe were the representatives of identified stakeholders and, by extension, their constituents. Even though the general public has an interest in worker protection and the safe operation of cranes, it would have little knowledge of the specific strategies for preventing cranes from toppling over or hitting power lines. Thus, for this case, "*civic*" refers to the citizen-representatives of crane-related stakeholders.

For the example of the abortion talks, civic fusion required only a small circle of pro-life and pro-choice leaders, who were able to take individual actions to protect the Massachusetts populace and jointly publish a consensus article in the *Boston Globe*.

The word "*fusion*" is borrowed from the process of nuclear fusion, in which positively charged protons are brought close enough together to engage nuclear forces that overcome their otherwise polarizing magnetic charges.

Think of an atom and its nucleus of protons and neutrons. The protons all have the same positive charge, which causes them to repel each other. (Figure 1.1) However, when brought close enough together, a nuclear force binds the protons and neutrons even as the protons retain their positive charge. The neutrons, lacking any magnetic charge, as well as the protons, contribute binding energy to hold the nucleus together. (Figure 1.2) Within an atom's nucleus are both the binding and repelling forces. (Figure 1.3) Thus, should something cause the protons to move beyond the bounds of the nuclear force, the magnetic force would cause the protons to quickly fly apart.

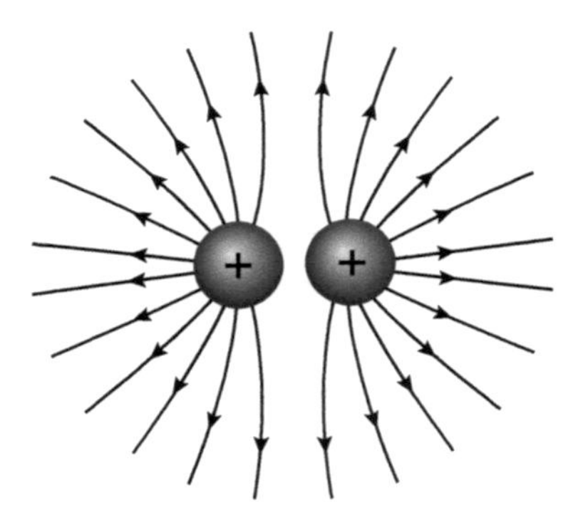

Figure 1.1
Protons repelling

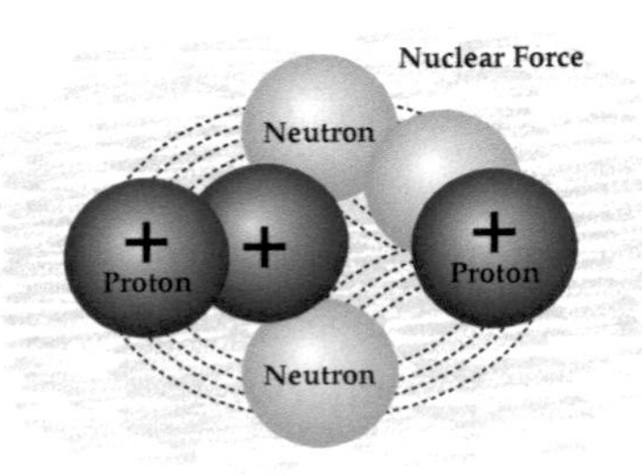

Figure 1.2
Nuclear force binds protons and neutrons in the nucleus of an atom

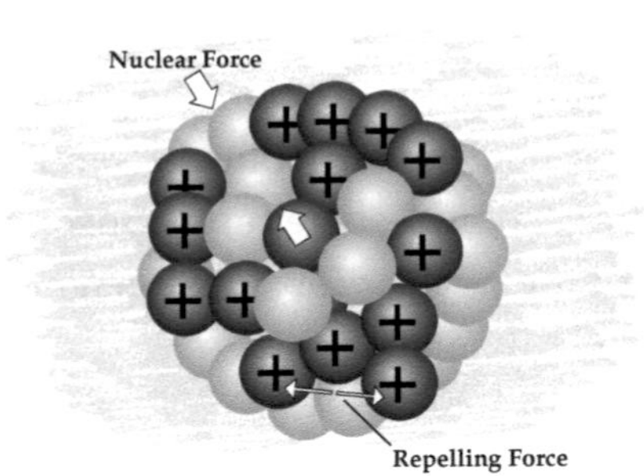

Figure 1.3
Repelling forces of protons remain even as nuclear force binds protons and neutrons

In this metaphor, the protons are the parties to the negotiations, for example, pro-life and pro-choice leaders. Each individual's passionate stance is a positive charge. Efforts to move the participants close together expose the polarizing forces that repel, for example, issues such as when life begins and the right of a woman to terminate her pregnancy. One quickly perceives a seemingly insurmountable gap between the two groups and the impossibility of achieving a stable bond amidst the polarization, like trying to force together the positively charged ends of two magnets.

The mediators, who do not contribute political passion on substantive issues, are the magnetically neutral neutrons. Without a magnetic charge, they do not contribute to the polarization.

By bringing diverse, politically active people close enough together, under particular conditions, mediators help disputants to bond. Note that just as protons retain their magnetic force even while bonded, people retain their passionate beliefs within the confines of civic fusion. The women of the abortion talks, for example, never veered from their deeply held positions: pro-life women continued to view abortion as the death of an unborn child and pro-choice women continued to view as paramount the moral capacity of a woman to choose to terminate her pregnancy. They connected through their shared humaneness and abhorrence of violence and their mutual recognition and understanding, although not acceptance, of the worldviews that underpin each other's positions.

Essential Conditions for Civic Fusion

Situations ripe for benefitting from civic fusion share certain essential conditions. Most importantly, the parties agree that the status quo is unsustainable and that none of the parties has enough power or knowledge to act unilaterally to solve the problem. Often the inertia of inaction has worsened the situation, as in our examples, Chelsea's public monies disappeared into the coffers of the corrupt, fatal crane accidents occurred with regularity, and individuals with extremist views attacked other adults to play hero to the unborn. As a result, a will to act emerges from somewhere within the political system or universe of actors.

Another condition is that past efforts to solve the problem failed, perhaps because existing government mechanisms and institutions available for pursuing resolutions proved inadequate to address the problem. Such past efforts, even when well-intentioned, often result in increased frustrations among the involved parties to the conflict, particularly those who believed they knew of workable solutions but were unable to persuade others to accept them.

In these situations, the people living the conflict need a forum within which to surface and acknowledge their deep differences and, at the same time, jointly build an agreement that encompasses those differences.

Civic fusion enables creative thought to emerge despite deeply held conflicting viewpoints. The seeming intractability, instability, and complexity of the public dispute may contribute the intense energy needed for people to transcend their ordinary thought patterns to acknowledge the legitimacy of others' beliefs and concerns, even as they may vehemently disagree with those pronouncements. A mediator tries to tap this energy to help people bond and at the same time, create space for jointly absorbing new information that conflicts with some of their usual assumptions about substantive issues and the intentions of other interested parties. Their newly gained understanding may enable them to create unique solutions that mutually satisfy the range of interests represented within the group.

When crane accidents accounted for the highest number of fatalities and serious injuries in the construction industry, unions and employers asked the federal Occupational Safety and Health Administration (OSHA) to revise its relevant national worker safety standards. The status quo was unsustainable. The existing standards, developed in the early 1970s, were obsolete because of changes in crane technology and work processes.

The OSHA Directorate of Construction, responsible for writing and enforcing regulations for all construction-related worker safety standards, does not and cannot have in-house expertise for all types of construction equipment. It often convenes work groups of stakeholders for advice on updating its regulations. The failure of a cranes work group established to propose solutions after four years of meetings and the continued reliance on safety standards that failed to adequately prevent accidents, created great frustration for workers and the industry. The work group's single consensus recommendation, that OSHA initiate a formal negotiated rulemaking, reflected a recognized need for a process adapted to the seemingly insurmountable differences among conflicting interests and values of the interested parties. By the time the negotiated rulemaking committee was convened, despite their differences, the parties were energized and determined to fix the broken system under which they lived. Conditions were ripe for civic fusion.

Design to the Obstacles

A carefully designed process, rooted in the mediator's assessment of the conflict's substantive issues, history, dynamics, stakeholders, and constraints, provides a foundation for achieving civic fusion. The process design is as critical to civic fusion as is the physical container in which nuclear fusion may occur.

Just as MIT's levitating donut is designed to eliminate known obstacles to nuclear fusion, public policy mediation processes are designed to account for known obstacles to civic fusion.[2] The process design maps out the steps needed to reach actionable consensus agreements. Perceived barriers can be converted into unique process components.

For example, when developing a new charter for self-governance in Chelsea, the politically unengaged populace was considered a barrier to building an actionable agreement. To meet this challenge, the process included the means for engaging people where they already congregated. We held meetings at popular local venues, such as social clubs, houses of worship, community residences, and schools.

Results

As a result of civic fusion, disputants find unique solutions to old problems and often forge new long-term relationships among past foes that support and sustain implementation of the agreements reached. Broad-brush disagreements on issues give way to nuanced understandings of complexities. The result is democracy in action: well-articulated, conflicting views merged for the public good, and strong support for agreed-upon solutions.

Civic fusion enabled OSHA and industry and union leaders to reach consensus on proposed worker safety standards for construction cranes and generated a deep commitment to the implementation of those standards. Negotiators' assumptions shifted on key issues, as did their judgments of institutions and other people's motivations. For example, employers, who previously had engaged with OSHA only over regulatory violations, expressed new understandings of OSHA's challenges in creating enforceable standards to protect workers. When their consensus proposal was stuck in a bureaucratic maze, many of the representative negotiators banded together to help move it forward

---

2. The Levitated Dipole Experiment, a joint project of the Massachusetts Institute of Technology and Columbia University, uses a donut-shaped magnet, suspended by an electromagnetic field, to cause 10-million degree-hot plasma to become more densely concentrated—an essential step in nuclear fusion, explains David L. Chandler in "Levitating magnet brings space physics to fusion," MIT News, January 25, 2010.

through coordinated strategies including press conferences, meetings with government officials, and testimony at a public hearing.

Similarly, the pro-life and pro-choice women came to respect, as individuals, those who held passionate positions intolerably different from their own, because of the strength of their bonds. Seeing each other up close and personal, made it impossible to see the other as an enemy, or as an individual lacking moral character. Members of each camp did not agree with the other sides' sense of morality, but they learned that no one was acting out of a purposeful immorality. Intense policy disagreements remained, but the demons disappeared.

Over time, each leader acted individually to achieve the group's joint goal of reducing the risk of future violence against abortion clinic workers. Choosing to promote healing rather than anger, during the memorial on the first anniversary of the clinic shootings, Nicki Nichols Gamble, then president of Planned Parenthood of Massachusetts, expressed gratitude "for the prayers of those who agree with us and the prayers of those who disagree," as two pro-life participants sat in the audience. Similarly, Madeline McComish, then president of Massachusetts Citizens for Life, told the Virginia-based spiritual mentor of the shooter and a proponent of justifiable homicide that he was not welcome in the state during the murder trial.

As civic fusion occurs, unexpected relationships develop and help sustain people as they journey into deeper understandings and mutual acknowledgement of opposing stances, in the effort to build and implement consensus agreements. Sometimes lifelong relationships are created. Many describe their participation as a highlight of their career because they were able to transcend petty disagreements to contribute to the common good.

The possibility of civic fusion offers a way out of the political polarization of public disputes. It takes awareness, intent, and commitment, but it can be done. The next chapters describe how public policy mediators can help to initiate and sustain civic fusion as well as how to help government and citizens reap its benefits.

CHAPTER 2

THE ENERGIES THAT BIND

We've all seen negotiations collapse. People make outrageous or humiliating demands, stiffen their resolve on principle, or miscalculate their actual power and overreach. They yell and point fingers at each other or simply walk out and refuse to return to negotiations. In such instances, the chaotic miscommunication of unbound passion, power, and conflict destroys opportunities for finding solutions when zones of possible agreement may exist. And yet, within that chaos may actually be the potential energy for achieving and sustaining civic fusion.

Productive use of the energies within passion, power, and conflict enables negotiators to engage, think, learn, contribute, civilly express interests, become cognizant of others' concerns, generate creative solutions, and essentially, overcome polarization to become unified around achieving a common goal. The challenge is to focus those energies in service of productive, deliberative negotiations. Below we explore each energy source separately to identify its potential for chaos and creativity.

Passion

Passion is the overwhelming emotion that trumps reason. It's a broadbrush stroke of emotion—like love, hate, or moral indignation—that simplifies all things complex and obscures doubt. It serves as a potential energy source throughout policy negotiations.

Once people have ventured into the world of passion, they fan its flames by giving credence to validating information and rejecting contrary evidence. Passion is affirming. Reason suggests the need for painful compromise.

For as long as possible, lovers will pretend not to see the irritants they will later use to rationalize their breakup. When demonstrators succeed in ridding their country of a hated leader, they will eventually wake up to the day-to-day challenges of eliminating corruption and creating jobs and opportunities for their citizens. Passion simplifies the complex until heightened conflict emerges to force a review of validating information and contrary evidence.

To experience passion feels good; the expression of passion is empowering, and the communal expression of passion is reinforcing. It is easier and feels better to express passion than to undertake the difficult work of reasoning agreement out of conflict.

Potentially chaotic and mind numbing, seething passion among negotiators can also be a great asset for the mediator. When lifted up out of the chaos and successfully harnessed, passion can fuel the civic fusion that helps move parties from a stagnant conflict configuration to the possibility of building something new.

The usual discussion of passionately polarized partisans is a heated nonexchange of ideas. Each person states and defends his or her position and offhandedly rejects what the other side says. Over time, either their disagreements escalate or they disengage out of frustration.

On the other hand, there is great energy in the passion people bring to the negotiating table when they discuss issues of central importance in their lives. It can power partisans toward sustained civic fusion—

creating a connection across their differences to deeper thought and understanding of their own and their opponents' beliefs—to innovate new solutions to their persistent disputes. Indifference, or the lack of passion, causes complex negotiations to falter because it fails to energize the emotional and intellectual activity needed to pierce habitual thought patterns that sustain a status quo.

To tap passions for productive use, the process has to allow for their expression. With the mediator providing a sense of calm in the room, parties can express some of the motivations that inform their positions. By slowing down the conversation, perhaps with gentle but prodding questions, mediators can help negotiators increase their own awareness of underlying assumptions that drive their passions and those of their polar opposites. A focus on intention and purpose, rather than on the outcome demanded, often reveals moral principles held by the parties. Sometimes these moral principles are shared but interpreted differently; sometimes they are different but can be respected or tolerated. And sometimes they are in great conflict, but can still be understood as forming the basis of another's morality. In essence, what emerges is an unexpected shared commitment to being moral, even if the parties disagree on what is moral. In other words, when negotiators realize that the other is not choosing to be immoral but rather also seeks to live a moral life, the conflict changes and the potential for productive conversation increases. The unexpected surprise may be that none of the parties is evil.

Developing a common public goal helps focus passions toward forging a consensus agreement. An articulated shared goal legitimizes substantive differences. It helps set aside questions of who is good and who is evil through a shared understanding that the intention of all the parties is to work on behalf of the good, however they define it. The policy complexities provide opportunities for the parties to tap the energy of their passions to creative innovative solutions that respect the values, different as they may be, of all the negotiators.

The abortion dialogue was highly energized by the passion the parties brought to the table. At its highest moments, with the participants' interactions deeply rooted in their passions, they experienced a heightened sense of connection. These bonds were strengthened by passions of love and the pain of unborn children, of women who died from botched abortions, of women forced, of women in mortal sin, of murdered young receptionists at women's health clinics, and from a profoundly deep chasm that kept the women of either camp apart from the other. As these passions were expressed, the activists' bonds fused. Reaching their shared goal of mutual understanding of "the other" led them to act to reduce the violent rhetoric of the abortion issue debate.

The six women who participated in the dialogue had met during televised debates, but had never learned of the legitimate, passionate, and moral basis behind the public positions of those on the other side. Passion provided the energy that sustained civic fusion over years of often painful, difficult discussions.

Unharnessed passion can lead people to negotiate against their better interests. The challenge is to channel the energy of discordant passion toward mutual progress on shared goals.

Power

Power enables a person to assert his or her will over another. Power forces the weaker to submit to the stronger. One who has absolute power over a situation has the capacity to act unilaterally rather than to negotiate. In the absence of such power, parties assert their relative power during negotiations to reach their goals. But how is relative power among negotiators determined?

Given our lack of a means for accurately measuring power in the way we use thermometers to measure temperature, we instead use the dance of negotiations to arrive at a mutually shared perception of power among negotiators. In public policy mediation, the back and forth of substantive proposals offered, rejected, revised, and refined are among the steps for determining relative power. Negotiations are completed when a mutually shared perception of power gets reflected in decisions on the substantive issues under discussion.

Power energizes negotiations. It keeps people alert and engaged as they seek to increase their own power and turn back that of others. Parties may overreach or may find it difficult to accept the limitations of their powers. Mediators often must untangle misperceptions of relative power and normalize the reality of power differentials even as they strive to provide equivalent opportunities for participation.

Every party to a public policy mediation has both actual power and perceived power. The mere fact that a negotiator's participation and consent have been deemed necessary for reaching an actionable agreement confirms a degree of power. Actual power derives from a multitude of sources such as institutional authority, position, leadership, access to power, resources, access to information, and an ability to initiate large-scale demonstrations or campaigns.

Perceived power has two components for each negotiator. The first is the negotiator's own perception of his or her power. The second derives from other negotiators' perceptions of an individual's power. Thus, the power of negotiators in the room is some combination of their actual power, self-perceived power, and their power as perceived by others.

Actual power is often recognizable by all negotiators, but to be useful, it must be effectively projected as support for particular proposals. For example, a negotiator may assert actual power by initiating a call to a member of Congress, who then causes a government negotiator to refine his previous stance on a proposal.

In negotiated rulemakings, the government agency responsible for developing and enforcing the forthcoming regulation has actual institutional power and, as a result, cannot be forced to knowingly create a rule that violates its mission or is inconsistent with its larger regulatory scheme. A statement by a government negotiator such as, "The Secretary is not willing to do that," is an assertion of institutionally based power. When such power is projected, mediators often need to engage other parties in reality testing to help them determine their options for challenging and/or accepting such power. A mediator might ask, for example: How important is the proposal to your constituents? If a coalition could be assembled, would it be strong enough to get the attention of the Secretary? Is the alternative to the preferred option a deal breaker? If there is no consensus, what is the likelihood that your preferred option will be in the future rule? What gains for you have been tentatively agreed to that might be lost if the negotiators fail to reach consensus?

Organizations with large constituencies of consequence to elected officials assert power. For example, during negotiations to develop rules regarding a grant program to pay for mentors, tutors, and college tuition for low-income students, some of the negotiators were in frequent contact with the senator who had sponsored the legislation that created the program and guided it through Congress to passage. Their ability to describe the law's intent and suggest possible clarifying changes in the law that favored their preferences were assertions of actual power.

In contrast, perceived power is accessible to all negotiators including those with little actual power. It is fluid and ever changing throughout a negotiation. A group of negotiators may form a coalition that increases the power of each coalition member or a person may provide information that reduces another's perceived power. Leadership qualities and a person's skill in generating options that link his or her interests to other negotiatiors with greater actual power may also increase perceived power. For example, in a past case, a representative of the environmental justice community successfully built her preferences into proposals that also satisfied banking and insurance interests. Her ability to effectively synthesize divergent opinions into mutually agreeable solutions helped her satisfy her constituents' concerns, and at the same time, increased her power in the eyes of other negotiators.

Power dynamics are affected by a consensus decision rule, transparency, and equivalent opportunities to participate that are provided in public policy mediation processes.

A consensus decision rule enhances deliberations because it requires all parties to listen and be responsive to each other. It requires everyone to express their interests and concerns, and challenges the team of negotiators to develop options to satisfy those concerns and integrate identified interests into a complex whole.

In contrast, with a simple majority decision rule, as much as 49 percent of participating parties may not have their interests met. Over time, if the same people and groups find themselves in the minority, they are likely to disengage after concluding that the forum does not provide adequate opportunities to satisfy their concerns.

With a consensus decision rule, each negotiator must listen carefully and work hard to understand the interests and concerns of the others because all must ultimately participate in the consensus. Dissent on a proposal effectively vetoes that proposal and triggers additional deliberation until a consensus emerges. A consensus rule stimulates lively deliberations and diffuses power among all the negotiators.

The consensus decision rule may appear to significantly reduce power differentials among the participating parties, but in actuality it simply reflects the conditions that make unilateral action ineffective and require coordinated action among all the parties to change the status quo.

Transparency enables access to information and protects against backroom deal making. Essentially, by ensuring access to information, transparency increases the power of the parties without resources to obtain or generate critical information, and it reduces the power of those who would seek or expect to gain from creating confusion and/or sweetheart deals.

Negotiators may request documents, reports, expert presentations, and any other means available to enable them to make informed choices. With multiple representatives from each stakeholder group, biases in the information provided are usually uncovered. If an issue is too complex to be effectively explained by negotiators, an outside expert or panel of experts is convened to educate the group on the issues. No one is ever asked or expected to consent to something he or she does not fully understand.

Attempts to increase one's power by obfuscating issues usually cannot withstand the effects of transparency. Inconsistent claims, biased information, and deception seldom survive a thorough review by stakeholder experts and the public. A few questions from other negotiators or the mediator can clarify confusions, thereby reducing the perceived power of the party effectuating such a strategy. Finally, transparency also helps people know what to expect from the process and ensures the parties they are building an agreement, and not acting merely as window dressing for preordained decisions.

With equivalent opportunities to participate during meetings, every negotiator may voice opinions and concerns, offer ideas, generate proposals, respond to others, consent or dissent, request caucuses, and otherwise engage in deliberative discussions. As participants indicate a readiness to speak, the mediator works to ensure that each is recognized and can speak without being interrupted. The use of a consensus decision rule and the goal of reaching an actionable agreement require active participation. Although this does not suggest that all negotiators get an equal amount of airtime during meetings—some people think out loud while others listen carefully before offering persuasive comments—if a party seems disengaged from the process, the mediator may check in with that party to ensure their interests and concerns get integrated into the eventual agreement.

Through participants' active engagement in substantive negotiations, power differentials are clarified and reflected in the details of emerging agreements. Negotiations provide the forum to test the limits of one's power and to assess the power of other negotiators. This dance provides energy for sustained negotiations.

Assertions of power in negotiations, if accepted among the negotiators, can ease the way toward agreements, and, if rejected, can lead to increased conflict during negotiations. Much of the time spent in negotiations is focused on clarifying issues, generating and refining proposals that are acceptable to all, and wordsmithing agreements. However, power is usually lurking below the surface ready to be wielded if necessary. It is a key force in play when people seek to assert their will over others to get what they and their constituents want.

Power dynamics can also contribute to chaotic miscommunication. Some negotiators decry assertions of power amid false expectations of power balances. Disregard for power differentials, combined with passionately held positions, have the potential to derail negotiations. For some, the acknowledgement of weakness may cause an insufferable humiliation. Such conditions may cause negotiators to reject agreements that significantly satisfy many of their interests even when such agreements promise more than can be gained in any other forum. The challenge is to help parties clarify actual and perceived power while sustaining the self-respect of all parties—especially the weaker and those who overestimate their power. In policy negotiations, an agreement that does not reflect the external power dynamics among the parties is not likely to survive critical constituent review.

A mediator tracks for power and senses it almost like an electrical buzz in the room. In most instances, it is subtly asserted but its impact on a developing consensus is palpable. Assertions of power and defending against power create energy among the parties. This becomes another energy source to tap in furthering sustained civic fusion.

Conflict

Conflict in the public policy arena is a clash of wills. People and groups line up on various sides of an issue and employ strategies and assert power to further their interests. Passionate conflict on issues is a hallmark of democracy, which is designed to provide opportunities to further political stances through multiple governance structures without resorting to violence.

With violence at bay, conflict helps to clarify issues and energizes its passionate antagonists. When no party can unilaterally assert its will over government, interested stakeholders, and the public, negotiations offer a forum for reaching agreements that satisfy the range of their wills. Conflicts bring focus to the set of issues that creates a context and motivation for negotiations.

In complex negotiations, mediators typically find three modes of conflict: positional and interest-based conflicts, conflicts of values, and conflicts of confusion.

Positional and interest-based conflicts are the substantive disagreements that require innovative solutions, difficult decisions, or compromise. For example, in Chelsea, the term length for city councilors elected citywide was a positional and interest-based conflict. Some citizens supported four-year terms to encourage long-range municipal planning, and others preferred two-year terms to avoid power imbalances with councilors elected by district, who were to be elected to two-year terms. Their positions were in conflict—two- and four-year terms—as were their interests—long-range planning and the avoidance of power struggles. In this case, resolution occurred when the negotiators learned the community feared the effects of power imbalances among city councilors more than it desired long term planning.

Conflicts of values are those disagreements rooted in differing worldviews and perspectives of right and wrong. An illustrative example comes from negotiations among fishermen and conservationists concerning endangered and protected species of whales and dolphins. The conservationists valued protecting endangered marine mammals. Some of the fishermen, on the other hand, stated outright that they did not care if mammals were killed as they fished; they valued their ability to safely deliver fish from the ocean to the public. Values are not negotiable. Mediators' efforts focus on helping negotiators explain their values and understand that the values of those with whom they disagree emanate from a different sense of right and wrong. The parties then work to develop acceptable, substantive options that reflect or contain their differing values within the complexity of negotiating scores of issues. Thus, in the above example, the parties created solutions whereby fishermen could safely and profitably fish and also effectively avoid mammals. The conflict of values remained unresolved.

A third type of conflict intrinsic to public disputes is conflicts of confusion. In this situation, discussion yields an alignment of interests and no actual dispute. Often people argue over an issue before they understand what others actually want. This form of conflict includes those in which the interests behind a position reveal a means for completely satisfying the disputing parties, but also include broader conflicts.

A famous story of two sisters fighting over an orange illustrates a conflict of confusion in which discussion yields the means for full satisfaction: One sister wanted to eat the fruit, and the other needed the rind to bake a cake. Their original dispute, where each demanded the whole orange, gave way after they successfully exchanged information regarding their interests.

A second example of a conflict of confusion is two men arguing vehemently over whether or not construction cranes must be fixed in place when working from ships, barges, or other floatation devices when operating in marine environments. The man who demanded cranes be tied down described an accident in which a crane fell from a barge and killed his friend. The other man used cranes to move heavy materials on aircraft carriers. After some discussion the mediator clarified their shared interest of preventing cranes from falling into the waters and highlighted an additional interest of transporting materials on a ship. In this example, the conflict of confusion stemmed from firm positions that obscured aligned and supplementary interests.

Beyond the confusion in complex policy negotiations, parties often find a convergence of interests. By peeling away layers of confusion surrounding broad issues, areas of agreement and differences in values as well as actual interest-based conflicts of more limited subissues come into focus.

Passion, power, and conflict all have the potential to cause the chaotic miscommunication that can derail negotiations, but they also carry the potential energy to sustain civic fusion for the productive negotiation toward an actionable agreement. Negotiations can and sometimes do give way to chaos, but they can be bound up again. Mediation is not brain surgery—there are margins of error, though they vary from case to case. In the next chapters, we'll discuss how close to chaos the cranes negotiations were in Las Vegas and sabotage efforts in Chelsea—and the strategies that got negotiations back on track.

Part II
Introduction to the Project Narratives

Introduction

The next three chapters tell the stories of three of my past projects: the Chelsea charter consensus project, the cranes and derricks negotiated rulemaking, and the abortion talks.

The following project narratives include the background, process components, substantive issues, and dynamics of each case.

Each project illustrates elements of the civic fusion process. Each describes the mediator's assessment and the process design, which we examine in detail in Chapters 6 and 7. They also touch on the concepts of Part IV, which focuses on the dynamics of managing complex negotiations. We'll draw on these cases later in the text to illustrate mediation and negotiation practices. The stories here should give you enough background to understand the details later.

The range of these stories is meant to illustrate the variety of public disputes and the need to design and tailor processes to account for each one's particular characteristics. There is no cookie cutter process. Of the cases described here, one was citywide, another statewide, and the third nationwide.

One process convened citizens, another representative stakeholders, and the third, activists. The Chelsea and the crane projects were more typical of public policy mediation whereas the abortion talks were a dialogue-mediation hybrid.

The consensus products of the first two cases became laws, and the third was published as a newspaper article. Outreach and consultation for each were completely different: Chelsea included innovative process mechanisms designed and managed by the mediation team, the crane representatives independently communicated with their constituents, and the pro-life and pro-choice participants informed their boards only on a need-to-know basis.

Included in each story are detailed descriptions of negotiations of a few issues to provide a sense of getting beyond long-held perspectives to embrace the complexity of issues. For some readers, the technical information may seem irrelevant and such readers may choose to skim some of those discussions.

The abortion talks stand apart from what many may consider to be a usual public policy mediation case. However, I include it because as a hybrid, it included a mediation component—six months to jointly draft a consensus article. The assessment it required offers lessons for starting a case without a defined goal or an initiating agency or organization. In addition, the abortion talks offer a magnified view, and therefore, an opportunity to reflect on the earliest stages of bringing disparate parties together, that is, facing polarization and initiating civic fusion.

It's important to note that I was not consciously working to achieve civic fusion as I mediated these cases. I understood my practice to be to assist diverse groups to reach actionable agreements that address complex policy disputes. I only came to the concept of civic fusion upon reflection on these cases. Although I had sometimes perceived a growing unity among people with unbridgeable differences, I hadn't put a name to it.

I've thought about and analyzed these projects for years. Many of my initial ideas failed when I tried to apply them to the cases as post hoc reflection. Because I live in the world of practice, I had ready tests for theories and ideas. Finally, I came upon the metaphor of civic fusion, which helps me understand what it takes to bring people from polarized positions close enough together to bond across the complexity of their situations to create something new.

As a practitioner, I've found that ideas illustrated through stories are easiest for me to integrate for improved mediation practice. For mediators, I hope these stories resonate with you and can help you reflect on your own mediation experiences. For people who are or were engaged in complex policy disputes, I hope these narratives help you recognize and better understand the dynamics of your situations. And for people concerned about the current state of politics, I hope these stories give you the hope and awareness that tools exist to take us beyond polarization.

CHAPTER 3

THE CHELSEA CHARTER CONSENSUS PROCESS

A diverse city of 28,000 residents located on Boston's northern border, Chelsea has been an immigrant city since the beginning of the twentieth century. During the late 1980s and early 1990s, City Hall was run by a clique of corrupt officials. To access public services, one needed to know the right people. Hiring practices hinged on a system of patronage, rather than on skill or expertise. Some policemen served as bagmen for the mobsters who ran illegal gambling clubs. Chelsea's government officials had become so autonomous that they were no longer responsive to the public they were repeatedly elected to serve. As a result, many Chelseans felt shut out of local government and lost faith in the city's ability to govern itself.

During this period, Chelsea was racked by fiscal mismanagement. Soon after a multi-million dollar state bailout, local officials couldn't make payroll and requested additional aid. When the mayor could not account for state funds provided to the city, state officials decided they'd had enough. Chelsea lost its right to self-govern, as the city was placed under state receivership.

The receivership legislation gave the state absolute authority over the city, suspended the authorities of the locally elected government, and called for the governor to appoint a receiver.

After a few years in receivership, the city started to recover. Some corrupt former city officials were put in prison, while others cooperated with federal authorities. New department heads assumed positions throughout City Hall, the gambling and strip clubs were shuttered, roads were paved, and the new police chief led his force to protect all of Chelsea's citizens. The receiver, Lewis "Harry" Spence, and his predecessor, James Carlin, had successfully stopped the hemorrhaging of the city's finances and stemmed the chaos of governance by a corrupt few.

It was time to think about creating a new, post-receivership, municipal governance structure that would bring stability and opportunity to the people of Chelsea.

Need for a Governing Structure

A critical element of the receiver's mission was to recommend to the governor a new form of government to replace Chelsea's 1903 city charter. This charter had been revised by hundreds of Special Acts of the Massachusetts state legislature, which, all combined, blurred the lines of authority and accountability of the mayor, the board of aldermen, the school committee, and the city's boards and commissions.

Although the receiver had the authority to draft the charter on his own, he believed that if the new government was to succeed, its structure had to be created by the people who would be governed under it. He saw the need for a new charter as an opportunity to increase citizen capacity for self-governance.

After my initial conversation with Harry Spence, I understood that to succeed, the charter process would have to accommodate the particular challenges posed by Chelsea's past. It would need to educate and motivate participation by old-time Chelsea residents, who were either politically disengaged or desensitized to corrupt practices, as well as immigrants with no history of democracy. The process would have to overcome a profound mistrust of outsiders, reach deep into a disenfranchised community, and confront the suspicions and frustrations spawned by past city administrations.

To prepare what became our successful bid for the project, I invited Roberta Miller, an expert in identifying and building local associational networks, to team with me. Central to our proposal was a comprehensive consensus process that would go to the people of Chelsea in the places they typically gathered to ask about their ideas and concerns for their new government. This input would be integrated into the new city charter. Roberta was primarily responsible for the outreach and consultation elements of the process, and I served as mediator.

The Mediator's Assessment

Interviews

At the start of the Chelsea process, I interviewed formal and informal leaders of the city. I met with elected leaders and members of the municipal boards and commissions, with the heads of the chamber of commerce and the Latin American Cultural Association, and even with the city Santa Claus, an Irish-American fellow who was president of the Polish War Veterans Club.

My initial interviews were with people culled from a conversation with Harry and his chief of staff, Steve McGoldrick. I found the rest by asking early interviewees to suggest others with whom I should speak. Among those recommended, certain names were repeated—they were the people with whom I knew I really needed to speak. After more than forty conversations, I developed a sense of the place called Chelsea along with an understanding of how to approach its citizens and how to assist them to construct a new city charter.

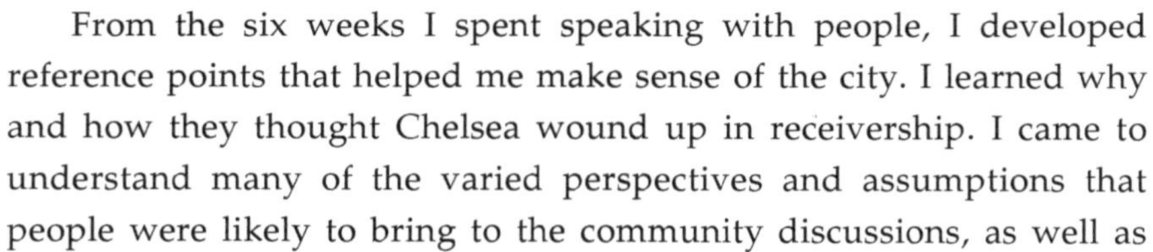

From the six weeks I spent speaking with people, I developed reference points that helped me make sense of the city. I learned why and how they thought Chelsea wound up in receivership. I came to understand many of the varied perspectives and assumptions that people were likely to bring to the community discussions, as well as what they thought a new government should do, what ideals they held for government, and where they thought the previous ones fell short.

Many interviewees believed that fiscal mismanagement led the state to suspend Chelsea's local democracy while others believed that the state took it over so that MassPort, the state port and aviation authority, could site an airport-employee parking lot in the city, which is adjacent to the airport in East Boston. Almost all called for fiscal responsibility as a crucial element of the new government, and many insisted that services be provided uniformly throughout the city. I learned that some people couldn't wait for the state receivership to end and others loved the receiver and hoped he would never leave.

I also learned that the people of Chelsea were suspicious of outsiders, as well as the receiver's decision to "give" them the authority to write their charter and the charter process itself. In addition, the community was skeptical of its own ability to work together to cause positive change. During the community leader interviews, many individuals spoke of the culture of the "stupid kid from Chelsea," which meant that no one should expect very much from them.

The interviewees also recommended individuals to serve as community meeting facilitators and citizen representatives to draft the charter. Many reminded me that the facilitators and charter drafters needed to be moral people highly respected by others. Chelseans had to trust that what they said would be accurately conveyed to and integrated by the charter preparation team.

Identifying the Charter Drafters

After the interviews, a round of community meetings, and a public forum, I faced the challenge of deciding who from Chelsea would serve on the committee that would negotiate the substance of the charter. From the first phase of the charter process, I had compiled a list of seventy individuals recommended by their peers.

Harry, Steve, and I decided to call the group of negotiators the charter preparation team to indicate that it would prepare the charter on behalf of Chelseans. We purposely used the term *team* to indicate a group with a common purpose rather than the sometimes cumbersome workings of a *committee*.

The question was how to get from seventy names to approximately twenty charter preparation team members to have a large enough team to be representative of all segments of the city yet small enough for deliberative conversations. The team had to be composed of people who were not considered morally compromised and assembled in a way that would not trigger the city's deep-seated skepticism. Knowing that this was a critical juncture in the process, but not sure of what to do, I called friends and colleagues for advice, including Howard S. Bellman, a trusted colleague and mentor. He said, "If it's too hard to choose twenty people, maybe it's easier to choose three." His suggestion, which I implemented, was to choose three people from the community, who would then choose the twenty team members. Based on suggestions from the receiver and his chief of staff, the selection committee was formed of Pastor Idalmis Garcia of the Mount Bellingham United Methodist Church; Stephen Quigly, editor of the *Chelsea Record*; and Susan Clark, founder and director of Choice Through Education, an alternative high school for at-risk teens. All were deeply respected citywide for their efforts and commitments to improve life in Chelsea.

At our first meeting, Idalmis, Steve, Sue, and I established criteria for selecting the team members. We decided that team members should be people who could think broadly enough to construct the best form of government for Chelsea instead of operating from a narrow agenda that benefited only those closest to them. Team members would need to be able to learn the mechanics of municipal government and to negotiate in good faith to build consensus agreements. And the group, as a whole, would need to reflect Chelsea's unique tapestry of people from different countries, ethnicities, experiences, and values.

We created a worksheet with twenty-four slots and filled eighteen of them from the list of seventy, based on our established criteria. As a result of my conversations with elected officials, we held three slots for sitting aldermen and one for a school committee member. Because the charter would eventually be subjected to a special election, we needed to include people who ran successful campaigns in pre-receivership days but not too many to make the people of Chelsea reject the charter because of fears that it would bring a return to old ways. In addition, one seat was reserved for the receiver's appointee and another for a state government official with charter and local government expertise.

Steve Quigley had the list of proposed charter preparation team members published in the *Chelsea Record* in an article that explained the charter process, the task of the charter preparation team, the process for selecting team members, and a request for Chelsea residents to nominate additional members to the team if they did not feel represented by any of the members proposed. Residents phoned in about fifteen additional nominees. The selection committee met again to consider these nominations and to add members to the team. We published the revised list and again asked for additional nominees from people who felt their interests were not yet represented. After a third round and no calls to the charter hotline, we finalized membership of the charter preparation team.

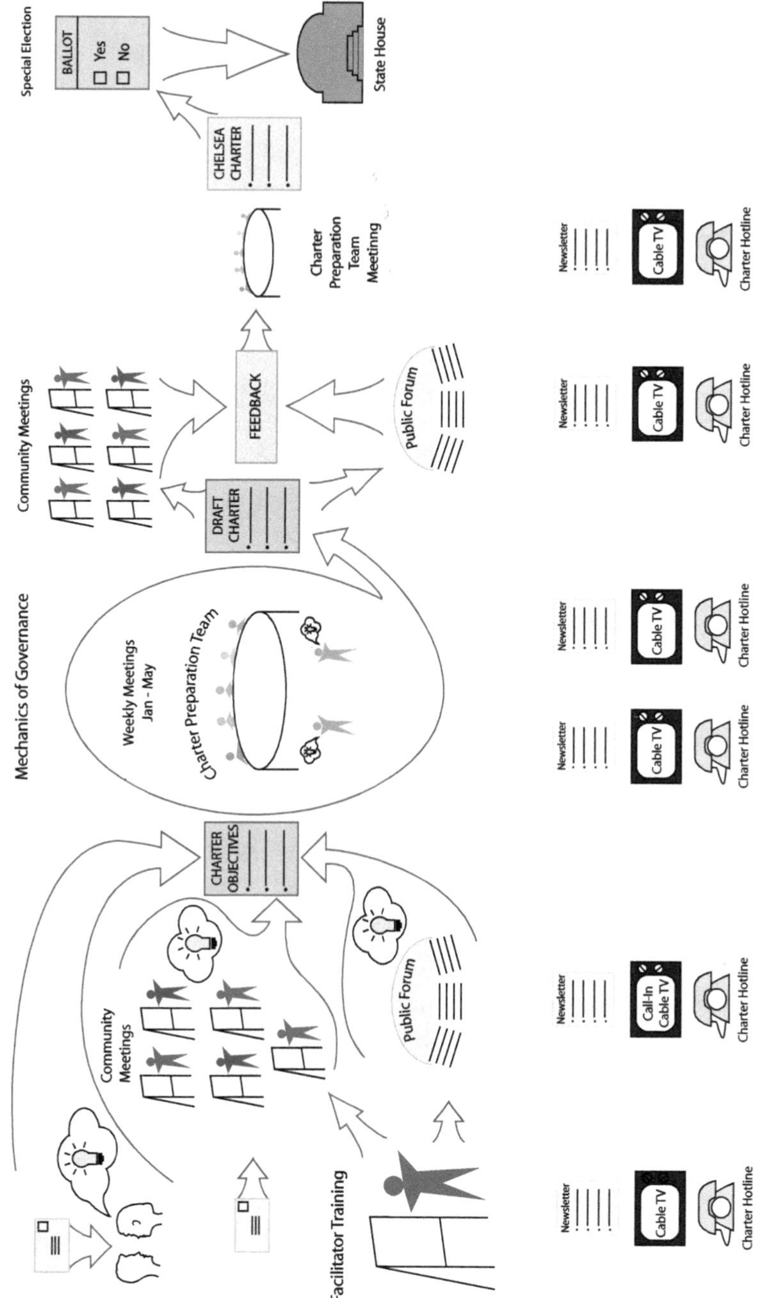

Figure 3.1
The Chelsea Charter Consensus Process Map

Deliberative Negotiations

The Preliminary Meeting

At the first meeting of the charter preparation team, with the help of the process map (Figure 3.1), I described the overall process, including the assessment interviews and the outreach activities that had already been completed. I also explained how the people present had come to be team members. We talked about their expectations of negotiating elements of the charter and clarified the steps for formalizing the charter as state law if they succeeded in reaching consensus.

A critical step in initiating civic fusion at the first meeting was an exercise in which team members added their names and significant Chelsea events to a time line of historic events that already included visits by George Washington and Abraham Lincoln, as well as two devastating fires that had burned through large parts of the city. Some used the dates they moved to Chelsea or were elected to office or started a job in town, but most put the dates their families immigrated to Chelsea. People began talking about their experiences of moving to Chelsea from faraway places and needing to learn a new language and a new culture, and how to find their way through an unknown and confusing system. As old timers recognized their family stories in those of Chelsea's newest residents, intimate connections began to replace the walls of difference among them. The diverse group of individuals that comprised the charter preparation team had begun to bond.

The preliminary meeting was also designed to educate the team about elements of city charters and to clarify procedural issues. Mark Morse, the professional charter drafter hired by the receiver's office after the Aldermanic Subcommittee on Governance selected him from among three candidates, provided a brief training on the mechanics of governance. He discussed the different forms of government from which the team could choose, for example, mayor/council with a strong mayor or weak mayor, or council/manager. He explained the required components of a city charter, including the elements required by the state for every charter. He then explained aspects of Chelsea's existing charter, which had been written and adopted after the fire of 1903, when the city's future depended on negotiations with insurance companies, and how the Special Acts of the state legislature that amended the charter resulted in confusion concerning the authorities and responsibilities among the different branches of the city government.

Next, we turned our attention to how the team would function by creating procedural ground rules to govern the deliberations. As they eventually would do with charter issues, the team members negotiated each element of the ground rules until they reached consensus on the complete document. They started with a mission statement and later addressed several other questions, including: What are the roles of the participants? What is the role of the mediator? How will we record meeting minutes and agreements? How will we deal with the media? What is the decision-making rule? Are we going to operate by consensus? (See Appendix C for the Charter Preparation Team's ground rules.)

After the team reached consensus on its ground rules, members talked about the information they would need to educate themselves about city charters. They asked for written publications, panels of experts, and visits to other municipalities to learn how other governments functioned.

Finally, during our logistics discussion concerning our schedule of meetings, I proposed team meetings every other week and work group meetings in the off weeks. I suggested that work groups could meet to develop proposals for the team to consider. However, the first time I asked for volunteers for a work group meeting, everyone volunteered. In retrospect, that everyone wanted to be at every meeting is not surprising given the level of suspicion and limited trust that was typical in Chelsea at that time. We wound up meeting weekly.

Months of Meetings

From January through May, the team met every Tuesday evening for three hours in the basement of the Chelsea Public Library. I prepared and distributed agendas in advance of the meetings and drafted summaries after each meeting for review and approval by the team. At each meeting, the citizen negotiators discussed a host of charter-related issues. The professional charter drafter translated the team's decisions into formal charter language, which they reviewed and revised at subsequent meetings. The general public was invited to attend, and sometimes Chelseans came to the meetings with suggestions and proposals.

The charter preparation team negotiated and reached consensus on all charter issues. This group of laypeople reviewed, revised, and approved every word of the charter, which covered issues including division of powers; legislative composition; school committee; city manager (appointment, qualifications, administrative powers and duties, and compensation); financial procedures (including annual budget policy, capital improvements program, and long-term financial forecast); and citizen participation mechanisms.

The typical progression of a deliberative consensus process is that team members initiate discussions in which various ideas get raised, and those that gain some traction are vetted, revised, and refined. As an emerging sense of agreement among the team comes into focus, people around the table nod their heads in agreement as others articulate support for the idea in their own words. Some individuals, who previously expressed concerns about an issue or proposal, settle back into their seats as their concerns are addressed. After noticing these indicators of consensus, to test whether or not we have an "agreement in concept," I may say something like, "If I hear you all correctly, it sounds as though you all support_________. Is that correct?" For the Chelsea charter process, after the team reached such agreements, we would ask Mark to draft text for the team's review. The draft text was distributed prior to the next meeting, during which it was reviewed and revised. (For more on managing substantive issues, see Chapter 9.)

Ongoing Education

To educate the charter preparation team and the general public, we held a televised meeting of an assembled panel of current and former elected officials from other cities with various governance structures. Charles Royer, then director of the Institute of Politics of Harvard University's John F. Kennedy School of Government and a three-term mayor of Seattle, Washington, moderated the panel. The panelists were Roberta Miller, my partner on this project who was also a former Watertown city councilor (council/manager), Edmund Tarallo, at-large Waltham city councilor (mayor/council) and Marilyn Contreas, the local government specialist of the Massachusetts Executive Office of Community Development.

We presented the panel with the subject of privatizing trash collection, a question Chelsea was considering at the time. The panelists explained how the issue would wind through the decision-making process in their communities based on the form of government they had. Team members asked questions and wrestled with the slight differences among government frameworks to get a good understanding of their choices for Chelsea. This televised panel went a long way in educating the charter preparation team members and Chelsea citizens.

It also had the unexpected effect of raising the status of the charter preparation team among Chelsea residents. Team members were impressively poised as they posed questions to the panel. They took the issues very seriously and expressed the weight of their responsibility. As a result, the team's stature rose in the eyes of the community. A buzz within the community—people were talking about the charter process in and out of City Hall—suggested a growing belief that Chelsea residents might actually be able to build a charter to govern themselves for the next 100 years.

Bumps on the Road to Success

Because the first meeting of the charter preparation team left me feeling hopeful and energized, I intended with the second meeting to score an early victory to create momentum and encouragement for slogging through six months of weekly meetings. The first item on the agenda was the preamble. I thought it would be a good place to start because it's typically a broad, flowery overview of the ideals of good governance. I expected the conversation to move in the direction of unifying, over-arching goals for Chelsea's future.

I thought the team members would read the distributed preambles from other city charters and constitutions, discuss elements of good government, write up comments on flipcharts, wordsmith a bit, ask Mark to turn it into "charter language," wordsmith a bit more, and quickly reach a consensus agreement on the charter preamble. I thought we'd spend about an hour on it at the next meeting, after which I expected to hear cries of "Wow! We already finished a section of the charter!" It seemed like a good plan.

To begin the discussions, charter preparation team members reviewed the preambles from town charters, as well as the Massachusetts and the U.S. Constitutions. To my surprise, after only a few minutes the team was engaged in a passionate discussion about whether or not God should be mentioned in the preamble. It became a major point of contention. One member insisted that God be mentioned in the charter, and another opposed such proposals on behalf of atheists residing in Chelsea. All agreed that the preamble should be unifying; they disagreed on whether including God would be divisive.

After going round and round, I cut off the discussion and passed onto another issue because spiraling around a decision to include or exclude God clearly was going nowhere near resolution. I was disappointed that what I had assumed would be an early victory to build momentum turned into a mess.

Before the next meeting, I met separately with the two women most engaged in the dispute because I thought that if they could develop language that both could live with, it was likely to be acceptable to everyone else. Eventually, Helen, the religious woman, offered language that Nadine, the presumptive representative of Chelsea atheists, accepted. I took the proposal to the next meeting confident it would be adopted.

When we got to the preamble issue listed on the agenda, I introduced the proposed text and asked for questions and comment. Although Helen had proposed the language, she rejected it!

I was shocked. I called for a ten-minute break during the meeting to give myself time to regain my composure, whereupon I began to realize the constraints of my theory in practice. Although I still believed that the people around the table had the best knowledge for creating Chelsea's charter, and I still believed that they had to do it for themselves, I had assumed too great an understanding of good faith negotiations. In retrospect, my mistake was returning to the preamble so soon. I should have waited until the team had gained more experience successfully negotiating agreements on other issues.

After the meeting, I talked with Helen and explained that she had just rejected the very language she had proposed and which, in the spirit of progress and compromise, Nadine had accepted. I suggested that this violated basic norms of negotiation. She said she understood, but continued to reject her own proposal because it didn't directly mention God.

I tabled the issue and moved on to other topics. I decided not to address the preamble for a number of meetings because it had begun to negatively impact our momentum. Months later, we considered preamble language similar to the "Great Legislator" of the Massachusetts Constitution, which can mean different things to different readers, but the team settled on confronting the issue head on, with the phrase, "under God with religious freedom."

To Have a Mayor or Not to Have a Mayor

At a later meeting, Marilyn Portnoy, a sitting alderwoman, proposed a mayoral form of government. The team responded with a resounding no! She then suggested a ceremonial mayor. She claimed it would be important to Chelseans to have "one of their own" to cut ribbons at new developments, inaugurate new fire trucks, lead cheers for the high school football team, and wish the graduates good luck. Team members expressed fears that anyone with the title of mayor would seek to grab power.

Surprisingly, Marilyn, referred to around town as the Fighting Lady, listened to the discussion of the team members. They gave due respect to her proposal but ultimately rejected it. It was quite extraordinary. The team actually employed deliberative decision making with the Fighting Lady. They had learned a way to discuss a passionate issue on which people held differing viewpoints, weighed the advantages and disadvantages of a set of options, and with respect and comity, had chosen from among their possibilities. It looked an awful lot like a functional democracy. Marilyn seemed to realize that her usual ramrod strategies would not intimidate a team of responsible citizens fused to create and protect self-governance in Chelsea.

School Committee by District or At Large

The most contentious issue was the composition of the school committee. Some team members strongly supported a school committee elected by district whereas others supported a school committee elected citywide, or at large. At the time of the Chelsea charter process, almost no members of the school committee actually had children in the school system.

The team members all wanted more parents with children in the schools to serve on the school committee, but they disagreed over how to accomplish it. Those supporting the school committee members elected by district believed it would be easier for parents of school-aged children and minority candidates to get elected if they had to campaign only in their neighborhoods rather than throughout the city. Others thought that at-large would be easier because to win the sixth and seventh slots, a candidate would need fewer votes overall.

This issue was passionately discussed and tabled at many meetings as team members tried to convince others to adopt their preferred option. More than a few people swayed back and forth between the two choices.

During a meeting with the receiver on unrelated issues, Harry told me that he supported a school committee elected by district. I reminded him that his representative on the charter preparation team had made that case on his behalf. In indicating his commitment to the people of Chelsea, he agreed that letting the team struggle to make its decision would ultimately increase the city's capacity for self-governance.

Because the team could not reach a consensus, after many hours of passionate discussion over multiple meetings, the issue was put to a vote in accordance with its ground rules.[1] Ultimately, by a vote of 80 percent, the team settled on a school committee elected at large. Still, according to the team's ground rules, final consensus on the charter

---

1. In its ground rules, the charter preparation team defined consensus as "no dissent by any member of the team." However, if a timely decision on a fully discussed issue needed to be made, "the mediator may acknowledge an impasse and will call for a vote. Proposals voted on will require 80 percent of the team members present for passage." However, consensus on the complete charter still needed to meet the "no dissent" decision rule.

would require the unanimous support of all charter preparation team members.

Confounding Political Attacks

As Chelsea residents increasingly came to believe in the legitimacy and potential of the Chelsea charter process, there were some who feared a loss of their own political power as a result of a new charter and an engaged citizenry. In particular, because the charter preparation team was leaning toward consensus on a council-manager form of government with no mayor, individuals in Chelsea who hoped to be mayor desperately tried to delegitimize the process. They were politically savvy enough to know that they could not publicly say they wanted a mayoral form of government. Instead, they tried to exploit the city's old tendencies toward distrust of outsiders for fear of being deceived. In one instance early in the process, during a televised board of aldermen's meeting,[2] an alderman reported that he had been to the State House and had seen people printing Chelsea's new charter. As he had expected, he informed his audience, the Chelsea charter process was a sham; it was window dressing to create political cover for decisions already made. His comments were published in the local paper and resonated throughout Chelsea.

To protect the legitimacy of the process against this particular attack, the charter preparation team, which had emerged as a respected, cohesive group by this time, selected five of its members to go to the next aldermen's meeting. They chose not to respond directly to the alderman's comments, but instead made statements regarding who they were, their roles on the charter team, the issues they were tackling, which issues they felt most strongly about, and how some had been resolved. Five people telling their credible charter stories effectively defused the alderman's impact. The responses to the attack against the process indicated that skepticism among team members was waning

---

2. Although the board of aldermen had no actual powers, the receiver continued to hold local elections, and the board of aldermen and school committee met regularly. Their decisions were considered recommendations to the receiver.

and that new norms of coordinated action on behalf of the city were taking root.

Another attack came just prior to the public circulation of the draft charter. At another televised aldermen's meeting, the Fighting Lady announced that she had received a copy of the charter in her mailbox, and it was dated almost two years prior to the start of the Chelsea charter process. "This proves," she said, "that it's a done deal." Her comments underscored everything she'd said from the beginning about the team's work: "This is all a joke. The state has something that they want, and that's what we're going to get."

The "mailbox charter" in the Fighting Lady's hand was actually a charter commissioned by the first receiver. Harry, his successor, and the Aldermanic Subcommittee on Governance, which the recipient of the mailbox charter had served on, had rejected it because it was written without public involvement. She had seen that charter two years before. It's possible that she forgot, or that the person who "dropped the charter in her mailbox" intended to set her up. In any case, her comments were quoted in the next day's edition of the *Chelsea Record*, under the headline, "Charter Is a Done Deal."

Once again, we all kicked into gear. I immediately wrote a letter to the charter preparation team members, explaining that the "mailbox charter" was a two-year-old draft already rejected by the receiver and the aldermen. Two days later, at its next meeting, the team developed its response strategies. They revised a letter to the editor of the local paper that I had drafted for their review, and they decided to send it with all of their signatures. They wrote a press release and a letter to the board of Aldermen. Team members went on cable TV and explained the differences between the draft charter they were working on and the mailbox version. The same five team members made statements at another board of aldermen's meeting. Behind the scenes, people tried to get the Fighting Lady to make a public apology. Although she didn't apologize, she made reference to her error at the next aldermen's meeting.

A third attack, which came very close to sinking the entire charter process, appeared without warning in the *Boston Globe*. The newspaper reported that, according to an almost-final version of the charter, Chelsea would have a fifteen-member city council.

The team had never even entertained that number. They had talked about seven and thirteen councilors, and every odd number in-between, but they never considered fifteen. And yet, on the front page of the Metro section of the *Boston Globe*, the headline screamed, "Fifteen Member Council for Chelsea." The paper quoted an unnamed source in the receiver's office.

At the next team meeting, many members themselves questioned the integrity of the process. I came to the meeting with a memo confirming Harry's intentions. A section of it read,

> I have received assurances that there is no "predisposed charter." The Receiver expressed to me his continuing confidence in this process. He believes that the charter you develop will accurately represent the wishes of the community and thus, is likely to be supported by the voters in a special election.

Midway through that meeting, after selecting three spokespersons to interact with the media on their behalf, team members were reassured of the legitimacy of the process and were able to turn their attention back to technical charter issues.

Eventually, we were able to get another article published in the *Globe* correcting the previous misstatement. Unfortunately, it was buried deep in the Metro section, but it was something we could distribute to the team and others.

In response to each attack, we had to quickly prepare and distribute information to the community. Steve helped expedite the information flow, and the city attorney provided legal opinions, as needed. The most powerful impacts resulted when local residents stood up to defend the process. The charter preparation team became a powerful, almost elite, force in the community. Even those opposed to the process dared not attack the team's credibility.

Outreach and Consultation

Given the unique circumstances of the city's situation, the Chelsea charter process included specifically tailored mechanisms for outreach and consultation. A city charter was the tangible product of the process and its complementary goal was an educated citizenry primed for self-governance. The status quo maintained a disengaged public that was highly skeptical of outsiders.

In response, the charter process provided numerous entry points for both passive and active participation. Roberta and I determined to take the process to the people of Chelsea in the places they typically gathered rather than to schedule charter meetings and wait for people to show up. To overcome the distrust of outsiders, we trained local people to facilitate meetings at social clubs and organizations.

The charter preparation team integrated the ideas, opinions, and concerns generated at the community meetings into their discussions and decisions.

In addition to the community meetings, the outreach and consultation components of the Chelsea charter process included public forums, educational newsletters sent to each household in Chelsea, call-in cable television shows, and two-way information via a charter telephone hotline.

Community Meetings All Over the City

The charter process included two rounds of community meetings: the first to discuss goals for the new charter and the second to review key elements of the draft consensus charter developed by the charter preparation team.

Local facilitators ran community meetings all over the city. The meetings were held at social clubs, houses of worship, and even peoples' homes—wherever a sufficient number of people could be brought together. They were held at places such as the Latin American Cultural Association, Historical Commission, Golden Age Club, Rotary Club, 14 Bloomingdale St. Elderly Housing development, Admiral's Hill Condominium Association, Kiwanis Club, Parent-Teacher Organization, Choice through Education, Hispanic Commission, City Hall (for city employees), and Chelsea High School. In place of community meetings among the Cambodian residents, a trusted person translated summary charter documents and discussed them with families in their homes. We were told that the community meetings were to these residents too reminiscent of forced participation at meetings of the Khmer Rouge that included executions of intellectuals.

Practically all the organizations in Chelsea had monthly meetings, which were listed in the local paper. Roberta contacted people from these organizations to ask if we could have one hour of their monthly meeting time to discuss the charter with their members. Many complied. Later, people called the charter hotline to ask for facilitators to come to meetings they wanted to arrange.

The key element of the community meetings was that we engage people on their terms and in their natural locations. In all, more than forty-five community meetings were held. Combined, they helped to connect the existing subcommunities of the city into a unified, municipal populace.

The facilitators were responsible for filling out feedback sheets after each meeting, which contained the thoughts, ideas, and opinions that they had heard and recorded on flipcharts during the meeting. The facilitators were paid when they returned a feedback sheet after a scheduled meeting.

The community meetings followed the formats that Roberta and I had designed. Roberta trained the facilitators and collected their feedback sheets. I synthesized the ideas and information the facilitators collected at the community meetings for use by the charter preparation team.

The first round of community meetings focused on the following questions:

- What characteristics would the new government need to have to serve us successfully for the next 100 years?
- What would make you feel that your local government worked for you?
- What would make you feel that your local government was fair to you and the rest of the community?
- Do you have any concerns about the charter process?

The second round focused specifically on support for and concerns about proposed charter elements such as the council/manager form of government, composition of the city council and school committee, terms of elected officials, residency requirement for the city manager, and public input into hiring of the city manager and key department heads such as the police and fire chief.

Because the schedule of meetings was published in the local paper, each group knew that others were involved in similar discussions. Individual citizens came together to deliberate about a collectively recognized problem and learned how together they could create a joint solution. I remember feeling incredibly charged when the community meetings were happening, and all the more so when I walked into the Dunkin' Donuts across the street from City Hall and heard two elderly gentlemen discussing the charter!

The Newsletters

Soon after I began interviewing Chelsea leaders, the receiver's staff, with input from Roberta and me, prepared and distributed the first in a series of newsletters that were sent to every household in the city. Each one was written in English and Spanish. The first described, in simple terms, what a city charter is, why Chelsea needed a new one, and how people could participate in the process to create it. It also explained that the Chelsea charter process marked the beginning of the end of the receivership.

It encouraged participation in the charter process stating, "You must speak up." In addition, the newsletter explained how a city charter organizes powers and authorities that invisibly affect people's day-to-day lives. It explained why the city had outgrown its 1903 charter, and how it had contributed to perpetual political gridlock.

Following the first series of community meetings, I compiled the input of those who had participated during the first phase of the process into a second newsletter called "What We Said."

The newsletter was organized according to the questions the facilitators had posed to people to elicit their opinions about Chelsea's charter objectives: "What do we want?" "What is fair?" "What is good government?" In addition, it included citizens' thoughts about why Chelsea was in receivership, along with ideas about various key charter elements, such as having a mayor versus a city manager and the size of the legislative body. Actual quotes from the people of Chelsea, without attribution, were sprinkled throughout the newsletter.

I specifically did not evaluate the responses in this newsletter, but merely compiled and synthesized them in a way that would be informative for the community and the charter preparation team. I think it was helpful and even fascinating for people to see the range of responses we received. It also gave people the beginnings of a willingness to believe that others were listening to what they said, and that what they said mattered. At various times and in multiple venues, I saw people point to quotes and heard them say something akin to, "That's exactly what I said!"

The responses regarding charter objectives showed an emerging consensus for good government, defined as fiscally responsible, protective against corruption, and providing for a fair and even distribution of city services and resources. The synthesis of residents' ideas provided the starting point for the deliberations of the charter preparation team. Its members took to heart the opinions of the people of Chelsea, and would often refer to the "What We Said" newsletter to inform their discussions. For example, many citizens believed that a larger council would result in more diverse representation and contribute to protection against corruption. In response, the team seriously considered councils only greater in size than the seven-member board of the old charter.

Call-in Cable TV Show

We regularly scheduled call-in cable TV shows to inform the community of the charter process. During the first charter-related show, part of a series called "Conversations with Harry," Harry explained the need for a city charter and introduced me to the community. I used the process map to explain all the elements of the Chelsea charter process.

As the process continued and the charter preparation team started to deliberate on elements of the charter, many more call-in shows were broadcast to let Chelseans know what the team was discussing and deciding. Preassigned runners brought the charter team panel dozens of questions from callers, covering all sorts of topics. They included:

- Will we be allowed to pick what form of government we want on a ballot?

- If we have a city manager, how will he or she be elected and how long will the term be?
- If, after the new charter is written and passed and there is an error, who will be able to change it? The board of aldermen or the state?
- The charter worked for eighty years, will it be better to add amendments to the existing charter? Why is it necessary to throw out the whole charter? Why not leave what is good and take out what is bad?
- Will nonresidents be allowed to vote? (The caller is against it!)
- I've heard some people say this is a done deal. Is it?
- How much does a city manager earn on average?
- Is it possible for the chief executive position to be two positions to try to lessen the chance of the corruption of one person?
- Can the state dictate the specific options we can adopt, like mayor or manager?
- Is Mr. Spence happy with his job?

The newsletters and cable television shows were a vital way of ensuring that the process reached every household, not just the residents who attended meetings. Because the local access channel had little material to broadcast, they repeatedly replayed the charter shows.

The Public Forum

In conjunction with the first series of community meetings, we organized a public forum for those people who were interested but were not members of any of the clubs or organizations where the facilitated community meetings were conducted. To promote participation, we held it at the high school gymnasium on the first night the public was invited to view its new parquet gym floor. Approximately 120 people attended.

After an introductory statement from the receiver and a walk through the process map, the facilitators led discussions of about ten people at each table. They followed the community meeting format. As I walked around the room, the entire gym was echoing with talk about governing

Chelsea. Some participants spoke in English, others in Spanish. They were contemplating, they were deliberating, and they were building hope for their city, which had fallen into the depths of corruption.

The Process Map

To help people understand the process the city was undertaking to work its way out of receivership, we used a process map—a 5 x 3 foot graphic of how each step in the charter process related to all others (illustrated in Figure 3.1). We took the map to cable TV shows, public forums, and charter preparation team meetings. The facilitators had 8 ½ x 11 inch versions of it to refer to at the community meetings.

Most importantly, the process map came to be an important tool for establishing and maintaining the credibility of the process. It challenged a persistent skepticism rooted in the broken promises of other outsiders. The power of the process map was that we could show people exactly where we were in the process, what we had already done, and what we were going to do. It enabled us to create and deliver on a shared set of expectations.

Circulating the Draft Proposed Charter for Public Review

After six months of negotiations, the Charter Preparation Team completed its draft city charter. It included a council-manager form of government with a thirteen-member city council of ten district and three at-large councilors, who would be elected to two- and four-year terms respectively. We sent out a newsletter summarizing the charter and published the summary in the local newspaper. It was translated into Khmer and distributed by a trusted member of the Cambodian community. Copies were available at City Hall, the public library, and many shops around the city. The following month, we organized twenty facilitated community meetings, a public forum, and several call-in cable shows to answer questions about the charter and to generate community feedback.

The community meetings provided another opportunity to engage people throughout the city. Everyone in Chelsea could review the draft document and provide their opinions on any aspect of it. The meeting format was designed to focus discussions on the key elements of the charter but allowed time for people to raise additional issues.

People could recognize the impact of their time spent offering opinions and advice on the charter at previous meetings. I compiled and synthesized the feedback obtained from the final round of community meetings, the public forum, call-in cable television shows, and the charter hotline to create a document for the Charter Preparation Team that provided section-by-section recommendations based on the community input. Some of the recommendations led to changes in the charter, and some were rejected, but the team discussed every aspect of every issue that members of the community had raised.

The community's input caused the team to reconsider some key decisions. For example, the draft charter proposed a thirteen-member council, but, as a result of concerns by many in the community that a thirteen-member council was too large, the team reduced it to an eleven-member council. Said one resident, "The meetings already go past midnight with a seven-member board, with thirteen, the meetings will never end—too much hot air." The team had proposed a larger council because public input from the first set of community meetings suggested support for more than the existing seven legislators to make it more representative and easier for residents to get elected from one of ten districts rather than the six districts under the old charter.

Another change to the draft charter was to provide two-year terms for all city councilors. The draft charter proposed two-year terms for district councilors and four-year terms for at-large councilors in response to community concerns that two-year terms motivated elected officials to seek short-term gains to ensure their reelection and limited opportunities to consider the longer term needs of the city. During community discussions of the draft charter, it became clear that the community feared the consequences of power imbalances among city councilors caused by differing terms more than it hoped for long-term city planning.

As a result of the norms established by deliberation among the fused members of the charter preparation team, they were able to articulate their choices and the benefits and disadvantages of each option and collectively choose among them.

Putting Chelsea in Its Charter

During the charter preparation team deliberations, team members had gradually taken ownership of the charter. As a result of their hard work, the charter had a decidedly local flavor to it, some of which reflected the pain, embarrassment, and distrust experienced by Chelseans because of former corrupt officials.

For example, to hire and fire the city manager, the charter requires an extraordinary majority of council members (eight of eleven). The charter also provides the public an opportunity to interview candidates. It explicitly denies elected office to convicted felons, and contains absolutely no mention of a mayor—not even a symbolic one.

Final Consensus

At our final meeting, we reviewed and revised the charter, section-by-section, based on the community feedback. After the team discussed the last set of comments, I asked the final question of the charter preparation team: "Is there any dissent from adopting this revised document as the proposed city charter for Chelsea?"

The silence meant unanimous support for the charter, consensus on the package of decisions that, when combined, created a governing infrastructure for Chelsea's future. Everyone in the room broke into applause.

Afterward, all the charter preparation team members signed the process map that had been propped up at the front of the room during every team meeting. They put all their names in a hat and drew out a winner—the person who got to keep the signed process map for posterity! (See Appendix B for the Charter Signature Sheet.)

This signature page, signed by all the members of the Charter Preparation Team, accompanied the proposed city charter when it was distributed throughout Chelsea prior to the special election.

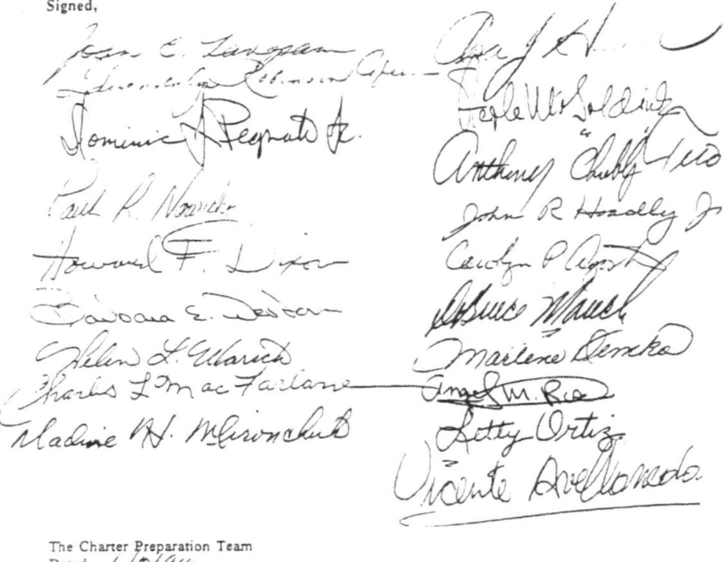

We, the members of the Chelsea Charter Preparation Team, present to you the city charter that we have prepared for you, the residents of Chelsea. We have met almost every week since February. We have listened to your opinions as individuals and used the input you have provided us at the community meetings, community leader interviews, ward meetings, public forums, survey, cable call-in shows and the charter hotline to prepare a charter that we believe will serve Chelsea well into the next century.

We believe that this charter accurately addresses many of the concerns that you, the community, have raised throughout the charter development process. The changes in the structure of Chelsea's government that would result from the adoption of the charter will provide the strong foundation for municipal management that is necessary to meet our challenges ahead.

Signed,

The Charter Preparation Team
Dated

Figure 3.2
The Chelsea Charter Signature Page

Special Election

In the three weeks between the team's completion of the final charter and the special election, "Vote No" and "Yes for Chelsea" campaigns formally registered with the city clerk. They raised money, distributed buttons and bumper stickers, and placed advertisements in the local papers.

On the day of the vote, I sat in my office completely unable to work because I was so anxious about the outcome of the special election. I felt the enormity of the responsibility I had taken on. Harry had taken a huge risk by turning the charter process over to the residents of Chelsea. Some state legislators and others thought he was crazy. It seemed that there were many people waiting in the wings to rejoice at our failure.

Finally, the numbers came in. Of the 30 percent of registered voters that cast a vote, 60 percent approved the charter and 40 percent opposed it. The charter was on its way to the Massachusetts State House where it would become law.

Transition to Self-Governance

In accordance with the transition provisions of the charter, a special primary election was held four months after the charter became law. Four weeks later in a special general election, the first city council and school committee were elected under the new charter. Thirty days after the council was sworn in, the president of the city council established a special screening committee to select a city manager. Thirteen months after the charter was approved, the Chelsea city council hired its first city manager, and the receivership ended.

CHAPTER 4:

CONSTRUCTION CRANES NEGOTIATED RULEMAKING

Background

I used to hate the sight of cranes on the urban horizon; it made things look unfinished. I preferred an uninterrupted skyline. But after 9/11, when I saw American flags flying atop the high perches of cranes, for me they came to symbolize the difference between us and them. We build—our enemies destroy. From then on, for me cranes were a symbol of hope and pride.

Not long after I experienced this new love for cranes, I was contacted by Noah Connell, director of Construction Standards and Guidance of the U.S. Occupational Safety and Health Administration (OSHA), to mediate a negotiated rulemaking to revise worker safety standards for construction cranes and derricks. The safety standards, referred to officially as 29 CFR part 1926 Subpart N—Cranes, Derricks, Hoists, Elevators, and Conveyors (Subpart N), were adopted in 1971 and based on industry consensus standards developed between 1967 and 1969. Everyone agreed that the existing standards failed to address the key safety issues of modern cranes and work practices. Accidents in, on, and around cranes and derricks caused an average of 89 deaths per year according to U.S. Department of Labor statistics, representing the greatest number of fatalities and serious injuries within a sector of the construction industry.

In 1998, OSHA convened the Crane Work Group of the Advisory Committee on Construction Safety and Health (ACCSH), and asked its members to suggest ways to improve the existing crane safety regulations. In its 2002 draft report, the work group identified some of the key hazards faced by crane operators and employers, but did not agree on how to fix things. They did, however, recommend that OSHA initiate a formal negotiated rulemaking process to revise Subpart N.

Overview of Negotiated Rulemaking

Negotiated rulemaking, sometimes referred to as regulatory negotiations (or reg neg), is a process for developing federal regulations that rely on stakeholders and government working together to develop consensus on the actual text of a proposed rule. A critical element of negotiated rulemaking is the forum it provides for government and stakeholder representatives to engage in complex negotiations. Reg neg offers an opportunity to integrate the differing perspectives and interests of national, state, tribal, and local constituencies that will be affected by the rule. Generally speaking, it brings a great deal of focus and resources to the issues embedded in the future rule. If successful, the nation benefits from publicly supported rules that achieve government and stakeholder policy goals.

Reg neg has been used since the early 1980s and was codified in the Negotiated Rulemaking Act of 1996. Many federal agencies have conducted negotiated rulemakings, but most still favor the traditional rulemaking process, in which the public is invited to submit formal comments on a draft rule prepared by the government. Government officials then evaluate the comments and determine whether or not to support, reject, or create alternatives to particular sections or subsections of their proposed rule. They do so on their own, without the benefit of deliberations with and among outside stakeholders and the public.

Reg neg uploads potential conflict to the front end of the rulemaking process, and provides early opportunities to resolve conflict rather than waiting for formal comments at the back end. In fact, participating organizations usually agree not to submit formal negative comments on the proposed rule if the sponsoring agency publishes their consensus text as the basis of its notice of proposed rulemaking (NPRM).

Importantly, the government agency retains jurisdiction over the final rule. As such, the agency may reject a formal consensus recommendation of its advisory committee. However, the government agency actively participates in the negotiations and provides its substantive expertise as well as its knowledge of regulatory enforceability. The final recommendation should, therefore, effectively incorporate all the concerns raised by the sponsoring agency, thus assuring the agency's willingness to adopt it.

The reg neg process is designed and facilitated by a public policy mediator, who is responsible for designing the overall process and managing the group deliberations to help them reach consensus on draft regulatory text for the proposed rule.

Cranes and Derricks Negotiated Rulemaking Advisory Committee (C-DAC)

OSHA initiated and conducted the cranes and derricks negotiated rulemaking in accordance with the Federal Advisory Committee Act and the Negotiated Rulemaking Act. In its July 2002 *Federal Register* notice of intent to establish a negotiated rulemaking committee, OSHA asked the public to nominate committee members from significantly affected stakeholder groups: crane manufacturers and suppliers, rental and maintenance companies, users (employers), labor organizations, crane operators, government/public entities, training and operator testing organizations, power line owners, and the insurance industry. (See Table 4.1 for the C-DAC Timeline.)

Table 4.1 C-DAC Timeline

July 16, 2002	*Federal Register* notice of intent to establish a negotiated rulemaking committee under the Negotiated Rulemaking Act (NRA) and the Federal Advisory Committee Act (FACA).
February 27, 2003	*Federal Register* notice of proposed negotiated rulemaking committee membership and request for comments.
March 31, 2003	Deadline for comments.
June 12, 2003	*Federal Register* notice of establishment of the cranes and derricks negotiated rulemaking advisory committee.
June 27, 2003	FACA charter signed by secretary of labor and filed with Congress.
July 3, 2003	*Federal Register* notice of final membership list for negotiated rulemaking advisory committee. *Federal Register* Notice of First Meeting of C-DAC.
July 2003–July 2004	C-DAC negotiations (11 meetings).
July 9, 2004	C-DAC reached final consensus on all issues.
August 29 & 30, 2006	Small Business Regulatory Enforcement Fairness Act panel.
October 9, 2008	Cranes and Derricks in Construction Proposed Rule published in the *Federal Register.*
December 8, 2008	Deadline for comments.
March 17–21, 2009	OSHA public hearing on the proposed rule for cranes and derricks in construction.
August 9, 2010	Final rule published in the *Federal Register.*
November 8, 2010	Effective date of final rule.

Identifying categories of stakeholders and selecting individuals and organizations to represent them are critical to developing an actionable agreement. (See Chapter 6,"Conducting the Mediator's Assessment.") From the fifty-nine nominations OSHA received in response to its request, it chose twenty representatives and published that list in a second *Federal Register* notice with a request for comments. Twenty-nine individuals and organizations commented on the proposed list: sixteen praised it and thirteen suggested additional members, sometimes the same person. In response to the comments, OSHA added three committee members to represent an additional crane manufacturer, an industry trade association, and the billboard industry. This process of requesting nominations, publishing the list of committee members in advance, and soliciting advice on the final composition of the negotiating team is essential for ensuring its public legitimacy and thereby, public acceptance of its consensus agreements. Ultimately, the twenty-three-member negotiating team, named the Cranes and Derricks Negotiated Rulemaking Advisory Committee (C-DAC), was composed of people hailing from government, the private sector, trade associations and unions, from across the country.

C-DAC met eleven times between July 2003 and July 2004. During thirty-one days of face-to-face negotiations, C-DAC members collectively grappled with complicated, divisive issues and worked through various nuanced options to reach final consensus on all the issues subject to negotiations. In addition to the negotiating sessions, the process included expert panel presentations, work groups, and caucuses.

Each meeting followed a formal agenda that was prepared and distributed prior to the negotiating session. Of the eleven C-DAC meetings, nine were held in Washington, D.C., one in Las Vegas, Nevada, and one in Phoenix, Arizona.

Virtually all the expertise needed for developing the worker safety standards resided within the collective wisdom and experience of the committee members and members of the public that participated on panels and work groups and provided public comments. In a few instances, C-DAC's knowledge base was supplemented by outside experts.

My associate mediator, Alexis Gensberg Robert, and I drafted summaries of each meeting to document C-DAC's agreements, identify key discussion points and proposed options for unresolved issues, and record public comments. OSHA staff reviewed early drafts of the summaries for technical accuracy, and C-DAC members reviewed, revised, and approved each summary. A team of OSHA regulation writers, led by Noah Connell, drafted regulatory text to reflect C-DAC discussions. C-DAC members reviewed and revised each section until it was acceptable to all the parties.

An Informal Mediator's Assessment

By the time I was retained for the cranes reg neg, C-DAC was already populated according to the FACA requirement of "balanced representation from affected and interested stakeholder groups."

After the C-DAC members were officially appointed by the Secretary of Labor, I conducted in-depth interviews with them before the first meeting. Over a three-week period, I learned of their key interests, issues, and concerns; the history of crane regulations and past efforts to revise them; expectations for the cranes and derricks reg neg; and for some, their experiences with a past OSHA reg neg: the Steel Erection Negotiated Rulemaking, usually referred to as SENRAC. (See Chapter 5 for more on mediator's assessments.)

I used the information gathered during these calls to design the preliminary meeting and later meeting agendas as well as to manage the negotiations. For example, because I learned that many C-DAC members knew little about negotiated rulemaking and the formal rulemaking procedures that would follow their negotiations, the preliminary meeting included overviews of both. Interviewees discussed the past efforts to revise the crane rules and referred to the draft work group report. It became a starting point in discussions for the issues it addressed.

The key issues were easily identifiable because virtually every interviewee discussed them. For those issues, I heard similar stories passionately told from different points of view. Participant willingness to discuss key issues afforded me the opportunity to ask questions to gain increased understanding of their personal assumptions, preferences, and fears and aspirations. For example, I learned about the U.S. method of testing crane prototypes using extensive physical analysis and the European computer modeling system. I heard horrific stories of electrocution deaths caused when cranes accidentally hit power lines. Almost everyone had strong opinions about crane operator qualifications, given the dearth of state and city licensing requirements at the time.

Of great interest to me was information related to the mental awareness required for safety and some of the tools, such as signs, ongoing training, and layered safety procedures, used to promote that consciousness and protect against a lack of it. From the interviews, I came to understand that maintaining worker safety is not static but is rather an ongoing, continuous process, and I became curious about how that would be reflected in the regulation.

I also used those early calls to learn about cranes and derricks. Prior to those conversations, not only did I not know the difference between a boom and a winch—I had never heard the terms! Some of the crane safety specialists sent me videos to watch. (Incidentally, if ever you need to leave the cab of a crane when the ground has been electrified, jump onto both feet and shuffle away so that you evenly distribute the amount of electricity each side of your body may get.) Based on recommendations, I bought and leafed through the *Mobile Crane Manual* (Construction Safety Association of Toronto, Toronto, Ontario, Canada 1982).

From the interviews and background documents, I learned the issues and the jargon and memorized the alphabet soup (acronyms) of the industry. Although I was clearly not a crane expert, I still needed to know enough to credibly manage the substantive negotiations. To gain additional information throughout the process, I asked many questions, sometimes during public negotiating sessions and sometimes quietly offline.

Upon completing the interviews, I knew highlights of each member's individual story. I synthesized what I'd learned to get a sense of where their interests were aligned and how that alignment might support potential agreements. I had an initial sense of which issues seemed to pose actual clashes across interests and which might be resolved by sorting through misplaced assumptions and clarifying confusions, or in other words, which were interest-based conflicts and which were conflicts of confusion.

The Preliminary Meeting

The preliminary meeting design reflected dynamics gleaned from the assessment even as it incorporated usual prenegotiation tasks. The two-and-a-half day meeting included a welcome from the OSHA Administrator; an overview of OSHA's goals for the revised safety standards; committee member introductions including statements about their goals, concerns, and thoughts about crane and derrick safety; an overview of the negotiated rulemaking process; discussion of ground rules and the list of issues to be negotiated; informational needs; logistics; public comment; and the beginnings of our discussion of substantive issues.

At the meeting, the OSHA administrator, Assistant Secretary John Henshaw, welcomed C-DAC members, thanked them for their willingness to provide their expertise to the agency, and assured them he would implement their agreements.

Noah Connell told the group that OSHA wanted and needed to increase worker safety. He suggested they identify the key hazards associated with cranes and then focus the regulations to protect against those hazards, and he explained that OSHA wanted the regulations to be clear, enforceable, and easily understandable for its users. In addition, Noah described the formal rulemaking procedures that would follow the C-DAC negotiations.

In my overview of the negotiated rulemaking process, I described the reg neg process and sought to address the concerns raised by those familiar with SENRAC. I used a generic negotiated rulemaking process map to illustrate all its parts and explain the core elements of the process (see Figure 4.1).

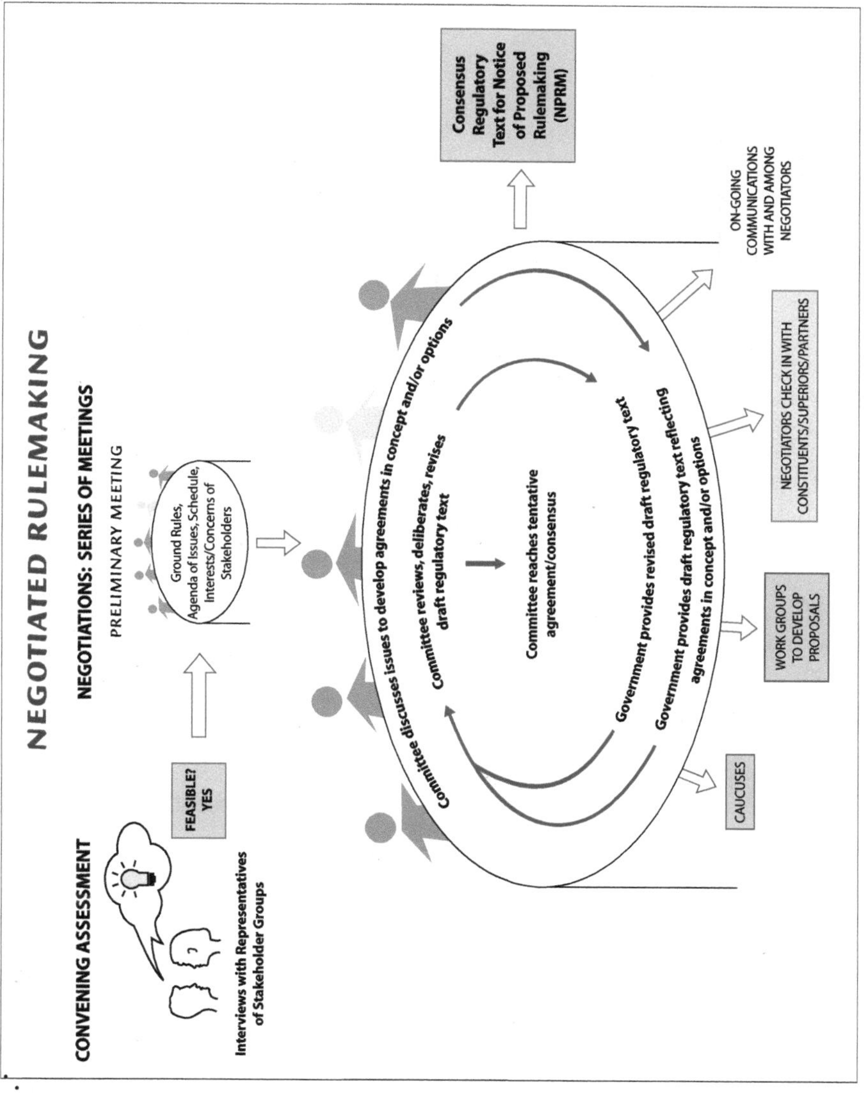

Figure 4.1 Negotiated Rulemaking Process Map

I explained that we would first "workshop" each issue, meaning we'd talk about the issue to get a sense of what it covered, people's thoughts on it, and what additional information we might need. I described how we would unpack each issue to identify its parts as well as to separate the confusions and underlying assumptions from critical disagreements. For many issues, we could expect to easily reach agreements in concept.

For tough issues, we would take the discussion as far as possible; if it became repetitive and void of new ideas, we would move on and leave the issue for another time.

They could expect OSHA to draft regulatory text reflecting their discussions. The group would then review and revise the draft text. We would do this repeatedly for each issue until the group reached a tentative agreement. If we had tentative agreements on all issues, we would review the entire package, make any necessary changes, and if all went well, we would reach final consensus on all issues. (For more on managing the discussions of substantive issues, see Chapter 9, "Keeping the Substance in Motion.")

Our next task was to negotiate ground rules. I provided a hybrid draft developed from those used during past consensus processes which included various options for issues.

Among the options offered for the decision-making rule were:

> **Option A:** C-DAC will operate by consensus, meaning that agreements will be considered reached when there is no dissent by any member; and
>
> **Option B:** C-DAC will strive for a consensus on all issues related to the NPRM. Every effort will be made to reach a unanimous consensus, meaning that there is no dissent by any member. However, consensus will be considered reached when there is a no dissent by more than [one, two, three...] non-federal negotiators.

Although I expressed a strong preference for unanimous consent, C-DAC was reluctant to set the bar so high.

Its members decided to define consensus as an agreement among all members but two. The ground rules set out that OSHA had to be a party to the final consensus to make the eventual agreement actionable, since officially, C-DAC's final work product would be a recommendation to OSHA. This led to a rousing discussion of OSHA having greater power at the table than anyone else, which, of course, was exactly right. (See Appendix C for the C-DAC ground rules.)

Negotiating the ground rules served as a practice run for building consensus on substantive crane issues in that the team successfully negotiated a consensus text, though at this time, only on procedural issues. It illustrated how they would later approach issues that were meaningful to them, even as they discussed issues such as how to add a member to the committee if they determined an interest group was not represented. As a first step toward eliciting cooperative bonds, the discussion of the ground rules transcended assumptions about expected coalitions among the negotiators. For C-DAC, it also became an opportunity to illustrate and address power differentials among the parties at the table. (For more on the value and impact of negotiating ground rules, see Chapter 8, "Facing Polarization.")

As in most cases, the parties expressed little interest in process issues, so the preliminary meeting included a considerable amount of time focused on substantive issues. After the ground rules discussion, C-DAC reviewed and revised a draft list of all the issues that would be addressed in the new regulations. Upon clarifying and agreeing on the scope of the negotiations, C-DAC members began to workshop crane safety issues.

It quickly became clear that all the negotiators supported increased worker safety—from both social and business perspectives. All agreed with the premise that workers have a right to expect to return home safely after completing a shift. Union and industry representatives expressed strong support for regulations that protect workers and prevent accidents. Some crane business owners told stories of visiting their hospitalized workers after serious accidents. Representatives explained that crane accidents are costly, and with increased insurance costs many crane companies do not survive major accidents. In addition, regulations contribute to level playing fields among companies and clarify employer and worker responsibilities and liabilities. The challenge was to develop standards that would effectively protect workers while ensuring that increased costs to the industry contributed to that goal.

The C-DAC Members and Mediator Entry

The committee members were drawn from all over the country and all sectors of the crane world. Some already knew each other. Billy Smith represented the largest crane company in the country. Doug Williams, a crane company owner, and Chip Pocock, his safety expert, were from the same company but represented different trade associations. Rob

Weiss owned a crane company with his father in New York City. Emmet Russell represented a union, as did Frank Migliaccio, Dale Shoemaker, and Stephen Brown. Darlaine Taylor was vice president of her family's crane company, and the others told me she knew more about cranes than anyone. Brian Murphy and Craig Steele were from trade associations of building contractors that used cranes during construction. Joe Collins, David Ritchie, Stephen Charman, and Stephen Wiltshire were safety experts from different companies. Peter Juhren, Michael Brunet, and Bernie McGrew represented crane manufacturers. Larry Means was the wire rope expert, Wally Vega was from a power company, Chuck Yurio worked for an insurance company, and Doc Weaver represented electrical contractors. Noah Connell represented OSHA.

With a predominantly male negotiating team and a list of issues that included post-erection inspections, it wasn't too much of a surprise that they tested my ability to adapt to their culture.

At the second meeting I was managing my comfort level as the only woman at an otherwise all-male negotiating table (Darlaine was absent and Alexis had not yet joined my team), when I started calling names from a sheet listing members of the public who had signed up to comment on crane issues. After a few public comments, I called for Ben Dover but no one came forward. "Ben Dover? Is Mr. Dover here?" I asked. By that time, everyone in the room was roaring hysterically. Sensing my confusion, Billy leaned over to me and said, "I think they got you, Susan." Still not quite getting the "bend over" joke, I replied, "That reminds me of something in high school." I was actually thinking of a practical joke the guys in my physics class played on me, but it didn't matter. I'd made it through their hazing. I thought it was fair for them to test me. If I had been among them, I would also have wondered if a woman from Boston could survive in crane culture.

With a negotiating team that consisted of one woman and twenty-two men, the gender dynamics and crane culture norms forced me out of my own comfort zone to mediate the C-DAC reg neg. In retrospect, it seems that we had something of an unstated deal: They were playful and protected me from aggressive behavior; I helped them effectively articulate their ideas and protected against humiliation. It is often the little things that build relations between people and make bigger things possible.

I'll leave Ben Dover as the sole example of teasing although, believe me, with this group, there were others! I did, however, appreciate the protection. During the public comment period of a meeting with an ambitious agenda, I limited each speaker to five minutes, including questions from C-DAC members. One speaker rose and argued that he needed more than five minutes and that C-DAC members would have a lot of questions for him. After an aggressive back and forth with me—frankly, I didn't know what else I was going to do to enforce the five-minute rule—one of the crane fellows said, "And now you have four minutes." The public commenter spoke and no one asked a question. We moved onto the next speaker. Clearly, someone took him out to the proverbial woodshed after that because at a later meeting, he prefaced his public comments with a "thank you to the facilitator for her help to the industry."

Other interactions also contribute to the relations between mediator and committee members. One day we went to lunch at a Japanese restaurant. The waitress brought only chopsticks to the table. When I noticed a great discomfort in one of the C-DAC members, I asked the waitress for forks. He was relieved; I was happy to protect him from potential embarrassment. It was the same orientation I used throughout the negotiations in which every idea deserved respect, and no one was made to feel embarrassed by his contributions. The result was that everyone felt respected and had the comfort necessary to offer his or her thoughts and to be open to new ideas during discussions of complex problems.

In working with C-DAC, it seemed that I had found an available bandwidth for success as a woman in a predominantly male world. It required a combination of competence and playfulness. I'm not suggesting that mediators must play into traditional gender roles, but I'm sure I would have been ineffective if I had insisted on a certain political correctness that ignored obvious gender dynamics. Personally, I felt respected and appreciated for bringing skills to the table that C-DAC needed. As with all the other dynamics in the room, the mediator needs to assess, understand, track, and effectively manage them to maintain productive negotiations.

The Negotiations

Each of our eleven monthly meetings followed a formal agenda prepared and distributed prior to the negotiating session. Members of C-DAC intensively discussed each issue in an effort to reach conceptual agreements, and OSHA representatives drafted regulatory language to reflect their "agreements in concept." Committee members thoroughly reviewed and revised the draft regulatory language until they reached tentative agreements on each section of the text of the proposed standard. The issues were technically complex. The proposed regulations often required built-in flexibilities to ensure worker safety and provide efficiencies for employers, given the need to accommodate varied crane types, sizes, and configurations as well as unknown future technological advances.

C-DAC members had the intrinsic wisdom, knowledge, and expertise needed to prepare enforceable and cost-effective standards to protect workers with limited unintended consequences. In sponsoring the C-DAC reg neg, OSHA called into public service people from across the United States with the greatest expertise on crane issues and equipment types. The power of negotiated rulemaking—and the potential for civic fusion—is found in the deliberations of such people. No one person can know everything needed to develop complex rules, not even with support from a team of consultants. But twenty-three passionate people with differing perspectives can meld their ideas to become sufficiently unified to develop effective national standards.

During their deliberations, the negotiators were passionate and persistent on their critical issues, but they seemed naturally at ease with resolving conflict and worked hard to find solutions agreeable to all. For difficult issues, when conversations became repetitive and failed to produce new ideas, I moved the group onto the next issue. Sometimes C-DAC members resisted these transitions, but as we rounded back to previously discussed issues, they came to trust my instincts for managing an iterative flow of the discussions.

In addition to their expertise, each C-DAC member enhanced the negotiations. To name a few: Noah, the OSHA negotiator, offered an open-mindedness and willingness to learn about matters he was responsible for regulating, even as he insisted on meaningful actions to protect workers. Billy, who had worked as a crane operator, OSHA employee, and safety and labor manager for a large crane company, contributed his multiple perspectives to help reach closure on many issues. Emmet, a union representative, offered reasoned approaches after listening to long stretches of discussions. Peter was the trusted go-to-guy for all things related to tower cranes. Rob, always passionate, kept our focus on NYC's 5,000 crane operators, and his detailed review of every word of the regulatory text greatly improved the standards. Doug's southern charm kept us in good spirits, especially when some of us began to tire of Rob's unending passion. And Joe provided not only expertise, but side-splitting stories of his wild son and his $50 wedding held during our meeting in Las Vegas.

Members of the public also attended most or all of the meetings. Some of them participated on specialized work groups. They helped on subjects such as derricks, floating cranes, navy issues, safety devices, operator certification, and electrocution hazards.

Every single person on the committee brought something important to the discussions. Some talked a lot; some talked less, but the sum total of contributions of each C-DAC member, and the trust that developed among them, resulted in the civic fusion necessary to reach consensus on the proposed regulations that met their goal of increasing worker safety with limited unintended costs and consequences.

Substantive Issues

Many needs and complex dynamics emerged during the process. Here we'll discuss the negotiations of two key substantive issues: testing and verification, and operating near power lines. In Chapter 9, we'll introduce a third issue, crane operator certification, to explain how to manage substantive issues.

Testing and Verification Criteria for the Structural Adequacy of Crane Components

Testing and verification of prototype cranes, among the most contentious issues for the ACCSH crane work group, engendered passions within C-DAC as well. To comply with the existing U.S. standards, American crane manufacturers verify the weights that prototype cranes can hoist by physically testing numerous boom configurations using what are known as strain gauges. In essence, the crane is set up and loaded with weight according to established testing standard tables. The resultant stresses are then measured and the data are used to help formulate the allowable lifting loads of the crane. Its allowable weight is then calculated as a percentage of what it was able to safely lift. In contrast, the European CEN (Comité Européen de Normalisation, also known as the European Committee for Standardization) standards only require computer modeling to verify allowable lifting weights for prototype cranes.

The question facing C-DAC was not only what the U.S. government would require in its new rules for future cranes built by American manufacturers, but whether European crane manufacturers should be required to physically test their prototypes according to the same guidelines in order for their equipment to be used in the United States. Some thought European companies should be required to comply with U.S. standards to keep a level playing field with American manufacturers. Despite the obvious conflicting financial interests, C-DAC's focus had to remain on worker safety, and so its members had to answer the following questions: Is the American method inherently safer than the European method? Or, is the European method unsafe?

Some C-DAC members strongly believed that computer modeling could not ensure the same certainty, and therefore safety, as physical testing using strain gauges. Others rejected the suggestions that European cranes were less safe and reminded C-DAC members that a European crane was deployed to clear the wreckage of the tragic 1999 Big Blue crane collapse at the Milwaukee Brewers baseball stadium, in which an American crane fell over, killing three workers and causing hundreds of millions of dollars in property damage. Both sides were emotional, and neither knew the intricacies of the European standards or the methods used to comply with them.

To fill the informational void, OSHA invited Hans-Dieter Willim, chief design engineer of German-based Liebherr Werk Ehingen, one of the world's leading crane manufacturers, and Craig Percy, vice president of U.S.-based All Test and Inspection, Inc., a well-respected strain gauge testing company, to provide C-DAC with exhaustive tutorials on procedures for verifying crane designs. With charts and graphs, video and graphics, and lots of questions and answers, C-DAC learned about American and European standards. Importantly, Mr. Willim explained that his company actually strain gauge tested prototype cranes with certain critical boom configurations to verify its computer model results.

At the end of the day, C-DAC members agreed that as long as the computer models were verified with strain gauge testing, both U.S. and European methods protected workers and asked OSHA to draft regulatory text to allow cranes to be used in the United States that had been tested and verified according to either U.S. or verified CEN methods.

However, this didn't entirely resolve the issue. At a later meeting, C-DAC members raised the issue of Japanese-made cranes, which followed yet another standard. This posed another problem: No one knew what the Japanese standards required because they had never been translated into English! And then there were questions about Brazilian crane manufacturers. Finally, with the focus solidly on worker safety, all C-DAC members agreed that they had to protect against the situation that had arisen some years back when cranes manufactured in a country without crane regulations entered the U.S. market and caused multiple accidents. Ultimately, the regulation allowed for testing and verification in accordance with the U.S. and verified CEN standards for crane manufacturers worldwide. This decision illustrates the often-stated principle of consensus processes: Don't let the perfect get in the way of the good. C-DAC members realized they could reach consensus on testing and verification standards without accounting for *every* possible contingency. They remained focused on meeting their essential goal of worker safety.

Power Lines

The United Brotherhood of Carpenters and Joiners of America welcomed us to their training facility in Las Vegas. Our meeting there was devoted primarily to addressing the hazards of operating cranes and derricks near power lines. The issue is of considerable importance: From 1997 to 2003, contact with power lines caused 27 percent of crane and derrick-related deaths.[1]

After a general discussion of power line hazards, we opened the meeting for public comments. Speakers included manufacturers and users of safety devices such as insulating links and proximity warning devices. We learned of a variety of strategies and best practices used by others, as well as requests for more stringent regulations and enforcement from an insurance company.

We also heard from the parents of Rory Moore, a young man who died when he touched electrified rigging while working on a construction site. First, his father provided a detailed account of his son's accident and asked the committee to protect workers from similar accidents. Their attorney then provided a PowerPoint presentation about the accident, including video of a distraught crane operator as he cried throughout his deposition. It was harrowing. Next, Rory's mother passed around a large framed photo of her son and, through her tears, described the pain she'd endured since her son's death. She asked the committee to help her find meaning in her son's death by requiring insulated links on all cranes.

It was heart-wrenching. It was 3:30 p.m., and though we had a full agenda of issues to discuss, we decided to call it a day. It was best to start fresh in the morning. Hearing about Rory Moore's death focused C-DAC and made its mission to protect workers tangible. It also made it inappropriate in that moment to engage in tedious discussions of various regulatory options.

With a fresh start in the morning, C-DAC members discussed the problems that contributed to electrocution accidents: operators may not see the power lines, may forget where they are or misjudge the distance;

---

1. J. E. Beavers, J. R. Moore, R. Rinehart, and W. R. Schriver, "Crane-Related Fatalities in the Construction Industry," *Journal of Construction Engineering and Management* (September 2006).

the boom may drift further than planned; time pressures may force operators to skip preplanning steps or push the envelope on proximity to power lines; or owners of power lines may not provide the requested information or assistance.

C-DAC discussed the latest safety devices, their effectiveness, and their potential to reduce operator awareness of hazards. They talked about the risks of various scenarios, such as working in the dark, traveling while lifting, and working under power lines.

The issue was both technically complicated and emotionally laden, although there was an indisputable consensus for protecting workers from power line contact deaths and injuries. Employer representatives were willing to invest resources but wanted to be sure that the required strategies effectively reduced worker risk. Furthermore, it was clear that no single strategy would work for all situations. C-DAC members needed to deconstruct power line scenarios to build an effective, multilayered approach to improve worker safety.

Ultimately, C-DAC decided to frame its power line discussions on eliminating hazards, avoiding hazards, and protecting against injury from contact. By the end of the meeting, they reached agreements in concept on the structure of the power lines section of the regulation. The negotiators agreed to think in terms of three zones: red zone for work areas where contact with power lines is likely or possible; yellow zone for work areas outside the red zone but in which there is potential for entry into the red zone; and green zone for work areas with no power lines nearby. Actual distances from power lines eventually replaced the colors.

In the rule, some actions are always required; others are dependent on the zone. In all instances, prior to initiating any crane activity, employers must determine proximity to power lines to determine the zone their workers will be in. In a green zone, for example, when power lines are underground, no additional actions are necessary. In the yellow and red zones, initial actions, such as determining the voltage of the lines, clearly marking the power lines overhead, and creating readily visible boundaries near the ground to identify the location of overhead power lines are mandatory. Additional safety measures are required within each zone. To comply with those requirements, the employer may select from a menu of strategies to create a multiple layering of safety features that when combined, identify the hazards, reduce the likelihood of contact, and protect workers if contact is made.

This agreement structure differentiated hazard levels and provided flexibility for accommodating different construction sites, crane configurations, and employer choices among available technologies. It increased support for the use of safety devices such as insulating links and proximity alarms. It also accounted for strategies to prevent contact with power lines as well as to protect workers if contact with the power lines occurs. Finally, the multilayered security scheme accounted for the possibility of human error and safety device failure by providing safety redundancies.

Close to Chaos in Las Vegas

In a room filled with active and potential conflict, I try to provide a calm and safe environment. To do that, however, I need to be at ease. Unfortunately, the swirling world of Las Vegas threw me off, so it wasn't a surprise when what felt like an attempted mutiny arose the third day. Although C-DAC had completed its initial discussions of most of the issues included in the scope of the negotiations, because of other responsibilities at OSHA, Noah's team had not yet produced draft regulatory text reflecting those discussions. Some members feared that all the work from their previous meetings had been lost and that we'd never complete our work in the one year allotted.

Noah caught wind of the flaring tempers during lunch break and told me what he had been hearing. Instead of reconvening at our planned time, Noah and I worked to develop a strategy for managing the strong emotions we knew were headed our way. The half hour we spent strategizing further enraged some C-DAC members who thought we were wasting their time.

When we called everyone back into the meeting room, tempers were high. I was met with severe anger. Some people tried to calm things, but their voices were outnumbered, and even they seemed to quietly question the veracity of the process.

As we had planned, Noah talked about his team's extensive notes for each issue C-DAC had discussed and the time frame for developing the draft regulatory text. He assured them that nothing would be lost and that his team would have the draft reg text available before we finished our initial review of all the issues. As planned, I asked Noah if it would be possible to get some of the regulatory text out to C-DAC before the next meeting to put participants at ease. Noah obliged. At the same time, I put up a slide of the original process map I used during my overview of negotiated rulemaking at our first meeting. I calmly showed them on the map what we had done and what was coming next. As I was doing so, Doc, an eighty-something-year-old, who brought an elder's charm to the group, said in his lovable way, "Now why didn't you tell us that before?" The tension was broken and everyone followed Doc's lead, which suggested we were right on track. To firm up C-DAC's comfort level, we also developed a schedule for completing our initial review of the remaining issues and an agenda for the next meeting that included regulatory text review.

I've thought a lot about that hour: It was the closest I'd ever come to losing a group to chaos. I regretted skipping the usual social time the night before. If I hadn't, I may have been able to address the concerns before they snowballed. We also should have had the draft regulatory text to the group earlier. It is reasonable for people to grow concerned about working hard with no results. Their fears threatened to move them outside the boundaries of their bonds. However, the dynamic leadership of the group, which allowed different people to take up the mantle of leader to guide the group through varied obstacles and the trust they had built, pulled the group back from the brink of chaotic disaggregation.

To sustain civic fusion, a public policy mediator must continually track the emotional comfort of the committee members. It's also critical to meet or exceed their expectations. In this case, that meant, to the extent possible, maintaining the same level of contact with committee members at each meeting, regardless of venue changes or inconvenience. For C-DAC, that meant being available for sidebar meetings, social events, and conversations well beyond the usual workday hours. I'd always enjoyed the social time anyway, but after Las Vegas, I made sure to never again miss going out for beers on the second night of each meeting.

Reaching Consensus

For one year, the committee had collectively grappled with complicated, divisive issues and worked through the nuances of various options. They clarified potential regulatory ambiguities and considered information provided in panels and in dozens of public comments. For difficult issues, we held work group meetings and conference calls between meetings and created proposals and counter-proposals until enough agreement emerged to reflect the prevailing sentiments of most committee members. Noah and his team turned C-DAC discussions into draft regulatory text, which members revised and refined into tentative agreements. C-DAC members consistently consulted with their constituents to receive input on new proposals and to educate them about the negotiations.

At the final meeting, eight subissues were outstanding. All but those related to operator certification required minimal attention. At least a dozen members of the public offered comments on the remaining issues. After a great deal of discussion, to accommodate concerns about a limited national capacity for certifying crane operators, C-DAC members agreed to provide a four-year phase-in period for crane operator certification. In addition, they developed alternative options for crane operator testing that allows employers to establish qualification programs that must be evaluated by a certified auditor. A provision was also made for the U.S. military to qualify operators and for government entities to license crane operators under specified circumstances. They rejected a proposal to allow for certification by an accredited educational institution or program.

All but two nonfederal negotiators agreed to the revised version of crane operator certification testing provisions. According to the C-DAC's agreed-upon ground rules, this met their definition of consensus. All other issues were agreed to unanimously.

With no dissent on turning all their prior tentative agreements into a final consensus agreement, C-DAC reached final consensus on all issues subject to negotiations. However, it would take more than six years and strong commitment and actions from C-DAC for the rule to become the law of the land. (For more on that, see Chapter 13, "Owning the Future.")

CHAPTER 5

THE ABORTION TALKS

Introduction

Amidst raging culture wars and calls of justifiable homicide, John Salvi, a self-proclaimed pro-life advocate, opened fire on two women's health clinics in Brookline, Massachusetts. He killed the receptionists and wounded five others. That evening in an anteroom of a television studio, Fran Hogan, president of Women Affirming Life, Inc., and Nicki Nichols Gamble, president of Planned Parenthood League of Massachusetts, who had lost a staff member that day, sat silently near each other as they waited to be called into the studio for their live interviews.

Within days, pro-choice supporter Governor William Weld and Boston Archbishop Cardinal Bernard Law issued a joint call for common ground talks—whatever that meant.

Just weeks before the shootings, I had met with Laura Chasin, executive director of the Public Conversations Project (PCP), to discuss her interest in the Chelsea Charter Consensus Process. Laura said that PCP had designed a novel approach to citizen dialogue on contentious issues and had piloted it with single three-hour sessions on the issue of abortion. Upon seeing Nicki quoted in the newspaper as saying she would only participate in the talks if they were professionally mediated, I called Laura.

We decided that our complementary skills made us a good team, particularly because we didn't know if the talks would focus on dialogue or consensus. Laura had experience designing and facilitating abortion dialogues. I had experience mediating consensus processes among representative leaders, and I had facilitated dialogues, though in the context of the Israeli–Palestinian conflict, not abortion.

With a nod from the governor's office, we initiated an intensive assessment to determine the feasibility of proceeding with and possible parameters for the talks. As extremists vehemently opposed the talks, Laura and I set out our first principle: Do no harm. I took that to mean that no one should get killed or injured because of the talks. At the time there was a palpable fear from people who threatened to harm anyone who would dare meet "with the devil."

The Assessment

With a blank slate, Laura and I considered the form the talks might take, the people we should interview, and the format of those interviews. We sought to identify achievable goals and possible participants, and maintained a willingness to abandon our effort if we determined there was too great a risk in moving it forward.

We had no idea what product would result from the talks although many assumed "common ground" might result in a set of agreed-upon policies. The governor's office furnished us with a list of possible topics including adoption, contraception, childhood poverty, prenatal care, and child abuse. We introduced the possibility of dialogue as an effort to humanize perceived adversaries by creating a safe environment for people to explore complexities and the values that inform their positions on the issue of abortion. Neither of us was comfortable with the term *common ground,* which seemed to point to a need to converge on similarities as opposed to respecting and maintaining differences. We opted instead for the more open-ended term *talks*.

We assembled an initial list of interviewees from known mainstream pro-life and pro-choice leaders. With each conversation, we added categories of stakeholders and names of new potential participants to our list. By the end of the assessment, we had spoken with more than twenty leaders across the spectrum of abortion-related issues. Over multiple conversations, activists, religious leaders, politicians, and representatives of related women's organizations explained what people expected and wanted, as well as their fears and hopes. From the interviewees, we identified goals and concerns about the talks and possible participants.

In our initial introductions with each interviewee, we made explicit our past positions on abortion. I told of my past membership in the National Organization of Women and of my participation at a pro-choice demonstration in Washington, D.C. Laura also told of her past associations with the pro-choice movement. I introduced myself as solidly pro-choice; Laura felt uncomfortable with either label as her understandings were evolving. We both knew we might need to find a pro-life facilitator for the talks.

As with all assessment interviews, we aimed to hear the narratives of each individual. We used a set of questions to guide the conversations, including:

- How do you generally feel about the convening of a dialogue of leaders of the pro-choice and pro-life movements?
- What is currently going on in your organization?
- What are your concerns about such a dialogue being initiated?
- What would you like to see members of a discussion group accomplish?
- What do you think are the obstacles to reaching your goals?
- What could these discussions contribute to the overall situation?
- Do you speak as an individual or as a representative of the organization you head?

- What conflicts do you see surrounding the dilemma of personal or organizational participation?
- On an organizational level, what would you need to do to participate and contribute to achieving the goals of the talks?
- Who should be involved? With whom should we speak?

The interviews were stressful. We conducted them in the context of fear and threats. Leaders of the pro-choice movement were in shock and reeling from the recent killings and their heightened sense of personal vulnerability. They were also angry about the shootings and believed the governor and the cardinal had politicized the incident.

The pro-life side was shocked that a pro-life person would kill. Still, the movement was split about participating in the publicly called for "common ground" talks, particularly in light of the cardinal's call for a moratorium on clinic demonstrations. One pro-life interviewee played us the hateful and rhetorically violent voice-mail message of Operation Rescue (OR) to illustrate the anger within parts of the movement and to show us what they were up against. The recorded message spoke about traitors to the movement sitting with the devil in common ground talks. At the same time, some pro-life activists wanted to reassert their humanity, and others wanted to break the stereotype of the crazed male pro-lifer.

Interviewees suggested the talks should go beyond the surface, "de-demonize" people, and develop a community of mutual respect. Some recommended meetings to promote ways of framing the issue to appreciate diverse moral and religious perspectives, create constructive changes in the public rhetoric, and help people understand that holding prayer vigils near clinic entrances, targeting doctors' homes, harassing people, and calling people murderers lead marginal people to believe they are doing a service to society by killing. Others advised that to build relationships and reduce the violence of the public rhetoric, the two sides would need to work together on a project, for example, to reduce unwanted pregnancies, make adoption easier, or prepare a joint press release for the anniversary of the shootings.

Within the interviews, we introduced the idea of setting terms of participation, which led some to suggest making the talks off the record, keeping the talks confidential, setting clear ground rules, providing professional facilitation, working with leaders or "people who count and can make a difference," and establishing a clear schedule of meetings.

From both sides, interviewees expressed a number of shared concerns. Many were worried about the potential for dividing their movement by participating in the talks. Some worried about an inability to keep the talks confidential, particularly given intense media interest. Others were concerned that the other side would be disrespectful or hurtful. Still others worried about draining energy away from their core organizational objectives. Within these commonalities, Laura and I saw the potential for productive talks. Some were later turned into principles of participation and others became topics for discussion.

To Interview or Not to Interview

During the assessment interviews, the question arose of whether we should interview a representative of Operation Rescue (OR), which at the time was considered extreme among the pro-life groups. OR had publicly expressed its vehement opposition to the talks.

My usual practice of speaking with individuals of varied opinions within each category of stakeholders suggested that we should contact OR. Yet, I was conflicted. I felt certain they would not participate in the talks, and I worried that having information about the talks would provoke OR to sabotage. It was also becoming clear that the talks would need to be confidential, in part because of threats others thought were coming from OR. Some refused to participate if OR was present at the talks.

To supplement my own thinking, I called a number of colleagues for their thoughts and expertise. Some reminded me of the principle of talking to everyone. Some suggested including the extremes in an effort to strengthen the moderates by reducing the impact of the extremes.

Two opinions weighed heavily on my mind. Howard Bellman advised that when convening a negotiated rulemaking [or other consensus process] there is the legal and theoretical notion "leave no stone unturned" with regard to identifying stakeholders. The reason for this is because the consensus that emerges will be an act of government, and interest groups may file lawsuits if they are not satisfied with the rule. Thus, in a negotiated rulemaking, the "leave no stone unturned" construct is requisite for an actionable agreement.

On the other hand, Howard suggested, the talks were expected to rely on informal associations among individuals. Any group that does not participate is simply not a party to the discussion; they cannot block private actions that members of the group may decide to take. Thus, he felt it was not necessary to include Operation Rescue given our general concerns about the potential harm OR could cause if informed of the dialogue at its earliest stages. Howard likened this situation to work he did with the AIDS community in relation to a group that had threatened and acted against members of other participating groups and so was left off the list of invitees.

I spoke with another colleague who worked at a think tank and was a former U.S. State Department official involved in Israeli-Palestinian negotiations. His inclination was to make a genuine effort to have some kind of contact with OR. He said he would always make such an overture toward any significant player with the thought that by remaining open, he might learn something. He suggested that since we were unlikely to invite OR to participate in the talks, we could keep the next steps of the process ambiguous and talk only about the exploration we were undertaking.

He said this was similar to his work on the Israeli-Palestinian conflict at the State Department during the 1970s. As a government official, he was restrained by policy from talking with the Palestinian Liberation Organization (PLO), but when he left government, he had a lot of contact with the PLO. (Hamas did not exist at the time.)

In the end, Laura and I agreed not to contact OR. We decided the potential damage it could cause outweighed the potential benefits we might gain. I was comfortable with the justification Howard had provided for refining the "no stone unturned" principle. The question of interviewing OR surfaced a key difference between dialogue and mediation, and our decision seemed to suggest the talks were moving in the direction of a conversation and not an outcome-based process.

Preparing for the Talks

Amid a swirl of hope and threats, we determined to hold secret talks with six women, who were all willing and available to meet for four 4-hour meetings over a one-month period.

We had already learned that Fran was ready to act to reclaim her humanity that she felt she'd lost after failing to approach Nicki at the TV studio the night of the shootings. And we knew that Nicki was motivated to participate to help revive her lost sense of security. The four other women were eager if somewhat fearful to meet the other side.

Criteria for Selecting Participants for the Talks

In considering who should meet for the talks, Laura and I hoped to identify people who really wanted to participate and had some commitment to learning about the other side. From many of the interviewees, we heard that an ability to maintain confidentiality, particularly in light of the great media interest, was essential. We believed the talks would be most beneficial if the participants felt free to fully explore new thoughts and ideas and did not feel constrained by a hierarchical relationship within their organizations or with another participant. Ideally, the participants would have a willingness and capacity to consider multiple interpretations of one idea, and, of course, the group would need to be balanced among the various perspectives on the issue of abortion.

Criteria for Facilitators

Although Laura and I both very much wanted to serve as the facilitators, we understood that the participants had the final say over who would serve in that role. Based on our past experiences and the assessment findings, we offered them criteria for selecting facilitators. We suggested that the facilitators should have a demonstrated ability to manage an interactive process competently, even-handedly, fairly, and without bias; a demonstrated ability to refrain from taking positions on the substance of an issue; not previously taken a public stand on the issue of abortion, where public stand was defined as making speeches, publishing articles, or signing public advertisements or documents supporting one side; served on a board of, or been employed by, an organization whose mission makes it a partisan in the U.S. abortion controversy. Of course, the facilitators would also need to be able to maintain confidentiality of the talks and be acceptable to all participants.

Despite the fact that Laura and I had both openly stated our past affiliations with the pro-choice movement, the participants felt comfortable with us as the team. (During the interview process, Laura learned that a board she served on was considered negatively by the pro-life participants. The organization was considered related to the issue, and Laura resigned from that board prior to the talks.) Whereas we had some expectation of a need for a facilitation team reflecting both pro-life and pro-choice stances, it appears that the trust Laura and I had built during the assessment phase made it unnecessary. The participants viewed us as process professionals and not as activists.

Goals

Based on the assessment, Laura and I developed possible goals for the talks. During consultations with us prior to the first meeting, the participants revised our draft into an agreed-upon set of goals. They were to

- Develop relations built on mutual respect and understanding that can contain differences about values and policies;
- Clarify differences and identify shared values and concerns;
- Help de-escalate the polarization among pro-life and pro-choice groups in Massachusetts;
- Exchange information on matters of mutual concern;
- Create channels of communications with leaders on the other side; and
- Identify possible joint activities.

The Participants

We had expected to have a larger and mixed-gender group, but scheduling ultimately had the last word. Laura and I decided that if we didn't get the talks started within nine months of the shooting, the effort would fizzle out. We decided to convene the talks with three women from each side.

The participants included the following:

- The Rev. Anne Fowler, then rector of St. John's Episcopal Church in Jamaica Plain and a past member of the board of directors, Planned Parenthood League of Massachusetts, and the board of the Religious Coalition for Reproductive Choice.
- Nicki Nichols Gamble, then president and CEO of the Planned Parenthood League of Massachusetts from 1974 to 1999. She was also a director of the Center for Reproductive Law and Policy and of IPAS, an international women's reproductive health care organization, and a volunteer for the Planned Parenthood Federation of America.
- Frances X. Hogan, a partner at the law firm of Lyne, Woodworth & Evarts, president of Women Affirming Life, Inc., and consultant to the Pro-Life Committee of the National Conference of Catholic Bishops.
- Melissa Kogut, then executive director of the Massachusetts affiliate of the National Abortion and Reproductive Rights Action League.
- Madeline McComish, a chemist, then president of Massachusetts Citizens for Life, chairman of the north suburban chapter of Massachusetts Citizens for Life.
- Barbara Thorp, then director of the Pro-Life Office of the Archdiocese of Boston and an executive board member of the National Office of Post-Abortion Reconciliation and Healing, the National Committee for a Human Life Amendment, and Women Affirming Life, Inc.

Prior to the first meeting, we asked all the participants to sign terms of participation. They covered the following issues: status of participants, confidentiality, communication, attendance, decision making, responsibilities of the facilitators, and record of the sessions. Perhaps most important, was absolute confidentiality. All agreed that even the fact that the meetings were being held was to be kept confidential and that only with a consensus of all the participants would this change.

Information about the talks was to be shared only with an approved list of people. Somehow, perhaps remarkably, even before they physically met, the participants trusted the others to keep their promises.

The Talks

After committing to four meetings over a one-month period, we began the talks. Never in our wildest dreams did we expect our secret talks would continue for almost six years and lead to the publication of a consensus article in the *Boston Globe.*

The earliest phases comprised a great exploration. The women discussed similarities and differences, substantive issues, and even the challenges of movement leaders. The middle years evolved into quarterly, relationship-sustaining meetings after they abandoned their initial effort to go public. The last phase of the meetings commenced with the decision to go public, and after agreeing that a joint article was the best vehicle for doing so, we spent our time together preparing the article.

Throughout the talks, the participating women spoke of being intellectually and spiritually stretched as a result of deep conversations with people of differing opinions. They observed that socializing primarily with those with whom they agree—rather than being with the "other side"—provides little opportunity for learning, even about their own positions.

The talks brought the participating women, originally polarized by their passionate beliefs, close enough together to unify for positive action. Their civic fusion resulted in actions that reduced the threat of activist violence in Massachusetts. It emotionally moved the people who witnessed it—from the worldwide readers of the joint article to those who attended their lectures and media events.

Civic fusion reached its zenith when we talked about highly divisive issues. Their passion intact, the leaders spoke with clarity and precision. They worked to understand each other. They asked questions and clarified any misunderstood phrases and concepts. And then they would get to the abyss—the deep, vast gap neither side could cross—and all would light up. I remember in those moments that I would look around the room and everyone looked beautiful. The abyss was painful because it was unbridgeable, but their civic fusion, rooted in deep respect and even love for each other, was sustained by their passion. For all of the participants, their beliefs about abortion are central to their sense of the world: The absolute truth that protects a child from the moment of conception and the absolute right of a woman to make her own choices about her body.

There was no way to overcome this central difference. And the more it glowed, the stronger the force that kept them together. When we finished the conversation and the dynamic passed, we all knew we had been somewhere usually out of reach. Some called it sacred; others called it mysterious. Now I describe it as civic fusion.

Getting to Know You—The First Meeting Series

When the six women who led the pro-life and pro-choice movements in Massachusetts sat together for the first time, it was with a great deal of both fear and hope. The pro-life participants prayed together just before the meeting.

From the assessment interviews, Laura and I knew that all the participants agreed that killing born people at health clinics is morally reprehensible. We designed the first meeting, in part, to surface this unifying connection because we expected it would give us an opening to gently coax the leaders to a sustained curiosity about the other.

The agenda focused on building relationships and identifying differences and similarities among the participants. We spoke briefly about a joint project. We talked about hopes and fears for the talks, the life experiences that had rooted their passions on the abortion issue, and how the shootings had affected them.

Each spoke when she was ready, what we called "popcorn style," rather than in a more formal circle around the table. We created metaphorical "bins" for noting subjects for later discussions. And we had an "ouch rule," which rerouted the conversation if a comment felt like a sharp jab.

We used many listening and anti-stereotyping exercises to improve the women's ability to listen to and hear each other, to create a sense of curiosity about the other, and to move the discussion of abortion beyond slogans to deeper understandings of similarities and differences.

My favorite was the hot button exercise. To start, we asked the participants to list every word and phrase of the abortion debate sloganeering that shut down anyone's ability to listen to the next word. These included murderer, justifiable homicide, anti-choice, fetus, pro-life, unborn child, products of conception. That was the easy part of the exercise. Then we asked the leaders to discuss the issue of abortion without using any of the words that were listed on sheets of newsprint that covered the windowless walls.

It wasn't easy. The women caught each other whenever someone pressed a "hot button." There was a lot of laughter as they all struggled to make their points without using their value-laden buzzwords. They came to realize they had been speaking in code. Many simple words—fetus, unborn child—were actually shorthand expressions for complex positions and moral judgments.

The need to discuss abortion without familiar terms forced the parties to explain themselves in new ways. They began to ask questions of themselves and to hear the "other side."

We negotiated a working vocabulary. For example, the words *fetus* and *products of conception* felt too clinical to the pro-life leaders. For the pro-choice leaders, *unborn child* incorporated the belief that life begins at conception or, at least, that what is growing inside a pregnant woman is a complete being. With reluctant consent, the group settled on *human fetus.*

During a de-stereotyping exercise, pro-life participants talked about their frustration of being characterized as religious fanatics taking orders from men, or as being indifferent to women in crisis and born children. The pro-choice members described their outrage at being called femiNazis and murderers and at the linking of abortions to genocide.

In keeping to their goals, the leaders considered the possibility of a joint project on adoption, helping teens with babies, sex education, or getting welfare benefits for single mothers. The ideas generated little energy. After some discussion, most of the participants considered such activities to be a distraction from their core missions related to abortion and noted that other groups were already doing this type of work. With a bit of annoyance, someone suggested that the governor and cardinal could devote more of their resources to such issues. With little effort, we achieved our goal of considering a joint project, even though this was rejected. Some people might be surprised at how quickly a lack of interest surfaced.

Between each of the meetings, Laura and I spoke with each of the leaders at least once. Although at the outset we had assumed the talks would end after the four meetings, we knew from our one-on-one conversations that all wanted to continue. We spent part of the fourth meeting reaching agreement on the basis for the next set of meetings. Over our years together, this became part of the routine for our last planned meeting.

In later meetings, the participants discussed substantive issues to deepen their understandings of their similarities and differences. They talked about the issues of partial birth abortions/bans on certain abortion procedures, and on the impact of abortions on women's physical and emotional health. They talked about feminism, women's rights, when life begins, the death penalty, euthanasia, sex education, and contraception. To support their conversations, both sides sometimes exchanged substantive information and research findings with each other.

At one meeting, they discussed the challenges of leadership during a protracted conflict—an area of common interest among the whole group. Although group members were on opposing sides of the abortion issue, their organizational dynamics had similarities. More than once during these discussions, the participants noted that others in their movements would have been shocked if they had known that their leaders were discussing organizational strategy with the other side!

The Need to Surface Differing Worldviews

As the meetings continued, a clash of worldviews emerged. Pro-life leaders explained that abortion is a mortal sin, thereby potentially condemning one to hell for eternity. With great exasperation a pro-choice leader asked why they weren't out there protecting women from damnation by aggressively promoting contraception. When they explained they were also opposed to contraception, the pro-choice leader was shocked. She was at a complete loss for understanding.

In that moment, I understood that in addition to the lack of a common vocabulary, their communications were constrained by their differing mindsets—their overall context of making sense of the world—within which are embedded assumptions of deeply held truths. As Catholics, the pro-life leaders view abortion, premarital sex, and contraception through the lens of an integrated religious framework. At least some of the pro-choice leaders would not deepen their understandings of the pro-life participants perspectives without comprehending their context or worldview.[1] (For more on creating space for not knowing, see Chapter 10.)

Uncovering, articulating, and understanding the worldviews of the pro-choice and pro-life leaders became the focus of the talks until we conquered that challenge. Laura and I asked each side to work together before the next meeting to write a couple of paragraphs describing their worldviews. Not surprisingly, this was a simple exercise for the pro-life side. They all agree that there is one universal truth and that truth informs their understanding of the issues of abortion and human sexuality. The pro-choice side, on the other hand, was seriously stymied by this exercise. They realized that they each came to the issue from a range of values and a cognizance of the complexity of life, relationships, and choices. Articulating these worldviews, which were eventually included as sidebars to the consensus article, enabled more productive communications and a deeper understanding of differences. (Their worldviews can be found in Chapter 10.)

---

1. Though pro-choice, I shared with the pro-life leaders a commitment to a faith-based life. My faith led me to a different answer to the question of abortion, but my considerations had similar roots in a faith-based infrastructure. The same could be said of the pro-choice minister in the group, although there was a bit of religiously based antagonism between her and the pro-life participants. I think the pro-life parties saw me as something of a fellow traveler even though I came from a different religious path. I'm sure that it enabled me to see the clash of worldviews and move to deviate from the planned scope of the meetings to clarify those worldviews.

Structure of the Meetings

After the first year or so, the meetings fell into a regular pattern. We began with a general update from each person, discussed a previously selected substantive issue, shared a meal, and ended with descriptive metaphors. With Laura and me at the head of the table, we sat the leaders between people with the opposing view.

Each series of meetings provided opportunities for observing, plateaus for resting comfortably, steady paths for forward progress, and occasional peaks to climb. The meetings were carefully designed to put everyone at ease and to foster productive conversations. The talks required difficult and complicated thought processes on the part of the leaders. They became open to learning about ideas they found reprehensible and to people they considered seriously misguided. In essence, by coming close enough together, they overcame their polarization and unified with their passionately held values and beliefs intact.

Before and after each meeting, Laura and I together spoke with each participant. We learned how they experienced the previous meeting, what had worked particularly well, and what had raised concerns. We queried their hopes and fears for the upcoming meeting, gauged the substantive issues of interest, and asked what was going on in their lives personally that related to the talks as well as within their movements.

Armed with that information, as well as knowing the terms for the next series of meetings, sometimes together, sometimes apart, Laura and I would develop the agenda for the next meeting. To design a meeting, I listed the substantive areas to address. Then, as I considered the dynamics of and among the parties, I would stare out my office window and visualize the meeting—not every specific comment, but the flow and energy of the meeting—and from these images, I drafted an agenda. I would repeat this until in my mind, the meeting flowed evenly and steadily. Fortunately, Laura had a similar capacity for "seeing" the meeting in this way. As a result, together we revised each meeting agenda until our visions were aligned.

I prepared in a similar way just before each meeting. With the agenda in front of me, I wrote out how to begin each agenda item and what I needed to remember about it. It usually took a few handwritten drafts to get the flow right. This exercise gave me the steadiness I needed to go into a meeting. Ultimately, most meetings require a mediator to think on her feet; the process design, the visualized meeting design, and the preparation get you ready for the spontaneity of the moment.[2]

The Metaphors

Every meeting ended with each participant offering metaphors that expressed their sense of the meeting. These metaphors gave Laura and me a shorthand way of understanding the meeting dynamics and results. Here are some examples:

- A tree with roots potted separately—deep down its roots are apart—but there is something we share.
- We are standing on holy ground.
- Stormy seas, we are in our boats, we see each other and wave.
- An old, very thick tree in a major storm. The lightning and storm are wracking it. It's not a young tree that can bend in the wind. Will it survive the storm?
- People leaning over a gulf trying to bridge it—trying to reach across with their hands.
- A crystal. When the light hits it, it goes off in many directions. I see this group as having the potential of spreading much light.
- A bird flying over an open ocean—carefree, beautiful, soaring. Then the bird starts to get anxious because she doesn't see any place to land.
- Image of the holocaust memorial behind Notre Dame in Paris. A long dark corridor with one candle at the end. This group for me is that candle. I dream we are part of the turning of the tide.
- Weaving. We have all been weaving a strand and we have the challenge and the gift to weave the strands together into a new product.

---

2. For more on this dynamic, see Howard Bellman, "Improvisation, Mediation, and All That Jazz," *Negotiation Journal*, vol. 22, no. 3 (July 2006).

You can sense in these metaphors the tensions between hope and fear. In the safety of a windowless room, the group members came to care deeply for each other as they developed an awareness of their differences, and a sense that their time together might have an impact beyond the change it created in their own lives.

Taking It Out of the Room

During the first year of the talks, the leaders gave serious consideration to "taking it out of the room." That was our code for going public with the talks. They discussed their concerns and fears, expected reactions, and possible vehicles they might use.

Many of the leaders, particularly on the pro-life side, expressed a great deal of fear of being misunderstood by others in their movement. They were worried about being branded as traitors or accused of accepting moral relativity, meaning reducing their clarity and commitment to a universal truth. And they were worried about causing a split in the movement, as some supported them and others rejected their efforts.

When a consensus emerged to go public two years into the talks, we discussed how to do so. We talked about a point-counterpoint or a consensus article. We considered a book and a film, and even invited an author and a filmmaker to a meeting to discuss the possibilities. The leaders also consulted someone who had been involved in a public abortion dialogue in another state, to discuss the implications of going public.

After a few months of planning, one of the participants decided that the conditions were not right for her to go public, based on internal conflicts within her organization. Some were relieved, others very disappointed, but their prior commitment to go public only with unanimous consent was sustained.

We shifted to meeting quarterly to remain in contact and maintain the possibility that future conditions would allow the group to make their talks public. The participants agreed to loosen the confidentiality constraints to allow them to speak publicly of their personal experiences in the talks while protecting the identities of the other participants. The meetings were designed around substance, often relative to the current issues of the time. Sometimes the majority of the meeting was taken up with the initial go round of what was happening in people's lives. We shared births and deaths, illnesses, challenges, trips, and changes.

About two years into the quarterly meetings, the discussions turned again to going public. The situation that had prevented the participants from doing so in the past had been resolved and a great deal of excitement emerged around the power of sharing their experiences with the public. Again, the leaders checked in with their boards and superiors. With a green light from all, they decided to go public with a jointly written article. Over a period of six months, and with the help of a former journalist, we drafted the article, which was published by the *Boston Globe* under the headline, "Talking with the Enemy." (See Appendix A for the article.)

In it, the participants described their experience of respectful discourse among people with deep value differences:

These conversations revealed a deep divide. We saw that our differences on abortion reflect two worldviews that are irreconcilable. If this is true, then why do we continue to meet? First, because when we face our opponent, we see her dignity and goodness. Embracing this apparent contradiction stretches us spiritually. We've experienced something radical and life-altering that we describe in nonpolitical terms: "the mystery of love," "holy ground," or simply, "mysterious." We continue because we are stretched intellectually, as well. This has been a rare opportunity to engage in sustained, candid conversations about serious moral disagreements. It has made our thinking sharper and our language more precise.

During negotiations over wording of the article, the pro-life leaders suggested including separate worldview descriptions alongside the consensus article to make clear their sustained differing values and beliefs for readers and their movements. The pro-choice activists agreed to do so.

Among the many challenges of writing the article was a mutual claim to the Declaration of Independence. Originally, the pro-life leaders cited it in their worldview sidebar as their core belief in an inalienable and self-evident right to life. The pro-choice participants objected because their side quoted it to support their claim to the right to life, liberty, and the pursuit of happiness. Ultimately, neither side mentioned it in its worldview sidebar. Instead, we described the episode as an example of their deep divide in the consensus article.

After discussing how to roll out the article, the group agreed to hold a joint press conference on the Monday after the article appeared in the *Sunday Boston Globe.* We sent out a press release and wondered if anyone would show up.

The Press Conference

We were shocked to find the room filled with journalists and camera crews from all the major networks. Even more shocking was the reaction from seasoned journalists. One cameraman thanked us for "doing this," as his eyes filled with tears. Having kept the talks secret for so long, we were not prepared for the reaction.

Emails from around the world, media requests, and invitations to speak at universities poured in. The great majority of people we heard from told of being inspired by the talks. They spoke of finding the courage to have difficult conversations that they had avoided in the past, including with family members.

The group received numerous requests for speaking engagements, radio interviews, and television appearances. Some media invitations expressed an appreciation for the innovative way to cover the issue of abortion rather than the same old angry debate.

After the article was published, we continued to meet to discuss public events and later, to check in with each other. We still meet occasionally, when someone suggests or requests we do so, often to support someone through a difficult life event.

Mediator Challenges

To say that my ability to sustain a safe, open, nonjudgmental space was tested, as that space was filled by passionate discussions of pro-life and pro-choice leaders, is an understatement. In the end, however, I believe my capacity to serve as a professional mediator expanded. In most of my cases, I do not have strong opinions on the substantive issues under discussion, but like most Americans, I do have strong and passionate views on the issue of abortion. To function effectively during the talks, I needed to self-manage stronger emotions and reactions than typically arise in my other projects.

As a mediator, my orientation is to create deliberative space to enable otherwise unlikely conversations among people who are passionate about an issue, who have spent a great deal of their lives living the issue, and most importantly, are in positions of power to act in favor of improving the status quo. In this capacity, I recognize that my passions and opinions are less than useless in the discussion; in fact, they can be detrimental.

In support of the participants' deliberations, I consciously worked to keep my own bursts of emotional energy from differentiating into particular emotions. Rather than feel, for example, hurt, angry, or frustrated, I tried to keep my inner energies undifferentiated, and then use that energy to sustain focus, intellectual rigor, and a capacity for sensing emotional and intellectual dynamics in the room.[3]

Still, the talks offered particularly trying moments and required greater concentration to support sustained open space for the leaders' conversations. When a pro-life participant compared the scale of aborted unborn children to the Holocaust of World War II, my mind reeled with the image of a born child torn from her mother's arms, tossed in the air, and caught on the bayonet of a Nazi soldier, compared to a woman walking with a companion into a women's health clinic and asking a doctor to perform a legal medical procedure. In that moment, my own thoughts took over, and I had to sit back and let my co-facilitator respond.

Co-facilitation was essential because both of us knew that we could momentarily withdraw if we needed to. During our debriefings after each meeting, Laura and I talked through what had been particularly challenging for each of us.

---

3. This is similar to the concentration required for certain physical activities. For example, in yoga, to sustain balance in a posture, one learns to focus his or her eyes on a nonmoving point and quiet the noise in the mind through awareness of breath. With distance running, to sustain a run, you sometimes need to breathe through a cramp or quiet the mind messages that tell you stop.

   For more on mindfulness and mediation see Leonard L. Riskin, *Beneath Yes: Mindful Awareness and Conflict*. (forthcoming)

Results

The talks among the leaders of the pro-life and pro-choice movements in Massachusetts contributed to a shift in the public rhetoric and increased security. In an article on the first-year anniversary of the shootings, *Boston Globe* reporter Don Aucoin wrote, "Has the past year brought the lowering of voices? . . . The answer seems to be a qualified yes, at least among some activists." As a result of their talks, each leader took actions that contributed to that shift. Madeline McComish dissuaded a supporter of justifiable homicide from coming to Massachusetts to attend the Salvi trial. Nicki Nichols Gamble alluded to support and concern on the pro-life side at the first memorial of the shootings. The leaders toned down letters and op-eds submitted by their movements. The pro-life participants warned Nicki and contacted the FBI about a credible physical threat to her.

The talks were a life-changing experience for each of these six women, who, over time, came to love and care for each other. They used to joke about how in another world they would be friends. They discovered many unique similarities. They were passionate activists, they were public leaders who managed organizations of passionate activists, they cared a great deal about women and women's health, and they agreed that fewer unwanted pregnancies were better for society.

Their differences were vast and encompassed questions such as: When does life begin? Is a human fetus a life or a potential life? Is there a universal truth that demands protection for the unborn or is a pregnant woman the moral agent who has a right to choose, within the context of her life's complexities, to terminate her pregnancy?

There was a painful recognition of the great gap between the pro-life and pro-choice participants. Yet, it was this gap, the pain it caused, and a shared struggle to understand that energized their bonds of civic fusion. Ultimately, the mutual affection that grew among the pro-life and pro-choice leaders enabled them to transcend their differences to connect across their common humanity. These bonds moved them to take actions that reduced the violent rhetoric of the abortion debate in Massachusetts.

Conclusion

After almost six years of talks, the pro-life and pro-choice leaders continued to vehemently disagree about when life begins and a woman's right to choose to terminate her pregnancy, but they ultimately recognized that both sides were rooted in a strong sense of morality. They did not agree with the other sides' moral basis, some made clear they could not respect or even tolerate the other's moral code, yet they learned that the other side was not acting out of a purposeful immorality. As a result, though their intense policy disagreements remained, the demons disappeared. The abortion debate was still about life and death issues for both sides, but the demons no longer informed the debate. Instead they were replaced with a warm, personal connection and a sad resignation for the gap they could not fill.

In the shared words of their article:

We hope this account of our experience will encourage people everywhere to consider engaging in dialogues about abortion and other protracted disputes. In this world of polarizing conflicts, we have glimpsed a new possibility: a way in which people can disagree frankly and passionately, become clearer in heart and mind about their activism, and, at the same time, contribute to a more civil and compassionate society.

PART III
BUILDING THE FOUNDATION FOR CIVIC FUSION

Before negotiations can commence, the mediator must lay the groundwork for effectively bringing the parties together. To do so, the mediator learns about the situation then designs a process tailored to its unique characteristics. These pre-negotiation activities provide the foundation to support productive negotiations among polarized parties.

In Chapter 6, I'll explain how to conduct a mediator's assessment, and in Chapter 7, I'll describe the components of a civic fusion process and how to think about assembling them to support negotiations to build actionable agreements.

CHAPTER 6

CONDUCTING THE MEDIATOR'S ASSESSMENT

Introduction

Hearing the same story from thirty or more perspectives is absolutely fascinating—and illuminating. When conducting the mediator's assessment, the mediator has his or her initial contact with the relevant parties. During exploratory interviews, the mediator distinguishes reference points that help orient him or her for entry into a complex system with the intent of building a consensus agreement. The information and dynamics uncovered during the assessment inform the process design and support the intense negotiations that follow. As a lover of jigsaw puzzles, I think of the assessment as opening the box, turning all the pieces face up, separating out the framing pieces, and discerning the myriad shades of color with which I'll be working.

In conducting the assessment, the mediator talks to people who live the conflict after reading a trove of publicly available background documents. He or she strives to surface nuanced information from in-depth interviews and synthesizes large quantities of often-conflicting information to frame the overall situation in terms that resonate with all the relevant parties.

The following information is gathered during the mediator's assessment:

- Product or intended outcome of the process
- Complementary goals
- Stakeholders, interested parties, and/or required participants
- Organizations and/or individuals to represent the parties
- Issues to be negotiated
- Key issues for each category of stakeholders
- Issues that are of key importance to all the parties
- Relevant history and dynamics
- Informational needs
- Outreach and consultation requirements
- Time and resource constraints
- Likelihood of reaching consensus, and
- Feasibility of convening negotiations, if required.

In this chapter, after a bit of assessment history and brief descriptions of project assessments, we examine the interview process, the information to be gathered, the synthesis of that information, and the early activities undertaken to begin to stimulate new ideas and thoughts.

The History of the Mediator's Assessment

In the field of public policy mediation, there has been some confusion over the descriptor to place before the word *assessment*. Historically, we conducted *convening assessments* to determine if it was feasible to *convene* representative negotiators to try to reach a consensus agreement. In those days, the mediator conducting the convening assessment was referred to as the *convener*. Nowadays, the entity that initiates a public policy mediation process is sometimes referred to as the convener of that process, which has created confusion around the term *convening assessment*.

Later, some termed it a *conflict assessment*, which was rejected by parties who preferred not to define their complex situations by its disputes. This gave way to the currently used term *situational assessment*. In practice, situational assessments tend to be formal assessments that include written reports. Dispute resolution professionals sometimes conduct situation assessments on behalf of the mediator, who is then furnished with their report.

In some cases, many decisions, such as the selection of the representative negotiators and the feasibility of proceeding to negotiations, are made prior to retaining a public policy mediator. Nonetheless, it is still necessary for the mediator to conduct at least a truncated or informal assessment to gain necessary reference points, build relationships, and begin to move the process forward. To do otherwise would be akin to asking a surgeon to step into the operating room without first meeting the patient or reviewing diagnostic test results.

I offer the term *mediator's assessment* to indicate the formal situational assessment, as well as the truncated or informal assessment, which does not include a written report. In addition, the mediator's assessment includes the component of building relationships with parties prior to the first negotiating session.

The Projects

As all civic fusion projects are unique, so too are their assessments. The assessments for the Chelsea charter consensus process, the cranes reg neg, and the abortion talks were all distinctly different.

In Chelsea, I met with forty formal and informal leaders to learn about the city's political history, why people thought the city was in receivership, and their goals for its future government. I also learned about the different sectors of the city and the challenges of identifying a team of negotiators that would have citywide legitimacy. Furthermore, it was important to introduce myself to city residents and give them an opportunity to get to know me.

For the abortion talks, the assessment was designed first and foremost to determine if talks could be safely convened and, if so, to identify participants and goals they would consider to be worthwhile and achievable. At the outset, we literally had no notion of what the talks might produce or even if they would occur.

By the time I was retained for the cranes reg neg, OSHA had already decided to initiate a negotiated rulemaking and had identified the advisory committee members. As a result, my assessment was primarily limited to telephone interviews with the appointed negotiators. From the assessment, I learned the basics of crane safety issues, relevant history, the status of the most difficult issues, and the stakeholder groups and their perspectives, and I began to build relationships with the negotiators.

None of these three projects required a written assessment report. For illustrative purposes, I will draw on two other previous projects that included written assessment reports: one for a negotiated rulemaking to develop federal standards in accordance with the Small Business Liability Relief and Brownfields Revitalization Act for environmental investigations of contaminated areas, often referred to as "brownfields"; and another for a reg neg concerning federal standards for drivers' licenses and personal identification cards as required under the 9/11 Commission Implementation Act of the Intelligence Reform and Terrorism Prevention Act (9/11 Act). (See Appendix D for these assessment reports.)

The Interviews

The Basic Protocol

A series of in-depth interviews is the central activity of the mediator's assessment. From conversations with representatives of all those perceived to be affected by or likely to impact the situation, mediators work to attain a sense of the existing status quo and its limitations as well as stakeholders' aspirations. The basic interview protocol is essentially a shorthand list of the information the mediator needs to gather. It is a tool to refer to during the interview for use as a guide to casually direct the conversation. Each question is likely to be asked in a slightly different way to fit it into the narrative of the interviewee. Though questions may be added to particularize the protocol for a given case, a starting point is usually the following list of questions:

- What are the issues to discuss?
- What are the difficult issues?
- What are the conflicting interests?
- What are the categories of stakeholders?
- What parties represent those interests?
- Can parties/organizations be identified?
- Are you interested, willing, and able to participate?
- Who must be included? Who else?
- What is your prognosis for consensus?
- How do you think others view the likelihood of reaching consensus?
- What dynamics are relevant?
- What is the history of this situation?
- What have been the past efforts to address this situation?
- What ground rules are necessary?
- If this process is wildly successful, at the end of it, what will have happened?

Background Information

Developing some background knowledge of substantive issues and the political implications of the situation before conducting the interviews helps the mediator better understand the information provided by the interviewees. During interviews, one asks for recommendations of additional background materials.

Mediators read official documentation, including reports and relevant laws. For federal cases, this sometimes includes Congressional Conference Committee reports, which clarify congressional intent. A review of articles that have appeared in the media and the trade press provide an understanding of the public framing of the conflicts. Comments on newspaper articles, blogs, and other social media offer information on how some individual's frame issues as well as the intensity of passions surrounding the situation. The background readings provide information about attitudes that may be recognizable in some of the interviewees, but it is important to keep an open mind to their individual, and possibly unique, perspectives.

In Chelsea, I read about the receivership, the receivership legislation, charter commission materials, Chelsea's existing charter, press articles about the run up to and the eventual placing of Chelsea in receivership, and demographic information about Chelsea.

For the abortion talks, I read newspaper articles about the situation in Massachusetts as well as pro-life and pro-choice publications. Like most Americans, I was painfully aware of the ongoing culture wars and their recent spillover into violence. The clinic shootings happened in my town.

In preparation for the cranes reg neg, I read the existing OSHA standards, data on crane accidents, and the ACCSH Cranes Work Group Report. I leafed through some of the 10 inches of ASME[1] industry consensus standards and crane safety books, and watched crane safety videos provided by interviewees.

For every case, I also memorize the "alphabet soup" of acronyms and related jargon. Becoming versed in this vocabulary helps one to work effectively within the substantive issues and gives me credibility among the negotiators. The policy mediator is usually not an expert on the substance that is under negotiation. The negotiators are the experts on various components of the substance or situation. However, the mediator needs a working knowledge of the substance to function effectively as the process expert in the room.

Interview Approach

My approach to conducting interviews is to draw out each person's narrative. People living a long-term conflict and those working to influence public policies willingly share their stories with a little encouragement. As they speak, I ask clarifying questions and work to frame questions that illustrate my understanding of their situation. Questions are a safer route than declarative statements because they project an openness, and asking meaningful questions makes people feel understood.

---

1. ASME was founded as the American Society of Mechanical Engineers.

The questions serve as a general guide for conducting the interviews. They should not be asked in the order they appear on the protocol as one might do when conducting a survey. To help get a natural flow to the interviewee's narrative, each question should be a bridge from the last statement to something related. Just as in a usual conversation, one speaker's comment triggers a related response; so too with these interviews. The mediator can gently guide the conversation to gather all the information needed by linking questions to past statements and connecting something from a prior statement to a new, but related, point.

By nature I'm tremendously curious. I really want to understand the myriad sides of a complex public dispute. And I am as interested in hearing from the MIT PhD gear specialist as I am in speaking with the fisherman, who has less than a high school education and an ability to read the ocean for marine life. One of the crane negotiators once described me as having an "ability to adapt quickly to the environment, the conversation, and peoples' personalities." In one-on-one interviews, preferably in-person, I strive to hear the individual stories of each party independently of the others and to listen without judgment. To do so, during the conversation, I presume that people are being honest with me, perhaps even speaking from the heart. It is best to try not to judge their truthfulness or think about what they might purposely be leaving out. To describe this mediator orientation during assessment interviews, my colleague, Howard Gadlin,[2] coined the phrase *positive gullibility*.

In conducting the interviews, I try to enter into each person's world to gain an understanding of what the situation looks like through his or her eyes. This is more than empathizing or trying to understand their frustrations and aspirations. I'm working to walk into or try on their experience of the situation. Trying on this person's experience helps me foresee how he or she is likely to engage during the negotiations, particularly on the most important issues. Later in the process, this helps me to both design the agendas of future meetings and manage the negotiations.

2. Howard Gadlin, PhD, is ombudsman and director of the Center for Cooperative Resolution at the National Institutes of Health.

Mediators also need to give people an opportunity to learn something about them. Interviewees likely make ongoing calculations about what information to share and what to withhold. I try to provide as much surface area for connection as possible so they will feel safe confiding in me because the more I know, the more effective I can be in assisting during the negotiations.

For example, in Chelsea, as people shared their stories of immigration with me, I shared my own family's immigration story. I wanted the informal and formal leaders I met with to have first-hand experience of meeting and asking me questions about the process and my background. I knew the interviewees would influence others' impressions of me—and the credibility of the process—within their circles. Thus, in Chelsea, it was important to conduct the interviews with the primary focus on learning about the community, but in parallel, sharing my own stories rather than present myself as a blank slate. This was particularly necessary in the Chelsea context because many of its citizens tended to be deeply suspicious of "outsiders."

I also use the interviews to help potential negotiators see aspects of their situation in slightly different ways. From the early interviews, I try to identify nuances in interests and concerns that could create fertile ground for new productive ideas. Pointing out these nuances to interviewees is my way of seeding the polarized ground for the future negotiations. Even as I empathize with the situation of the interviewee, I sense whether or not to begin a discussion of the perspectives and situations of others. It can be helpful to ask about barriers to agreements to test out ideas for alternative framings or even options that might bridge controversies.

Identifying the Interviewees

The agency that initiates the process is the first stop for identifying interviewees. Officials usually have a sense of some of the key interest groups. At a kickoff meeting, the mediator usually develops a list of initial interviewees. To determine who should be on the list, consider the following questions: Who are the interested parties? What categories do they fall into? For example, crane manufacturers and unions were two of the categories of affected stakeholders for the cranes reg neg.

Who will the product affect, and who will impact its implementation? And, to put it bluntly: Who will be able block an agreement from being implemented?

Finding the right people to interview is an iterative process. I ask all the interviewees for advice on whom to interview and listen for redundancies. Individuals and organizations identified by multiple interviewees should be strongly considered for the next round of interviews. I strive to speak with a *minimum* of three people within each category of stakeholders. It usually takes three iterations of interviews to gain confidence in the completeness of the information gathered.

The most challenging question of the abortion talks assessment was whether or not to interview the leader of Operation Rescue (OR), an organization, which held daily demonstrations at abortion clinics. Clearly, OR was an interested party and, under the usual circumstances of a policy mediation, I would have requested an interview. However, from the early interviews Laura and I had already conducted, we knew that potential participants did not expect the talks to forge a consensus abortion policy and that the talks were likely to be private and confidential. OR publicly opposed the common ground talks, and many interviewees refused to participate in talks with OR. For these reasons and because of security concerns about the talks, we did not interview OR. (For a more in depth discussion of this decision, see Chapter 5, "Abortion Talks.")

Gathering Useful Information

Ultimately, the information the mediator needs to gather during an assessment is the political will or intent to change the status quo, background and substantive information, the product and complementary goals, a list of who needs to be considered for participation in the deliberations, a list of issues to be negotiated, history and dynamics of the conflict, and time and resource constraints.

Affirming an Intent to Act

Without political will and intent to change the status quo, the system lacks the dynamic necessary for civic fusion to occur. The commitment to act, coupled with a need for cooperation in order to act effectively, creates the dynamics necessary for a slight shift in assumptions, allowing for new thought patterns and the emergence of creative ideas. It is critical that the affected citizens as well as the relevant government agency have a desire and commitment to alter the status quo.

Usually, a government agency indicates its intent for a process by informing the interested parties that it plans to act. They offer parties an opportunity to influence decisions that will affect them but put them on notice that a failure to engage effectively will eliminate or reduce their impact on the future product. Under such circumstances, if the negotiations are successful, the government action will be rooted in the consensus agreement reached. If it fails, the agency will still act to alter the status quo, but it will do so with more complete understanding of the issues, outstanding conflicts, and the consequences of its decisions.

In kickoff meetings with initiating government agencies, I ask if officials intend to act regardless of whether or not consensus is reached. During assessment interviews, mediators learn of the status quo and related future aspirations from the interested parties.

In the cranes reg neg, OSHA and the affected parties were committed to revising the federal worker safety standards for cranes and derricks. In fact, OSHA initiated the negotiated rulemaking process in response to a joint request of the crane industry and labor unions. High fatality and serious injury rates from crane accidents made the status quo intolerable.

In Chelsea, the receiver was required by legislation to submit a new city charter to the governor to replace Chelsea's past form of government. During interviews with community members, I repeatedly heard the refrain, "We want our democracy back."

In the abortion talks, which were initiated at the request of the Massachusetts governor and the Boston archbishop, the participants were committed to protecting born people from future violence. Their agreement to meet to achieve the goals they identified implicitly suggested a willingness to shift from the polarized rhetoric of the status quo.

Determining the Product

Typically, but not always, the initiating agency or organization identifies the product or written outcome it seeks well before it retains a public policy mediator. Sometimes a complementary goal is apparent as well.

OSHA contacted me to help develop proposed revisions to the worker safety standards for the use of cranes and derricks in construction. The receiver in Chelsea sought a consensus process to develop a city charter. He also identified the complementary goal of building citizen capacity for self-governance.

For the abortion talks, however, Laura and I responded to a call for common ground talks—a process without a stated product. The goals for the talks emerged from the assessment. The idea for a written product, the consensus article, emerged as a result of the connections forged among the participants over years of meetings.

Identifying the Issues for Discussion

In an assessment, the mediator seeks to determine if there is a rich enough agenda of issues to discuss, the key issues for each interviewee, and which issues are expected to be the most difficult to resolve. Often the initiating agency identifies a fairly comprehensive list of issues to be negotiated. An agenda of issues is considered appropriate for policy mediation when its complexity is likely to create potential opportunities for mutual gains.

When given an opportunity to tell their stories, people usually identify the issues that are most important to them as well as the dynamics and parties that have prevented them from reaching their aspirations. They tend to be eager to talk about the difficult issues, which are often the issues that contributed to failure in past efforts.

In the cranes reg neg, OSHA proposed a comprehensive scope of issues in the federal register. The most difficult issues, I learned from the interviewees, were operator certification, ground conditions, contact with electrical power lines, and testing and verification of crane prototypes. Most interviewees identified some or all of these among their key issues.

For Chelsea, the table of contents of a city charter constituted the list of issues to be negotiated. Some of the key items identified during interviews were chief executive of the city (e.g., mayor or city manager), size of the council, terms of office, and public participation in hiring the police and fire chiefs. However, most of the interviewees spoke at a more abstract level about the government failures that led to receivership and ideals for its future government. These ideals would later be reflected in the city charter.

For the abortion talks, the goals drafted and refined as we conducted the interviews became the issues we would discuss. Because we started with the intention to meet only four times, we began with a modest list of issues including similarities and differences among the participants, actions to reduce the violence of the rhetoric, and a possible joint project.

Gathering the Relevant History

It is difficult to fully understand a situation or conflict without understanding its relevant history, including past efforts for resolution.

By the time mediators get involved, there is often some history of failure, and it is helpful to learn how the situation evolved over time. People are usually frustrated with the status quo and infuriated that no one can unilaterally improve it. They may realize that they must cooperate with others to release themselves from their Gordian knot, but they may be completely uncertain about how to make that happen.

In Chelsea, the perceptions of why the city was in receivership provided a lens into community dynamics. The theories expressed ranged from the rational—because of fiscal mismanagement—to the conspiratorial—because the Massachusetts Port Authority wanted to put an employee parking lot in the city. From the narratives people shared, I also learned of the community's existing healthy infrastructure of social clubs and organizations.

The crane interviewees told me of the C-DAC precursor, the crane work group, and its recommendation that OSHA initiate a formal negotiated rulemaking process. I also learned that unions and the crane industry jointly asked OSHA to revise the cranes regulations because both sides believed the existing standards did not fit with modern equipment or current work conditions and therefore were a contributing factor in the high number of crane accident–related deaths and serious injuries.

For the abortion talks, Laura and I learned of the invisible, yet impassable, wall that existed between pro-life and pro-choice leaders as they testified on opposite sides of state bills and met for media debates. We also learned a great deal about the evolution of each movement; the Herculean efforts undertaken to change the status quo, sustain gains and protect against future losses; and the multiple issues that fell under the abortion issue umbrella.

Considering Consensus

One of the questions I enjoy posing during assessment interviews is whether or not people think consensus is possible. Interviewees often say they think consensus is possible but then express certainty that their opponents do not. People on the other side offer mirror image responses. An affirmative expectation of consensus doesn't by itself guarantee an agreement, but without the will to succeed, people may not engage in the work necessary to shed new light on assumptions, allow for curiosity where there has been fear, create new paradigms for agreements, and make tough choices.

Most C-DAC members were cautiously optimistic about reaching consensus on revised standards, although they expressed considerable concern about the controversial issues of operator certification, ground conditions, and testing and verification, which had toppled the work group effort.

In Chelsea, people were generally resigned to the effort. Some were ready to get their democracy back, and if the charter process was the way forward, they supported it. Many were skeptical. Still others unrealistically wanted the receivership to continue indefinitely.

Identifying Timing Issues and Resource Constraints

As the outlines of a situation emerge, a mediator should also consider timing and resource availability. Reasonable deadlines promote efficient negotiations, and statutory calendars or elections may set deadlines.

Because negotiations sometimes balloon to fill the time available, an open-ended time frame may have a negative effect on the negotiations, whereas allotting too little time for a complex set of issues will result in failure. Feasibility, in part, depends on securing the required resources, such as government staff time, negotiator availability, and funding for the mediator and logistical needs.

In Chelsea, the statutory end of the receivership provided a hard deadline. Before democracy could be restored to Chelsea, we would need to complete the charter negotiations, and the citizens would need to hold a special election, have their legislators introduce and pass the charter as state legislation, elect a new city council, and have the council hire a city manager. When I was selected for the project, we had one year for the charter process. Contracting confusions cut that to nine months.

For the abortion talks, Laura and I decided that starting the meetings more than nine months after the shootings would diminish momentum for the talks. We held the talks with six participants, rather than our expected eight, because aligning schedules proved too difficult, and we determined we couldn't wait any longer to get started.

OSHA originally suggested eighteen meetings for C-DAC over as many months, which seemed like an unnecessarily long time for sustained, productive negotiations. OSHA agreed to my suggestion of twelve meetings over a period of one year. My contract end date became our hard deadline.

Synthesizing the Interview-Gathered Information

When a mediator hears the same story from many perspectives, common ideas and themes emerge, but the stories also reveal countless shades of gray between poles of black and white. He or she finds misunderstandings and nuances that promise opportunities for resolution within issues perceived as unbridgeable impasses. Hearing the perspectives of as many as forty or sixty people concerning the same situation provides a good indication of what the negotiations will look like.

The entire interview process is very fluid. The synthesis begins with the earliest interviews and continues throughout the series of interviews.

As mediators conduct interviews, they continually refine their views, which then inform the questions asked during later interviews. The barriers and dynamics identified by previous interviewees become opportunities for testing the potential for new understandings regarding difficult issues. Subsequent interviewees can be asked about issues from the perspectives offered in the earlier conversations. As the thematic dynamics begin to emerge, the mediator refines initial discernments during later interviews.

When the interviews are complete, I sit and think or go for a walk. I imagine my mind as a computer into which I've tossed tons of information, and then wait for it to sort that information into thematic categories. Then I begin to write, which helps clarify what I've heard. After I've written all that comes to mind, I go through the raw data of the exhaustive notes taken during the interviews and add in any themes and understandings missed. Because my initial thoughts reflect a continual synthesis over the course of the interviews, the last step of checking my notes is crucial to ensure that I've accounted for all I heard from each party.

The synthesis helps to determine the categories of stakeholders and who might represent each group, as well as their key interests and concerns. The synthesis process also highlights any concerns shared by multiple stakeholders, key dynamics, informational needs, expected outreach and consultation activities, as well as the likelihood and feasibility of consensus.

Selecting Negotiators

After completing the interviews, a mediator can recommend who should sit at the negotiating table to the initiating agency. He or she identifies the categories of stakeholders who have a large enough set of interests to engage in mutual gains negotiations or enough power to be able to block an agreement, or both. Stakeholders with very limited interests should be excluded because they can hold the process hostage and participate in distorting coalitions to achieve a limited agenda. However, sometimes politics suggest inclusion of such a party.

It may be counterintuitive, but often a larger than expected team makes for better negotiations and may increase the likelihood of reaching an agreement. My preference is to include at least three representatives within each category of stakeholders.

Because the solutions to complex policy questions are often found as a result of increasingly nuanced understandings, it is helpful if representatives within a stakeholder category do not have a uniform sense of the issues. Their differences enrich the negotiations and provide more opportunities for agreements. In addition, representatives within a stakeholder category are often able to persuade peers to consider proposals they might otherwise reject outright.

Although mediators always ask interviewees if they are willing to participate in future deliberations, one must be careful to state that the question is not an invitation to participate but an affirmation of their willingness to be considered.

For the brownfields negotiated rulemaking referred to previously in this chapter, I met with EPA officials to identify categories of stakeholders and initial interviewees within those categories. The initial categories included other federal agencies, state government, local government, tribal government, developers (residential, commercial, industrial, for-profit, not-for-profit), bankers and lenders, environmentalists, environmental professionals, environmental attorneys, and insurance professionals.

As the assessment unfolded, it became clear that the interests of the environmental justice community deviated enough from the environmentalists to be considered a separate category of stakeholder. In addition, the categories of environmental attorneys and other federal agencies posed challenges for participation as negotiators. Environmental attorneys included all the other stakeholders among their clients at any given time. Thus, as a group, environmental attorneys did not have their own distinct set of interests but rather attorneys' interests were those of their clients of record at the time.

To be able to tap the environmental attorneys' depth of knowledge relevant to the enforcement of environmental regulations and their ability to analyze the impacts of various options across multiple stakeholders, I created a new and distinct category of participation called resource participants. Resource participants engaged in the deliberations but not in decision making; they had no right of dissent. Real estate brokers and representatives of the environmental insurance industry also participated in this capacity. This construct enabled the negotiators, the process, and the eventual standards to benefit from the expertise of these parties. At the same time, they could participate without the complications of needing to reach an internal consensus among their constituents that a formal decision role would require.

To accommodate the other federal agencies with related interests but without the authority to regulate under the brownfields law, the EPA team created a federal work group. It consulted with its members to carry their interests into the negotiations and to vet proposals. Sometimes federal work group members attended plenary negotiating sessions and provided public comments.

For the abortion talks, we started our assessment with a list of leaders from the pro-life and pro-choice organizations in the state. From our initial conversations, we generated a second list of interviewees, which included politicians, clergy, and leaders of organizations for which abortion was related but not central to their missions, for example, the League of Women Voters. These interviewees provided us with a great deal of context, although none participated in the talks.

Mediators need to be comprehensive in identifying categories of stakeholders during the assessment. However, because the composition of a negotiating team is central to achieving an actionable agreement, it is useful to utilize available checks on proposed participation via public review. In Chelsea, this public check was accomplished by publishing the proposed list of negotiators in the *Chelsea Record.* For C-DAC, OSHA published the proposed list of committee members in the *Federal Register* for review and comment. In contrast, the abortion dialogue specifically did not require any such review given that the talks were both secret and confidential for security reasons.

Key Issues by Stakeholder

After interviews with multiple individuals within each category of stakeholder, the mediator synthesizes the information across those interviews for the key interests and concerns of each stakeholder group. One discovers key issues for the first interviewee in each category, and then listens for similarities and differences from the others. One can test their initial findings as he or she moves through the interviews.

Knowing the key concerns of each stakeholder group and where their interests intersect with others helps make the negotiations efficient. For example, during the drivers' licenses reg neg, a member of law enforcement spoke of the benefits of having a federal database of combined motor vehicle data from all fifty states. Afterward I turned to the representative from the American Civil Liberties Union for his response, as I knew from the assessment interview that this proposal would raise significant concerns for him.

Key Issues across Stakeholders

Another part of the assessment analysis is to determine the key issues that are important to all or most of the stakeholders. Some of these will be binding issues in that all parties are concerned that an issue be properly addressed. In other instances, these may be difficult issues that represent a clash of interests but are of crucial concern to many. It is helpful to know the varied interests tangled in such issues to design the meeting, manage the negotiations, determine informational needs, and identify nuance.

For example, in the brownfields reg neg, many stakeholders expressed a general fear of change and industry disruption. At the time of the assessment and before the new standards became law, environmental assessments of brownfields were conducted in accordance with a voluntary industry standard developed by ASTM International.[3] The stakeholder groups that used this standard were concerned about the potential for disruption of transactions as the industry moved from a known to a new set of procedures. Another shared issue was the shelf life of an assessment. Questions were raised about how long an assessment would be considered valid for establishing an all appropriate

3. ASTM International was formerly known as the American Society for Testing and Materials.

inquiry liability defense.[4] Some thought the shelf life of an assessment should be six months, others one year, and still others, longer. This is especially relevant when a site has groundwater contamination and/or migrating plumes but also affects the costs to purchasers and impacts the size of the environmental assessment market.

In the drivers' license reg neg, to protect against counterfeiting drivers' licenses and personal identification cards, all parties supported a layering of overt and covert security features, continuous upgrade of security features to keep ahead of sophisticated counterfeiters, and the development of standards for the transliteration of names spelled with non-Roman alphabet letters such as Chinese and Arabic. In contrast, combining state motor vehicle data systems, also a key issue for most stakeholders, emerged as a multifaceted issue: law enforcement supported the capability of identifying criminals across state lines; civil liberties organizations worried about privacy and access to confidential information; data security groups were concerned that a single database provided too great a temptation for identity theft; state motor vehicle agencies were concerned about protecting their databases; and state legislators and governors were concerned about costs.

Key Dynamics

Whereas key issues are those items that will eventually be negotiated, key dynamics are the situational factors that are likely to influence and affect the negotiations. Examples of key dynamics include time-related items such as statutory deadlines or upcoming elections, requirements for information or particular analyses, and community characteristics. Generally, if these dynamics are not woven into the process design, they are likely to become barriers to building actionable agreements.

---

4. All Appropriate Inquiries (AAI) is a process of evaluating a property's environmental conditions and assessing the likelihood of any contamination. All appropriate inquiries must be conducted to obtain protection from potential liability under the Comprehensive Environmental Response, Compensation, and Liability Act (CERCLA) as an innocent landowner, a contiguous property owner, or a bona fide prospective purchaser. Every Phase I assessment conducted with EPA Brownfields Assessment Grant funds must be conducted in compliance with the All Appropriate Inquiries Final Rule at 40 CFR Part 312. (From http://www.epa.gov/brownfields/aai)

The key dynamics in Chelsea included a disengaged citizenry, a deep-rooted skepticism of outsiders, and many non-English-speaking residents. In response, the process design included sending bilingual, local facilitators to hold charter meetings in places where people naturally met. To overcome a fear of outsiders with hidden agendas, in implementing the process, Chelseans played visible roles, for example, as media spokespersons.

For the abortion talks, a key dynamic was the requirement of absolute confidentiality. We needed to identify participants who would agree to and maintain confidentiality for the entirety of the dialogue and possibly, far into the future. Fears for physical security, another key dynamic, sent us into a nondescript windowless basement for our meetings.

Informational Needs

Conflicts grow deeper when a lack of good information leads people to fill in the blanks with false assumptions. To be useful, information provided within a civic fusion process must be perceived as balanced by all the parties. Informational needs emerge during the mediator's assessment, as well as throughout the negotiations. The parties and the mediator work together to identify and secure suitable information prior to the negotiations and as needs arise throughout the process.

The charter preparation team members had little background in the nuts and bolts of city charters, and I knew from the assessment that we needed to provide them with trustworthy information. Fortunately, the National Civic League prepares unbiased information for charter commissions across the country, and we used its materials. The professional charter drafter hired by the receiver's Office provided a tutorial on the required elements of Massachusetts' city charters. In addition, to illustrate the otherwise abstract decision-making processes of various forms of municipal government, we convened a panel of local government officials from different cities and towns to explain how they would approach a proposal to privatize trash collection.

Expected Outreach and Consultation Needs

The assessment interviews also yield information on outreach and consultation needs, which are directly linked to the question of who, in addition to the negotiators, must participate to ensure an agreement will be actionable. After these groups and individuals are identified, outreach and consultation mechanisms are created for their effective participation.

Outreach and consultation activities vary across cases: organizational representatives must consult with their superiors and/or boards of directors and constituents. Projects that affect a broad public may require means for engaging it. The feedback generated from these modalities must be compiled and integrated into the decision making of the negotiators. That said, it is never helpful to create a more complex process than necessary. Outreach and consultation activities should be included when they are essential for reaching an actionable agreement.

In Chelsea, from my very first interview with the receiver, I understood that the effort would require unique participation mechanisms to achieve consensus on a city charter that would pass in a special election. I also understood that people, particularly those historically shut out of City Hall, would not be likely to go to political meetings.

For the abortion dialogue, outreach and consultation was an internal question: Who absolutely needs to know of the talks and under what terms can they be told? It was the opposite of the usual questions related to outreach and consultation. The dynamic of absolute confidentiality would drive the need to develop precise terms for the participants' consultations with their boards and superiors. All the participants needed some level of assurance that all those informed would keep the talks secret.

Determination of Feasibility

In the early days of public policy mediation, cases moved to the negotiation phase only after a positive determination of feasibility. As the field has evolved, political leaders often make that determination prior to a mediator's assessment. For example, some of my past cases were congressionally mandated negotiated rulemakings in laws such as the Amendments to the Higher Education Act, the Native American Housing Assistance and Self Determination Act, and the 9/11 Act.

For the brownfields reg neg, the EPA requested that the assessment include a determination of feasibility for convening negotiations to develop the standards. The usual factors for determining feasibility are as follows:

- A reasonable number of relevant stakeholder groups for sustained productive negotiations;
- Representation of stakeholders is possible;
- Issues to be discussed are complex and diverse;
- Issues are ripe for decision making;
- Outcome is in doubt—no one can act unilaterally to resolve the conflicts or significantly alter the status quo in their favor;
- Parties believe it is in their interest to negotiate because they will attain more from negotiations than they can from actions in other forums; and
- The initiating agency has the resources and a willingness to participate.

One can never predict the outcome of negotiations with absolute certainty, particularly when multiple perspectives must be reconciled. However, based on the assessment, I determined that the aforementioned conditions existed for the brownfields reg neg, and that it was therefore, feasible to initiate negotiations.

Prior to establishing the abortion talks, Laura and I undertook an extensive assessment to determine their feasibility. Given the potential for violence for participating in common ground talks, our first test for determining feasibility was to see if it was possible, at a minimum, to do no harm. By this we meant that participants would not face physical threats or injury as a result of the talks. Once we found that there were ways to initiate the talks safely, we worked to identify potentially achievable goals, the terms of participation, and leaders who were willing to participate.

The Assessment Report

Although every policy mediation requires an assessment, written reports are not requested in every case. However, the mediator's assessment report is a powerful tool in that it can be used to frame the overall conflict in terms that are understandable and that resonate with all the parties. If the situation can be described in a report that legitimizes the reader's concerns and also provides an increased understanding of the others, the conflict begins to look manageable. Parties have reported that seeing the situation effectively described in terms of the parties, issues, and dynamics helps them "get their arms around it" and reduces their sense of being overwhelmed by the conflict.

The mediator's assessment synthesizes great amounts of information into a comprehensible and resonant framing of the conflict. To do so requires a studied understanding of conflict, power dynamics, negotiation theory and practice, as well as the curiosity that enables one to learn about alternative worldviews and to hold varied perspectives in one's mind simultaneously.

CHAPTER 7

DESIGNING THE PROCESS

Introduction

Tailored to the unique characteristics of the conflicts they are built to resolve, process designs provide an overall plan for the mediated negotiations and related activities needed to develop actionable agreements. Informed by the mediator's assessment, the process design integrates the public goals, the diverse group of stakeholders and others who must participate, the issues they will address, the relationships that must be built, and the dynamics that will influence the negotiations.

All civic fusion processes share assumptions and basic building blocks, but the design of each must account for distinctive needs embedded in the situation. The process design is summarized in an easy-to-understand process map, which enables participants to track their progress. Because new dynamics emerge during mediated negotiations, process designs must be flexible enough to adapt to the unexpected. The process design is, in itself, a way to begin to show people a way out of their morass. Its structure delineates an understanding of the complexity and the identified barriers. The process map looks complicated but is understandable. It legitimizes the refrain of how difficult it will be to make progress, but, as many participants have noted, it provides a structure that people can grasp.

Assumptions

As a young college student hitchhiking across the United States, I was impressed by a wisdom that seemed inherent in the people I met. I recognized this impression again during my studies of Plato's *Dialogues,* particularly concerning the soul's opportunity to contemplate true being and the human recollection of innate knowledge.

These studies and experiences informed the underlying premises of the processes I design: People living a conflict have unique knowledge and wisdom to contribute to resolving their complex situations. This knowledge sometimes needs to be drawn out and compiled so that it may be integrated into comprehensive deliberations.

My experience in studying and mediating disputes also helped me to uncover another premise: People involved in a conflict hold substantive and world view assumptions that are embedded in their perspectives of the situation and sustain the status quo. Those assumptions need to be surfaced and examined to create opportunities for new ideas to emerge.

In other words, parties to a conflict hold some of the key insights and knowledge required for its resolution, but at the same time their proximity to the conflict causes and sustains beliefs that limit their ability to access and contribute their wisdom to develop innovative solutions.

Building a policy mediation process on these premises may change the orientation of the parties from polarization to civic fusion. If parties can retain their values and commitments to their interests while embracing the complexity of their conflict, they may find ways to engage with others to jointly solve the problem. The need to create this dynamic is reflected in the process design and is layered into its implementation.

In addition to the process assumptions about people in conflict, like those I work with, I have assumptions about human nature, which influence the processes I design and are part of why I am drawn to this work. I assume that human nature includes the potential for a broad range of action, thought, passion, and emotion. Circumstances can impact what is expressed, and societies can be built to create systems of circumstances that lead toward virtue and away from evil.

In my mind, as I design processes to address complex public issues and conflicts, I seek to foster a temporary society that encourages the expression of virtue—the highest aspects of human nature—and relies on the capacities of all its members to address their common public problem.

Basic Building Blocks

The basic building blocks of civic fusion process designs are its product, complementary goal, negotiating sessions, outreach and consultations, trusted information, and logistics. We will look separately at each of these process components. A process may include some or all of the basic building blocks and each is specifically molded for the situation. Unique process elements may also be required.

You can think of process components as rooms in houses. Most houses are likely to have kitchens, bedrooms, and bathrooms. Some may also include other elements like living rooms, dining rooms, offices, and porches. And just as a New York City apartment's kitchen will look different from one in a large farmhouse, so too will the elements of a particular civic fusion process, as each is designed to fit its context.

The Product

The primary goal of the process is the desired result. The product of most processes is the written consensus agreement that is the vehicle for attaining the primary goal. It can take many forms, such as a proposed regulation, a city charter, a plan, a memorandum of understanding, or an article.

In most cases, the intended product is clearly identified by the government agency initiating the process, but not always. For C-DAC, the primary goal of the effort was to protect workers in, on, and around cranes. The product was a proposed revision to the worker safety standards for cranes and derricks used in construction that would form the basis of a notice of proposed rulemaking.

In Chelsea, the primary goal of the charter consensus process was the long-term restoration of democracy to Chelsea. The intended product was a new city charter. It would be subjected to a special election, and if approved by its citizens, would form the basis of state legislation to be adopted by the Massachusetts state legislature and signed into law by the governor.

In an emergent process like the abortion dialogue, the primary goal was to protect against violence resulting from the abortion debate. However, we were not trying to develop a specific written product at the outset of the process. A consensus article emerged only years after the talks began. Additional products in this case can be said to be the individual acts taken by the participants to further the primary goal.

The Complementary Goal

The complementary goal supports implementation of the product. The complementary goal may or may not be articulated as such by the sponsoring agency. It sometimes becomes apparent in response to one of my favorite assessment interview questions: If this process is wildly successful, at the end of it, what will have happened?

The complementary goal must be integrated into the process design in those cases in which the product will only be actionable if the complementary goal is achieved.

In Chelsea, the complementary goal was an engaged citizenry to promote self-governance. Without its attainment, the city charter would fail to secure a functional democracy.

For C-DAC, there was no initially articulated complementary goal, but as often occurs with a negotiated rulemaking, it resulted in a team of experts with intimate knowledge of the standard and the ability to explain the rule to their diverse constituents. The people who negotiated the standard have since presented at crane conferences and safety meetings, and their associations have fielded calls and questions. As a result, OSHA will likely receive fewer letters requesting clarification of the standards. Individuals are likely to go first to their unions or trade associations with their questions, leaving OSHA to answer those questions that require formal interpretations. These post-negotiation C-DAC activities are a helpful support but are not essential for implementing the product. Thus, the process design did not include components specific to a complementary goal.

The Negotiating Sessions

To develop the product, every process includes a series of meetings of people with varied perspectives and interests relative to the intended outcome. The negotiating sessions begin with a preliminary meeting during which the team negotiates ground rules to govern their interactions and works to finalize the list of issues to be negotiated. We then typically "workshop" each issue, which means we have an open discussion to see where people generally fall relative to the issue. We then dissect it into subissues, clarify any confusions, and identify where interests conflict and coincide.

During the negotiation sessions, mediators help to uncover each stakeholder's interests behind their positions, and then help integrate those interests into a meaningful whole. Consequently, the negotiations are rooted in interest-based[1] and integrative negotiations.[2] Mediators also assist the parties as they develop and assess options, identify opportunities for mutual gain, and trade off on issues valued differently among stakeholders. The mediator helps to appropriately sequence and break issues down to component parts to differentiate actual interest-based conflicts from confusions. Although compromise may be necessary at particular points in the negotiations, well-reasoned solutions tend to emerge from participant deliberations to resolve most issues.

---

1. For more on interest-based negotiations, see Roger Fisher, William Ury, and Bruce Patton (1991), *Getting to Yes*, New York: Penguin Books.
2. For more on integrative negotiations, see Lawrence Susskind and Jeffrey Cruikshank (1988), *Breaking the Impasse: Consensual Approaches to Resolving Public Disputes*, New York: Basic Books.

A designated person or small team that may or may not include negotiators—it could be government officials, a consultant, or the mediator—writes draft language to reflect the discussions. The draft text is then distributed to the negotiators for review and revision.

The negotiators review the text related to each issue in an effort to reach tentative agreements on each one. The agreements are tentative because their acceptance is contingent on reaching agreement on all issues. Tentative agreements may be reconsidered if they are affected by subsequent discussions of other issues. Otherwise they are only revisited after all issues have been preliminarily decided. Throughout the negotiations, the text provides a helpful focus for the discussions.

For difficult issues—and there are always at least a handful—tentative agreements may not be reached until the final negotiating session. Discussions on those issues usually occur across multiple negotiating sessions. As the team runs out of ideas and discussions become redundant, they move to another issue, with the expectation of returning to the outstanding issue at a later date. At the final meeting, these issues may require compromise to reach closure. When successful, the negotiation sessions end when final consensus is achieved.

Outreach and Consultations

Within a civic fusion process, outreach and consultations are necessary to engage people beyond the negotiators. The form these take depends on who must be involved to develop an actionable agreement, that is, to reach consensus on a product that will be implemented. Outreach and consultations may range from negotiators checking in with their constituents, for example, through conference calls, to formal mechanisms for engaging the public that are designed and implemented by the mediation team. Outreach may include ongoing activities throughout the negotiations or planned events at particular process milestones.

Ongoing consultations are critical for preventing representative negotiators from agreeing to proposals their constituents may later reject. Through such mechanisms, negotiators gain increased awareness of their constituents' preferences and obtain feedback on proposals and emerging ideas. In addition, negotiators often need to explain the situational constraints that may limit their ability to achieve all their aspirations. Finally, continuous consultation improves the actionability of the agreement in that constituents are informed of the evolving proposals and solutions over the course of the negotiations instead of being surprised at the end of the process.

Apart from the public comment requirements of the Federal Advisory Committee Act (FACA), C-DAC members conducted all of the necessary outreach and consultations on their own throughout the negotiations. Most members checked in with superiors and held conference calls with their constituents. Many were assisted by staff from the organizations they represented.

The Chelsea charter consensus process, on the other hand, was built around its complementary goal of engaging the public and teaching self-governance. The process design included a series of community meetings at social clubs and organizations throughout the city. The initial round of community meetings was held before the negotiations commenced, a second set of outreach activities was initiated after the negotiators reached tentative agreements on key charter issues, and upon completion of the draft city charter, another round of community meetings was held throughout the city.

My colleague Roberta Miller and I designed the community meeting format. Roberta then trained local people in the facilitation techniques needed to implement that format. During the community meetings, the facilitators recorded the ideas and opinions generated and returned those to us on feedback sheets we had provided. I compiled and synthesized the opinions and ideas collected from each series of meetings for use by the charter preparation team.

In addition, we held public forums for people not affiliated with local clubs or organizations. Our other outreach and consultation mechanisms included bilingual newsletters sent to each household, call-in cable television shows, ward meetings, a survey, and a charter information hotline. The team members also informally consulted with those they viewed as their constituents. This range of activities extended civic fusion well beyond the boundaries of the negotiators.

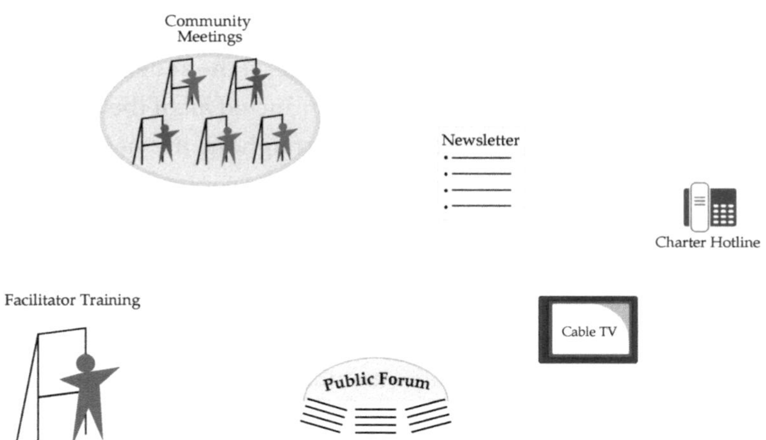

Figure 7.1
Chelsea Charter Consensus Process: Outreach and Consultation Mechanisms

Because the talks were secret, public outreach was forbidden during the abortion dialogue. Still, all the participants needed to obtain permission from their organizations to participate, as well as to go public with their experiences. For some, this meant going to their boards of directors, for others to a bishop or cardinal, but whoever was consulted also needed to keep confidential any and all information about the talks.

Meeting Logistics

Timing

In designing processes, it is important to account for relevant logistics. First and foremost are timing issues. Some cases have statutory or other hard deadlines; some have none. Some deadlines occur as a result of contracts or available budgets. When Congress mandates a consensus process, it usually includes a statutory deadline for enactment of the regulation or other product. For example, in reauthorizations of the Higher Education Act over the past decades, Congress has set dates for implementing new regulations. The time available for negotiations is determined according to the calendar of activities that must follow the regulatory negotiations, including preparation of a preamble and cost analyses.

With public disputes, the next relevant election is often a crucial timing element. New administrations frequently reject the work of past administrations as they often do not feel compelled to implement policies they did not influence or do not support.

Number and Frequency of Meetings

The number and frequency of meetings are estimated based on the time available and the scope of issues to be negotiated, as well as the outreach and consultations needed.

The amount of time needed for negotiations increases with a larger scope of issues, greater complexity, and higher intensity of conflict. The number of meetings or meeting hours will be less with fewer issues, less complexity, and/or moderate conflict. The amount of time needed for negotiating sessions may also be affected by the amount of time available and expectations of likely negotiators.

The location of the negotiators affects the length of the meeting. Locally based projects usually consist of frequent short meetings. If the negotiators travel from across the country, it is necessary to have fewer but longer meetings. Location may also affect the public's ability to attend meetings and participate in the process.

Meeting frequency is linked to the ability to sustain civic fusion over time. If all the necessary tasks can be accomplished between meetings, it is best to meet at least once per month. Meetings may be more frequent if hard deadlines limit the overall time available. Waiting more than six weeks between meetings can slow momentum and reduce the efficacy of the established norms of deliberative negotiation from meeting to meeting.

In Chelsea, we met one evening per week for six months. Our deadline was driven by the legislatively mandated end of the receivership.

The C-DAC meetings ran between two-and-a-half to four days. Nine of our meetings were held in Washington, D.C., and the other two were held in Phoenix, Arizona and Las Vegas, Nevada, to give people from the West an increased opportunity to attend the meeting and address the C-DAC members.

Resources Available

Public policy mediation cases are labor and resource intensive. It is important to determine if the necessary resources are available during the assessment rather than initiate negotiations and find the process severely constrained by a lack of available resources.

The sponsoring agency must make staff time available for the process, as well as resources for retaining the mediator. Government negotiators, who perform the majority of the work, may need reductions in their usual responsibilities, as new and demanding tasks of the mediation process are added to their workloads.

Trusted Information

Conflicts often deepen when there is a lack of good information and when people rely on biased information to support their positions. In contrast, when negotiators are well informed about the issues, they are better able to develop innovative solutions. When negotiators are insecure about their grasp of issues, they hold tighter to known positions. Solutions are most likely to emerge from increasingly nuanced understandings of difficult issues.

There is a range of mechanisms for providing information to the negotiators. It may be a matter of finding existing written materials or experts that will be considered credible by all the negotiators. Or the process may require a comprehensive review of biased materials or presentations from a diverse panel of experts. Some informational needs are clear at the outset of the process, but others become apparent during negotiations.

In Chelsea, we relied on the National Civic League for unbiased information about city charters and local governance. It publishes materials specifically to support city and town charter commissions. In addition, we retained a professional charter drafter, who provided a presentation of city charter elements at the preliminary meeting and clarified issues throughout the negotiations.

For key information in the C-DAC case, we relied on panels of mutually recognized experts as well as industry consensus regulations supplied to C-DAC members by ASME.

During the abortion dialogue, when we discussed controversial issues, such as the impact of abortions on breast cancer rates, each side provided the other with research that supported its views. In this instance, we weren't seeking consensus on policy, but rather were searching for a deeper understanding of pro-life and pro-choice perspectives and concerns.

In all three projects, the parties required significant amounts of information. Some informational needs were identified during the assessment, but many more became apparent during the negotiations. If mutually agreeable unbiased information was available, the groups used it. In the absence of such materials, panels of experts and/or multiple reports and articles were used to provide a range of relevant opinions and perspectives on the issues under discussion. Participants jointly identified informational resources.

The Art of Building the Process

Every civic fusion effort requires its own process design; no single design will work well for all mediations. The information gathered during the mediator's assessment can be used to tailor a process and each of its building blocks to the unique characteristics of the situation.

Tailoring to Specific Aspects of the Situation

To begin the work of organizing and synthesizing thoughts and gathering information into a process design, mediators may begin by considering set of reformulated assessment questions:

- What is the problem?
- What is the product required for progress?
- What, if any, are the complementary goals, particularly with regard to actionability of the agreement?
- What is particularly challenging in this situation? What do people believe are the barriers to success? What makes people think this situation is difficult or even impossible to solve?
- What are the healthy aspects of the community and the stakeholder groups?
- Are there structures to build on from past efforts at addressing this problem?
- Who must participate to ensure successful implementation? Who else? (Did I miss anyone?)

- What are the time and resource constraints?
- What history and dynamics are relevant?
- What were the surprising pieces of information I heard?
- What information and expertise is needed?
- What are the related laws, if any?
- What ground rules are necessary?

To get a feel for the deeper situation and underlying dynamics beyond the issues, one needs to look for the human stories behind the political stances and try to get an overall sense of the configuration of the situation. What are its unique characteristics? What is identifiable within the shared story of the interviewees? What is fascinating and interesting about this situation? How did the situation evolve to where it is? Who were the past players? Are they still engaged or have they given up on chances for solving the problem?

When people say it will be impossible to succeed, what do they mean? In Chelsea, people actually laughed when they learned of my efforts there. What about the situation makes it seem intractable to people? What do they consider the barriers to success? What are the emotions they attach to these barriers? What are the human stories that make it safer to hide behind barriers than to overcome them? What narratives contribute to getting beyond them? What metaphors do they use to describe their situation?

In designing processes, rather than be intimidated by the barriers like many of the participants, barriers should be considered challenges to design to. Imagine an architect that is brought to a steep hill made of bedrock by potential clients who want to build a house on it. The barrier-averse architect would say, "You can't build here. The hill is too steep." But another would suggest stairs or ramps, with steel pins in the foundation to secure it. It may be challenging to get the building materials way up there, but the builders can use a crane or conveyor belt. It will be more expensive, but if they succeed, the house will have great views and the rooms will be bathed in natural sunlight.

The Process Map Planner

The process map planner (Figure 7.2) illustrates the overall infrastructure of a civic fusion mediation process. It shows how the basic building blocks might fit together and how they are informed by the mediator's assessment. However, one cannot work chronologically through the planner to build the design because each process component is dependent upon aspects of the others. For example, decisions about the negotiations are linked to outreach and consultation.

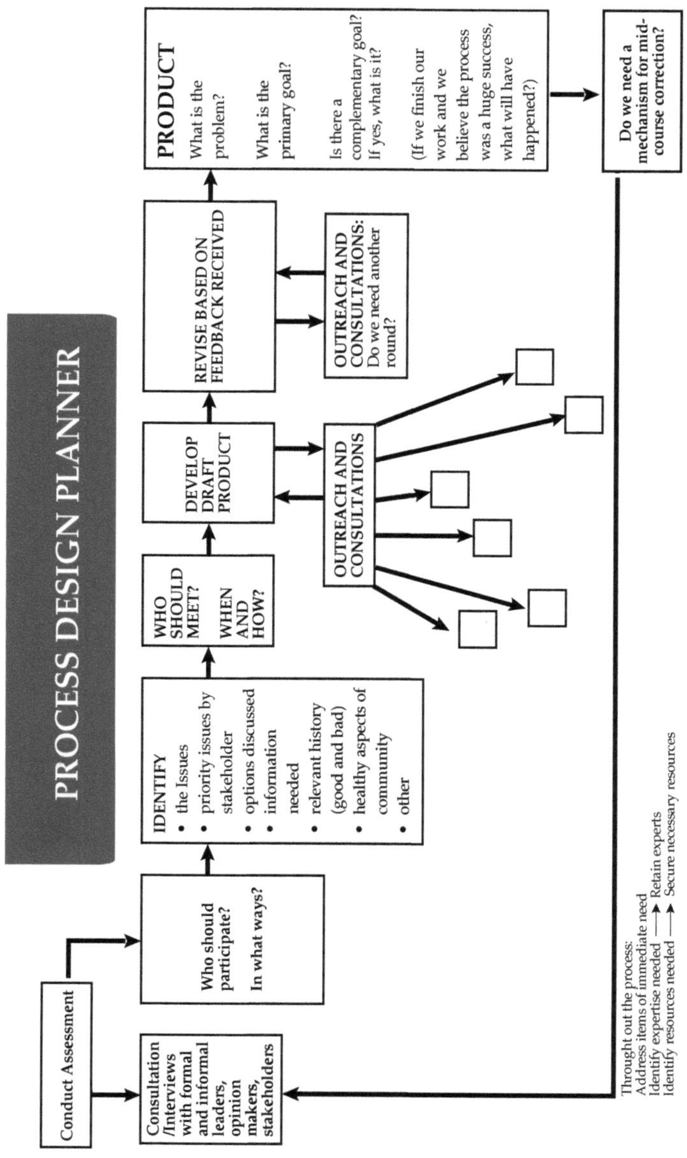

Figure 7.2
The Process Map Planner

After thinking through the process design, one can use the process map planner to draw the process map to illustrate its components. The process map will help people understand and remember the planned sequence and integration of activities. It will also provide the overall context for the negotiations and generate momentum as participants progress through the process.

Constructing the Building Blocks

Building the process design requires going back and forth among the process components to revise one as another clarifies. It usually takes many drafts to complete. My approach to process design is to consider questions pertaining to each basic building block coupled with information gathered during the mediator's assessment and thoughts for tailoring to the situation. Illustrative questions follow as well as suggestions for sequencing one's thought on process components to form the design. Figure 7.3 summarizes one way to think through a process design.

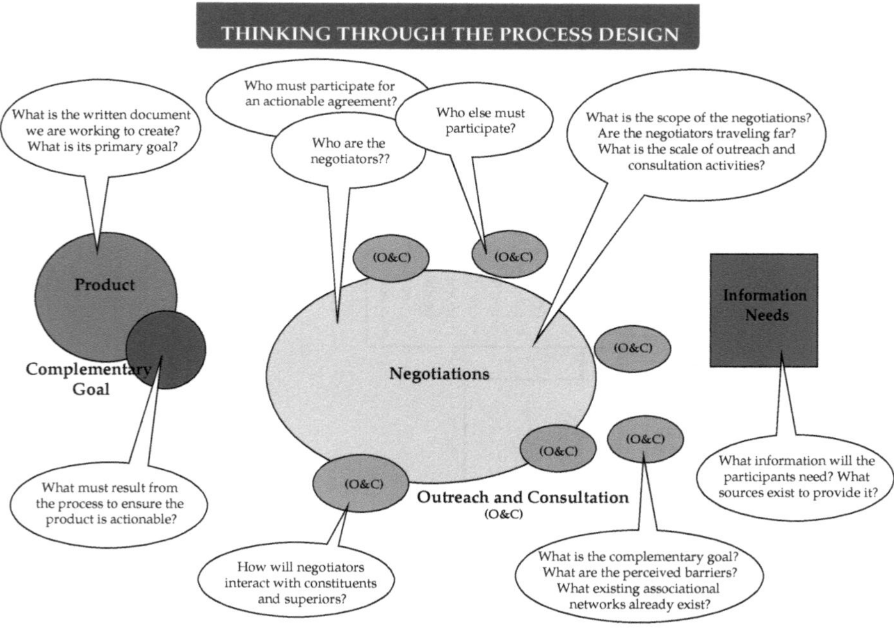

Figure 7.3
Thinking Through the Process Design

Since the product is usually apparent, it is a good place to begin: What is the consensus document that is meant to result from a successful process? For example, is it a draft regulation, a charter, or a memorandum of understanding? Corollary to the product is the goal. What is the product meant to accomplish? What is the complementary goal? What outcomes, in addition to the product, must result from the process to ensure implementation of the agreement?

Next, determine who must participate to build an actionable agreement. Participation is divided into 1) negotiators and 2) other participants. Most of the information for determining the negotiators is apparent from the assessment: Who will the product impact? What are the key categories of stakeholders? Who will effectively represent the stakeholders? Who will be required to act to implement the agreement? Who will be able to block implementation of an agreement?

In some cases, the groups and individuals that will participate in the negotiations will be known from the assessment, as in the abortion talks or from even earlier activities, such as the already appointed C-DAC negotiators. In other situations, as in the Chelsea case, during the design phase it may only be known that a group that is representative of the community will need to be identified.

With the negotiators known, consider the non-negotiators whose participation will be integrated through the outreach and consultation components of the process: Who will the negotiators need to consult with—superiors and/or constituents? For the agreement to be actionable, who else needs to be involved? Is achieving a complementary goal necessary for implementation of the product? If so, who needs to participate to achieve it? Whose opinions will be influential? Who in addition to the negotiators will need to be on board and/or able to block implementation of the agreement? Who in addition to the negotiators will have an active role in implementing the agreement?

After clarifying participation, one may determine the number, length and frequency of the negotiating sessions and the necessary forms of outreach and consultation for integrating the advice and education of non-negotiator participants into the process.

To estimate the number of negotiating hours needed consider the following questions: What is the scope of the negotiations? How many issues will be negotiated? How complicated are they? What are the difficult issues? How deep are the conflicts surrounding them? How might the history of the situation and/or past efforts to resolve the conflicts affect the process?

The amount of time needed for the negotiations increases the larger the scope of issues, the greater the complexity, and the intensity of the conflicts. To determine if the meetings should be multiple hour or multiple days, consider the questions: Where are the negotiators located? Are they local? Will they have to travel significant distances to get to meetings? Another factor affecting frequency of meetings is time required for outreach and consultation, which may occur throughout the negotiations or at particular milestones.

Outreach and consultation activities include negotiator feedback mechanisms and when necessary, engagement with a broader set of non-negotiator participants. If the negotiators intend to initiate consultations with members of their organizations, the process design may need only note those activities, and the mediator may periodically inquire about their occurrence. If not, the design may need to include mechanisms to ensure feedback interactions, for example, as regular conference calls or occasional facilitated meetings between negotiating sessions.

Perhaps the most complicated process design component is outreach and consultation when intensive participation by non-negotiators is required. Outreach and consultation to integrate the advice, opinions, and education of a broader range of non-negotiating parties may require unique process mechanisms. If such participation is essential for creating an actionable agreement, one may begin the design of such mechanisms by considering questions such as: What is the complementary goal? Why is it critical to actionability? What are the perceived barriers? Why do people think it will be so difficult or even impossible to build an actionable agreement? What existing associational networks exist? What strengths in the system/community exist that can be built upon?

Answers to these questions coupled with knowledge of the situation may suggest a range and scale of outreach and consultation mechanisms as well as the dynamics they must reflect. For example, because Chelsea residents were skeptical of outsiders, the process needed to put locals front and center. People were not expected to attend blatantly political meetings, but the city had a healthy infrastructure of social clubs. To integrate those challenges and dynamics, we trained people from Chelsea to facilitate hour-long conversations at the usual monthly meetings of social clubs around the city. Because Spanish was the first language for many residents, Spanish-speaking facilitators were among the trained group. Such process design elements helped overcome perceived barriers of skepticism, lack of trust, and language constraints, as well as to achieve the complementary goal of reaching deep into the community for participation and to teach self-governance.

The final element of the process design is to identify information the participants are likely to need and available sources for obtaining such information. Some needs are clear from the assessment but additional informational needs usually emerge during the deliberative negotiations.

Resilience and Adaptation

The process map may give a slightly false sense of security regarding the route to a consensus agreement. Unlike a road map, which indicates every road to a destination, the process map provides the main junctions but not every detailed step. It is a guide, but many unexpected situations and design needs arise throughout the process that could not have been contemplated at the outset. For this reason, the process design must allow for adaptation throughout its implementation. The mediator, in conjunction with the negotiators, must respond to challenges that arise in real time to sustain civic fusion long enough to build an actionable agreement. The clarity of the process map may, at some points in the process, give way to the disarray of reality.

In Chelsea, as we plodded along our intended path, some old timers tried to sabotage the process in an effort to retain their receding powers. Every incitement required a detour in response. Had we continued as planned and ignored the incitement, the provocation might have succeeded in derailing the charter consensus process. In addition, we had to develop an alternative outreach mechanism when we learned of resistance to the community meetings within the Cambodian community.

Working with a Emergent Process

Each meeting of the abortion talks was meticulously planned, but the almost six years of meetings were not drawn from a larger template. It was an emergent process. We did not know at the outset where it was headed. For each set of meetings, we obtained input on goals and topics. To keep the group from veering off course and back toward polarization, we provided ongoing process design expertise.

As a group, the participants were somewhat resistant to "talk process." They wanted Laura and me to design the meetings on our own, but we felt strongly that we needed their input and so we continued to consult them.

Once the participants decided to go public, the talks turned into a mediated process. Its focus shifted first to deciding on the appropriate vehicle for going public. After they agreed to write a consensus article, the next six months of meetings were devoted to jointly preparing the article.

The three projects discussed in this text illustrate how different civic fusion process designs can be. There are basic building blocks, but each situation requires its own arrangement, models, and often, unique process components. They are arranged across time to fit particular circumstances. To try to find a cookie-cutter approach fails to respect the complexity of the situations that would require such intensive civic fusion processes.

In drawing from accumulated understandings derived from a mediator's assessment, process designs may be constructed to accommodate the unique characteristics of the situations they are designed to address.

PART IV
INITIATING AND SUSTAINING CIVIC FUSION

Introduction

Complex public policy challenges reflect a blend of passions, values, interests, emotions, self-interest, and altruism. This chaotic mixture often becomes configured as confusion, gridlock, and conflict, which is sustained by assumptions of interested parties and maintained by a steady flow of selective perceptions that continuously support the positions taken and defended.

When the existing configuration of positions, interests, and conflicts—the status quo—is no longer sustainable, a government agency may initiate a public policy mediation process. A mediator helps parties to de-construct and re-build as much of the existing configuration as is needed to create an actionable agreement.

In this part of the book, I bring you into the negotiations. I describe the key dynamics in play that mediators must anticipate and manage to initiate and sustain civic fusion. To mediate polarized public disputes, the mediator continually and simultaneously tracks multiple dynamics, with some requiring primary attention at times and others needing only a guiding touch to stay on course.

CHAPTER 8

FACING POLARIZATION

Imagine people walking into a room for the first time to negotiate a solution to a problem that has vexed them for years. They enter and look around. Maybe they see some familiar faces, perhaps they sit down next to someone they know to be likeminded. They may observe strangers, people they've tangled with in the past, and others they've never met, but whom they know hold positions antithetical to their own. People are rather tense, anxious, and uncertain.

Initiating civic fusion amidst polarization requires critical preliminary activities. First, the negotiating parties need to understand the overall process and be assured it will be worth their time and effort. Next, they will generate a common public goal along with procedural ground rules, which will govern their negotiations. Developing the ground rules provides negotiators with an opportunity to experiment and succeed with consensus decision making. After reaching consensus on process issues, the negotiating team will begin discussing substantive issues to identify the scope of their negotiations.

Confirm Impact

The parties must be assured that they have a real opportunity for meaningful impact on a solution to their long-standing problem. They need to know that if they succeed in reaching a consensus agreement, the initiating agency will implement it.

Among the ways of making this clear and apparent to the parties is for the head of the sponsoring government agency to tell them so directly. These leaders champion the process by letting the parties know their efforts are appreciated, and most importantly, confirming the future impact of their work.

Harry Spence, the Chelsea receiver, repeatedly—in speeches, on cable television, and at meetings—told the community that if they reached consensus on a city charter that passed in a special election, he would send that charter to the governor.

The head of OSHA, Assistant Secretary John Henshaw, kicked off the first C-DAC meeting. He welcomed the C-DAC members, thanked them for their willingness to provide their expertise to the agency, and assured them he would implement their agreements.

Because governing always requires balancing diverse interests, it is helpful for government officials to make explicit their overall goals for the product, usually with nods to a range of the interests of stakeholder groups represented. In addition, the government negotiator provides information about the required formal processes that will follow the negotiations to ensure appropriate expectations.

From the assessment, Laura and I knew that the abortion talks, although focused on a hotly contested political issue, would be rooted in more personal than overtly political interactions. As a result, even though the governor and the archbishop provided the impetus for the talks and knew about them, we decided it wasn't necessary for them to directly launch the talks.

Review the Process

To slowly draw together the negotiators, a mediator must ensure the participants understand the entirety of the process, including their roles and responsibilities as well as those of the mediator. The explanation should include a clear, comprehensive process plan and provide assurance that someone is steering the ship. This contributes to building confidence in and establishing the legitimacy of the process.

For the preliminary Chelsea charter preparation team meeting, I placed a 5-foot-wide version of the process map at the front of the room. As I pointed to the appropriate symbol on the process map, I explained that we had already conducted the assessment interviews, had already sent out newsletters and had cable television shows, trained facilitators, and held a round of community meetings. I also explained to the participants how they were selected as members for the charter preparation team. (Refer to Figure 3.1, the Chelsea charter process map.)

Next, I detailed the steps they would undertake to prepare the charter. I described the community meetings to come and how they would integrate the community input into the charter discussions. Knowing that most brought with them a deep skepticism rooted in a history of outsiders' broken promises, I wanted to show them explicitly that we'd done precisely what we said we would do. I hoped this would build confidence for the next phase of the process.

For C-DAC, I provided an overview of the negotiated rulemaking process. I used a process map embedded in a PowerPoint presentation to illustrate the negotiation dynamics as well as their responsibilities for consulting with those they represented.

For the abortion dialogue, we started similarly, by situating the talks in the context of the initial exploratory activities. Laura and I described the assessment phase and the transition from the interviews to the decision to move forward with the talks. We again explained how they came to be the participants. We described the process in terms of its focus on agreed-upon goals, our work to design meetings to achieve those goals, and the exercises we expected to use. In addition, we differentiated the characteristics of dialogues from those of debates and deliberations.

During process overviews, I describe the principles of consensus and the responsibilities of negotiators working under a consensus decision rule. For example, I explain the difference between consent and support: If you actively support something, you would be willing to carry a sign at a demonstration to tell the world that you love that policy decision. On the other hand, you may consent to a proposal that you can live with. I describe the following as enlightened self-interest: understanding that to get what you most want, you need to ensure that others' interests are also satisfied.

In addition, I describe the responsibilities of negotiators engaged in a consensus process. For example, they must articulate their opinions and concerns so they can be woven into the overall agreement, and they must assist in developing solutions to satisfy their objections to proposals put forward by others. It's not sufficient for a negotiator to hate a proposal. He or she needs to tell the group why, and how to revise it to meet the desired objectives.

Negotiators clarify their responsibility to consent to livable proposals and to block consensus for serious objections. Because the goal is to create an actionable agreement, the latter is as important as the former. A participant's dissent on a proposal effectively vetoes that proposal and triggers additional deliberation until a consensus emerges. It can be hard to be a lone holdout, but if that participant's constituents will vehemently reject the proposal, then it is vital to dissent. It doesn't help anyone to finalize an agreement that will be shot down as soon as it's out of the room. For this reason, it is crucial for representative negotiators to maintain ongoing contact with both superiors and constituents throughout the negotiations.

Beginning to Bond

After the brief introductory activities, it's time for the mediator to engage the parties in a way that slowly brings them yet closer together.

In most cases, participants introduce themselves by providing their names and organizational affiliations, as well as say a little about their goals, concerns, and thoughts about the issues before them. During the first C-DAC meeting, each person spoke for a few minutes about key issues of crane safety. Many said they were hopeful that the group would reach consensus on rules that were sorely needed.

In Chelsea, at Roberta's suggestion, we tried something different. We asked all the team members to place themselves, via a Post-it note, on a Chelsea historical time line. Then each person described his or her significant Chelsea event. This exercise proved extraordinarily effective as people bonded across time, many through similar immigration stories. (Chapter 3 provides a more in-depth description of this exercise.)

During the abortion talks, a question about how abortion came to play a central role in participants' lives spurred them to share deeply personal stories of abortions, women's health, and protecting the innocent. By exposing vulnerabilities, the women drew closer to each other. The group dynamics would have been different if there had been male participants. Laura and I would have framed different initial questions because the women would likely have been less willing and able to share such intimacies in a mixed-gender group.

These initial interactions were the first steps in bringing people close enough together to bond across their differences. They learned something about the individuals they had considered "other," and perhaps felt some assumptions shift as a result. Their core beliefs remained intact, even while early bonds of civic fusion formed among them.

Discern the Common Public Goal

The common public goal significantly contributes to a group's transition from polarized gridlock to joint problem solving. Amid frustrations over being tied together by their disputes, a shared goal provides a construct within which all have the potential to get what they want, as well as to protect against their nightmare scenarios.

People in conflict often view themselves in a zero-sum game in which every gain for one is a loss for another. When the status quo is unsustainable and no party can solve a problem unilaterally, all must begin to think about the range of negotiator interests in terms of "and" rather than "or." Their task is to attempt to satisfy the primary interests of all the stakeholders. The naming of that task is operationalized as a common public goal, sometimes referred to in the ground rules as the mission statement.

A simple illustration of this is from a past project to develop a consensus plan to reduce the incidental deaths of whales and dolphins from commercial fishing operations. Though they entered the room assuming their interests were diametrically opposed, the stakeholders essentially agreed to work together to protect marine mammals *and* ensure viable fisheries. The participants came to realize that their individual interests could not be treated as mutually exclusive, and they became bound by the necessity of determining the means for achieving their comprehensive goal.

The common public goal provides a unifying framework for placing negotiators' interests in relation to each other. This provides a level of comfort by making explicit that the solution will need to satisfy all parties' overriding interests, and leverage for the mediator to tap throughout the negotiations.

Parties derive a level of security from seeing their interests articulated in writing and legitimized as part of a consensus statement. It helps to reduce their fears of failing to persuade others of the validity of their interests.

Finally, the common public goal provides the mediator with a source of leverage. Throughout any negotiations, I refer to "our goal," and use the term to remind the negotiators that everyone must get what they need for the effort to succeed.

In Chelsea, our common public goal was to "develop a charter document that has the future of Chelsea in mind, not just current issues, and reflects and wins the support of the people of Chelsea." The latter phrase alluded to gaining the support of local power brokers. Chelsea needed a new way of self-governing, but to pass the new charter also had to win the majority of votes in a special election.

Negotiate Procedural Ground Rules

One of the first formal tasks of the negotiators is to develop ground rules to clarify process issues and expectations. The procedural ground rules, also referred to as organizational protocols, are a set of agreements among the negotiators that govern their process. (See Appendix C for examples of ground rules.)

Ground rules usually include about ten topics and run from three to five single-spaced pages. Of great importance, the ground rules spell out what constitutes an agreement and the status of that agreement relative to its implementation. They are more comprehensive than a usual agreement to mediate, and they do not include the behavioral rules of civil discourse that are common to ground rules of some public engagement processes, such as one person speaks at a time.

The procedural ground rules typically include

- Participation
- Decision making
- Agreement
- Confidentiality
- Communication
- Roles and responsibilities of the negotiators
- Roles and responsibilities of the mediators
- Record of the sessions
- Attendance
- Media

To begin the discussion, I provide a draft set of ground rules, usually a hybrid set created from past cases. Each section includes draft text, options, and white space to indicate that additional elements may be added.

The ground rules help to sustain civic fusion by preventing process conflicts. More than once I've had participants ask to skip the ground rules discussion to get to the substantive issues sooner, with the idea that we would deal with ground rule issues as they arose. Of course, by then it's too late. Process conflicts amidst substantive discussions become means for political gain, which are likely to fuel mutual aversions and push people too far apart to sustain civic fusion. For many parties, process issues seem irrelevant compared to the substantive issues. Organizational infrastructure, however, is the equivalent of substantive issues for mediators, who at times, may need to negotiate with parties to assure a productive and transparent process framework.

The following discussion illustrates ground rule negotiations, including additional detail related to discussions of participation, decision making, agreement, and confidentiality.

Participation

The participation sections of the ground rules clarify who will be seated at the negotiating table and who will be obligated under an agreement. Sometimes members are identified only by the organizations represented; in other cases, the names of the negotiators are listed in the procedural ground rules with their affiliated organizations, which they are authorized to obligate. If the participants are present only in their capacity as individuals, then only their names are listed.

The participation section also typically includes a section describing how to add members, varying levels of participation, if applicable, and if primary negotiators can appoint alternates to serve in their absence.

Decision Making

The decision rule section is critical because it indicates what will constitute a decision. Civic fusion processes typically rely on consensus decision rules defined as unanimity. My preference is always to negotiate until all parties agree. Doing so, in my experience, makes everyone work harder and take responsibility for the complexity of the situation, including the reality of limitations. However, negotiating teams sometimes decide to define consensus as something less than unanimity. In such instances, it may be necessary for the mediator to remind the negotiators that an agreement reached with a less than unanimous definition of consensus may not be actionable if a dissenting party can block its implementation.

The consensus decision rule for the abortion talks was absolute. The participants agreed that information about the talks—even their existence—would be made known to the public only if they reached consensus agreement to do so.

The Chelsea charter preparation team agreed to operate by consensus, defined as unanimous agreement, with respect to the complete charter. However, they also agreed that during their negotiations, if the team had fully discussed an issue, reached impasse, and did not expect more discussion to lead to any new proposals, I was empowered, as the mediator, to call for a vote. To pass, a proposal would need to be supported by 80 percent of the team members present. This decision rule enabled the team to reach tentative agreements on issues with a vote, but such tentative agreements were reviewed as part of the overall package that was the charter. The complete charter had to be adopted by unanimous consent of all parties at the negotiating table. Thus, the 80 percent rule served to create an efficiency during deliberations but not a means for allowing an extraordinary majority to prevail over dissenters.

Agreement

Ground rules also make expectations explicit regarding agreements reached. For example, the product or written agreement, may be a recommendation to a government agency. It cannot be considered a final decision because the government cannot transfer its authority to a citizen or stakeholder group, and therefore, must retain its authority to accept or reject recommendations. In such cases, the ground rules may speak to an expected quid pro quo: If the negotiating team (of which the government is a part) reaches a consensus agreement as defined by the ground rules, the government will act on that agreement. However, officially, the agreement is a *recommendation* to government.

For example, the consensus reached on crane safety standards was a recommendation to OSHA, which then used the agreement as the basis of its proposed rule. In Chelsea, legislation stipulated that the receiver was responsible for recommending to the governor a new form of government for Chelsea. Thus, the ground rules of the charter preparation team defined the agreement as a recommendation to the receiver.

The government retains the right to reject the recommendation, but rejecting a consensus agreement built by a fused group of diverse stakeholders may have negative political consequences. However, the ground rules do not legally bind the government to act on the recommendation.

Confidentiality

Most mediated public disputes are governed under open meeting laws, which require plenary sessions to be open to the public and all documents to be publicly available. However, they allow for confidentiality among the negotiators and the mediator. The ground rules usually state that the mediators will hold information in confidence if asked to do so by a negotiator and that private caucuses may be held at the request of any party to the negotiations and/or the mediators.

In contrast, as described previously in Chapter 5, the ground rules for the abortion dialogue specified absolute confidentiality of all aspects of the dialogue to protect the participants. The existence of the talks was only made known to a list of people the participants were required to inform. Spouses were included in the list of informed people; assistants were not. (After the *Boston Globe* article appeared, one participant's assistant told her she was relieved to learn that it wasn't an affair that had led her to repeatedly slip out of the office without telling anyone where she was going!)

Managing Procedural Conflict

If a negotiator violates an inferred but not explicit ground rule, the written procedural agreements can be used as a means for solving procedural conflicts that arise. Revising the ground rules can be a means for resetting the negotiations.

In the marine mammal case, a politically connected party contacted the office of a senator to discuss a proposal he strongly supported. A staff person from the senator's office then called each negotiator to pressure her or him to support it. Some were absolutely livid at the political intrusion and the assertion of political power.

The negotiator apologized to the team and said the calls were not made at his urging but rather at the initiative of a staff person. The proposal was withdrawn. To assuage the strong anger of the parties and to protect against a repeat occurrence, I proposed relevant additions to the ground rules. After the negotiating team discussed, revised, and agreed on changes to the ground rules, we were able to turn our focus back to the substantive negotiations.

Negotiating the ground rules illustrates and provides a low-risk opportunity for learning how to function in a consensus process. The parties are provided with a draft list of issues that constitute the scope of the ground rules negotiations. They may add or subtract issues. They work from draft text, which they review and revise until they reach tentative agreements. The entirety of the ground rules is not agreed on until the entire document is complete.

The negotiators carefully discuss each section, propose new options or revisions, and discuss them until they achieve consensus on the changes. When an issue is linked to a previous one, the negotiators return to the earlier issue and review it for consistency with later decisions. After all sections are tentatively agreed on, the negotiators review the document section by section, and upon completion, the mediator asks if there is any dissent to accepting the ground rules as the group's governing document. When there is none, they have successfully negotiated a consensus agreement. This is similar to the methods they will use to address their substantive issues.

The ground rules discussion is something of a dry run for the substantive discussions. It builds confidence in the parties' abilities to participate and succeed in a consensus process. It is also typical that support for particular ground rule elements may cross the usual lines of coalitions and interests. This starts to stir up negotiators' previously fixed assumptions about those parties with which they strongly disagreed in the past.

Upon successful conclusion of the ground rules deliberations, the negotiating team has a common public goal that frames the deliberative discussions for producing the product, a set of mutual agreements for governing the process, clear expectations of procedural issues, a sense of how to operate productively in a consensus process, and the beginnings of safely shifting assumptions. These are early movements toward civic fusion.

After such initial process activities, the tone of the discussions tends to be measured and even. Although people usually want to delve into substantive issues, the process discussions are an opportunity to teach restraint and foster respect for fellow negotiators. Process issues generally do not stir passions in the ways that substantive issues sometimes do and so serve as a useful starting point.

Substantive Issues

The initial step into a policy conflict is to review the list of issues that will form the scope of the negotiations. As with the ground rules, the negotiators work from a draft list compiled prior to their first meeting. Again, they add, subtract, discuss, and revise until they reach consensus on the list of issues. The conversation is limited to whether or not an issue should be part of the scope. The negotiators do not get into difficult substantive discussions at this point. If an issue raises their passions, the mediator confirms agreement that it falls within the scope of the negotiations.

This limited foray into substance accomplishes bonding in a variety of ways. First, at the end of the discussion, they have achieved consensus on another written document—the list of issues that forms the scope of their negotiations. The scope creates boundaries for the conflict, which makes it less overwhelming. In addition, during the scoping discussions, some people probably found themselves in agreement with others they expected to spar with.

The specifics of negotiating the scope of the negotiations will be described in greater detail in Chapter 9, "Keeping the Substance in Motion."

Social Time

Seeing people outside their formal roles helps them to bond. Social time may help break down negative stereotypes, and it may build relationships that provide goodwill during the negotiations. As negotiators face difficult and complicated issues, the social bonds may give them the necessary patience to stay with an issue to find a mutually agreeable solution.

To encourage socializing during national meetings, I usually recommend two-and-a-half or three-day meetings. With people tired from travel on the first night, the second night usually provides convenient opportunities for informal conversation and social interactions.

For the year of C-DAC meetings, we always met for beers for an hour or so on the second evening of the meeting. People got to know each other more personally on these occasions and sometimes debriefed aspects of the meeting. During the abortion talks, every meeting included a shared meal. Whereas formal meeting time was designed to create bonds across difference, the shared meals allowed for easy connections through life and family stories.

CHAPTER 9

KEEPING THE SUBSTANCE IN MOTION

Keeping the substance in motion is like juggling balls. Like the juggler, the mediator keeps numerous issues in the air at the same time. Each issue is discussed, tossed back into the mix, discussed again, tossed back in the air again, and so forth, until the negotiating team tentatively agrees on a solution. Tentative agreements reduce the number of issues in play, although a previously resolved issue may be added back into the mix if it is affected by later decisions on a related issue. Similar to a juggler, the mediator consciously controls motion that seems to border on chaos. Luckily, mediation allows for margins of error: If the balls drop, you can pick them up and start again. And the mediator does not work alone but rather has a room full of negotiators that help keep the issues in motion.

To give a sense of substantive scale, the Chelsea city charter covered sixty-seven issues in a 60-page document. The proposed worker safety standards for cranes and derricks used in construction addressed forty issues in a 122-page document. In both projects, more than twenty parties negotiated and reached final consensus on every word and punctuation mark on all pages of the product.

When working with up to twenty-five negotiators on a vast range of issues, a mediator always faces the problem of where to start when many issues are interconnected and priorities vary widely among the parties. And yet, the mediator has to start somewhere.

The way forward is to identify the scope of the negotiations, "workshop" each issue to identify its subissues and particular dynamics, subject all items to deliberative negotiations to reach tentative agreements, and ultimately, to achieve final consensus on all issues.

Identify the Scope of the Negotiations

The first time substantive issues are raised is usually during the first meeting. This is when the group identifies the scope of the negotiations, which is the complete set of issues that needs to be addressed to complete an actionable agreement. Often a draft set of issues is identified during the mediator's assessment and/or outlined by the initiating entity.

For the cranes reg neg, OSHA published a draft list of issues in the *Federal Register* and revised it based on comments received. In Chelsea, the professional charter drafter introduced the list of issues required for city and town charters under Massachusetts law. The goals identified during the abortion talks assessment formed the scope of issues to be discussed.

Typically, participants refine a draft list of issues to confirm the scope of their negotiations. The group clarifies, adds, and subtracts issues. At the end of the scope discussion, there is general agreement—consensus—on the list, with the caveat that it will be revised as the negotiations proceed if new issues emerge or if listed issues do not require further attention. As I often say about the list of issues, "When we finish all of these, we get to go home."

During discussion of the scope of issues, I restrict the conversation to a simple determination of whether or not an issue will make it onto the list. If discussions grow passionate, I agree to put the contentious issue on the list, and then move onto the next issue. Sometimes the negotiating team adds an item to the scope even when it interests only a small number of parties. If an issue is on the list, the parties will thoroughly discuss it sometime during the process.

Preventing further conversations on substantive issues at that point contributes to fostering deliberative negotiations. To sustain productive negotiations of complex issues among twenty or more people, the mediator needs to be able to assert control over the agenda, timing, and intensity of the discussions. The negotiating team will get to every issue, but appropriate timing and sequencing of the issues increases its productivity.

Workshop the Issues

Once the parties reach consensus on the scope of their negotiations, they "workshop" the issues. My colleague Howard Bellman and I evolved this concept for promoting open negotiations and protecting against early impasse. In workshopping an issue, the negotiators discuss its subissues, dynamics, key interests and concerns, and possible ideas and options they've considered. It is a time to broadly discuss the issues without the pressure of trying to reach an agreement or focusing on a written document. It is a time for early joint exploration and learning about the interests, concerns, and perspectives of all the negotiators.

At this stage, the negotiators typically reach conceptual agreements on some issues, clarify others, and identify areas of actual interest-based conflict. Soon after an issue is workshopped, the negotiating team is provided with draft text reflecting their discussions.

In the early days of public policy mediation, government agencies often presented draft products as a starting point for the negotiations. The effort to develop and internally vet these drafts made government negotiators defensive amid a reluctance to significantly revise their work. Stakeholders responded negatively to what seemed like constraints on the scope of the negotiations and predetermined resolutions. Although draft text brings focus to the deliberations, it is essential that the text emerge from the negotiators' discussions. The workshopping method produces credible draft text.

As with the scope discussion, the workshop deliberations are also constrained, although less so. These are not yet full-blown efforts to negotiate disparate interests. With early, perhaps tenuous bonds fused, the group jointly walks through each issue to determine what lurks within it. The parties publicly surface their key issues and interests, and the mediator helps separate confusion from actual conflict and inhibits impasse. It is a time to air out the issues.

The opportunity to share one's concerns and learn of those of others, without attempts to persuade or a need to defend, often causes glimmers of hope to flicker. People begin to sense the possibility that something different and positive may actually result from their deliberations.

Though initially perceived as broad and intractable, many actual conflicts center on a limited range of subissues. In workshopping an issue, the negotiators work toward an agreement on its component parts. Sometimes, clarifying confusions that surround assumed conflicts leads to agreements in concept. On other issues, actual interest-based conflict is identified as a subissue amid layers of general agreement. In workshopping issues, the group also identifies its future informational needs, which helps to prepare for later sessions.

The complexity of issues and the expected time required for the negotiations affects the time allocated for workshopping the entire scope of issues. Typically, negotiators workshop the issues in the order they appear listed in the scope. For a negotiated rulemaking to develop student loan regulations for the U.S. Department of Education, we workshopped all the issues in one meeting and completed the remainder of the negotiations in two more meetings. C-DAC used six of its eleven meetings to workshop the forty issues that comprised its scope of negotiations.

From the workshop discussions, I get a deeper understanding of the veracity of each issue. Later, this will help me determine a productive timing and sequencing of issues at future meetings.

In essence, through the scoping and workshop discussions, the participants slowly draw closer together. For issues with actual interest-based conflicts, I keep a gap that I don't yet want them to cross. Early in the process, the parties want to dive into the issues they care most about, but I try to prevent them from doing so until they have enough curiosity and credible information to engage in productive negotiations. Curiosity suggests a journey for new understandings and prospecting for innovative ideas. (For more on encouraging curiosity, see Chapter 10, "From Certainty Through Not Knowing to Curiosity.")

The opposite course would be simply to open the floor for people to raise the issues they cared about most. Without a meeting structure and norms of deliberative negotiations, people would most likely quickly reach an impasse coupled with anger, frustration, and confirmation of the other's inability to work toward consensus, or simply put—polarization. Such conversations are familiar, and interrupting the usual and expected dynamic creates dissonance and space for the hope of resolution.

Typically, after workshopping the entire list of issues, the group has reached conceptual agreements on the easiest issues, clarified the subissues embedded in complex issues, created a shared sense of the difficult issues, and even made some proposals for resolution. For example, early on in the Chelsea negotiations, the charter preparation team decided on a council/manager form of government, considered two- and four-year terms for city councilors, and knew they had deep disagreements over school committee composition.

Following the workshop phase of the negotiations, the negotiators are provided with draft text that reflects their discussions. They then spend the rest of their meetings negotiating, adding to, subtracting from, reworking, and revising the draft text to develop the final written agreement.

Reaching Tentative Agreements

After all the issues within the scope of the negotiations have been workshopped, they continue to remain in play; nothing has yet been agreed to. As there is no agreement until everything is agreed to, negotiation teams work to reach tentative agreements on each issue and then thoroughly review the entire draft product prior to achieving final consensus.

The interconnectedness of the issues makes choosing the post-workshopping starting point of the negotiations rather complicated. Obviously, it is impossible to talk about and track forty or sixty issues at once. The timing and sequencing of the issues impact the tone and productivity of the negotiations. Mediators work to balance the need to have sufficient time for multiple passes at difficult issues with the usefulness of building momentum by reaching tentative agreements on easy and moderate issues. For example, I usually begin meetings with complicated issues in the early mornings when everyone is fresh and fully caffeinated. Then, I may put more emotional and potentially explosive issues on the agenda immediately after lunch, when people feel more inclined to take a siesta than fight! It may be helpful to discuss related issues on the same day and to follow a difficult issue with a host of completely unrelated and easy issues.

To design the agenda for each meeting, I envision the negotiation dynamics inherent in each issue and blend them into a productive agenda. From a high level of abstraction, and based on the assessment interviews and past interactions with the parties, I imagine how the parties' energies are likely to clash and merge during discussions of a given issue. In building the meeting agenda, I consider how to smooth out those energies and sequence issues to foster increased unity and comfort during the negotiations.

The draft written document, reflecting the parties' workshop discussions, provides a focus for the negotiations. This initial text[1] prepared for the negotiators includes agreements in concept on easy issues, outlines options discussed for moderate issues, and for the most difficult issues, something akin to an outline of the subissues identified along with a great deal of white space on the pages to indicate the hard work to be done. The white space is also meant to assure people that those issues, although already discussed, have not been resolved because we did not yet find a way to satisfy their identified interests and concerns. Thus, the document is an emerging agreement meant to provide focus, sustain momentum, record progress, and denote work remaining.

---

1. This is different from the single text method described by Fisher and Ury in their book *Getting to Yes*, whereby a complete agreement is drafted by the mediator and provided to each side. The parties then provide their proposed revisions to the text, which the mediator, working offline, integrates into the next draft. The mediator repeats the revision process until final agreement is reached.

   In the process referred to above, the negotiators, with assistance from the mediator, repeatedly refine the draft together; they jointly wordsmith the document during plenary negotiating sessions.

Agreements in concept do not indicate resolution of an issue. There is great distance between the spoken and written word. Before the initial draft text is circulated, I explain to the negotiators that there is a significant difference between what they believe they agreed to in concept and what they will find as written words. I ask them to read the text with an eye toward fixing it, and remind them that we will revise the draft text until it conforms to their agreements. Nevertheless, I've come to expect calls and emails from a few outraged representatives because of the usual disparity between verbal and written agreements.

The parties negotiate their way through the draft document to reach tentative agreements. An issue that is tentatively agreed on does not appear again on a meeting agenda until the final review, unless it must be changed because of its relationship to another issue. With so much substance in motion, this method provides a means for progressing on the product without closing off the possibility of future revisions.

While some issues resolve with surprising ease after confusion over positions gives way to shared interests, many do not. It often requires a great deal of effort to sustain group focus on divisive issues. As the bonds of civic fusion take hold, parties seem to want to connect with others despite their differences. To avoid the discomfort of their conflicts as well as information that contradicts long-held views, they tend to raise tangential and unrelated issues. The mediator needs to sustain focus to help parties embrace their differences to innovate mutually satisfying solutions.

One of the challenges of keeping the substance in motion is ensuring that discussions of each issue stay separate from others, and sometimes, sustaining focus solely on parsed subissues. The interrelatedness of the issues makes it hard for the negotiators to keep to the boundaries of an issue, but crossing those boundaries makes it more difficult to unravel conflicts and confusions to build solutions. It is like untangling a knotted, thin, gold chain. You have to loosen up the tangled mass and then carefully separate and follow each strand through its loops, twists, and snarls to free it up.

An overall strategy for getting control of the vast scope of the negotiations is to continually reduce it by reaching tentative agreements on as many issues and subissues as possible to decrease the number of outstanding issues. Throughout the negotiations, the list of issues in motion grows shorter until the group has a handful of the most difficult issues, which will require the intense attention described as the march to closure in Chapter 12.

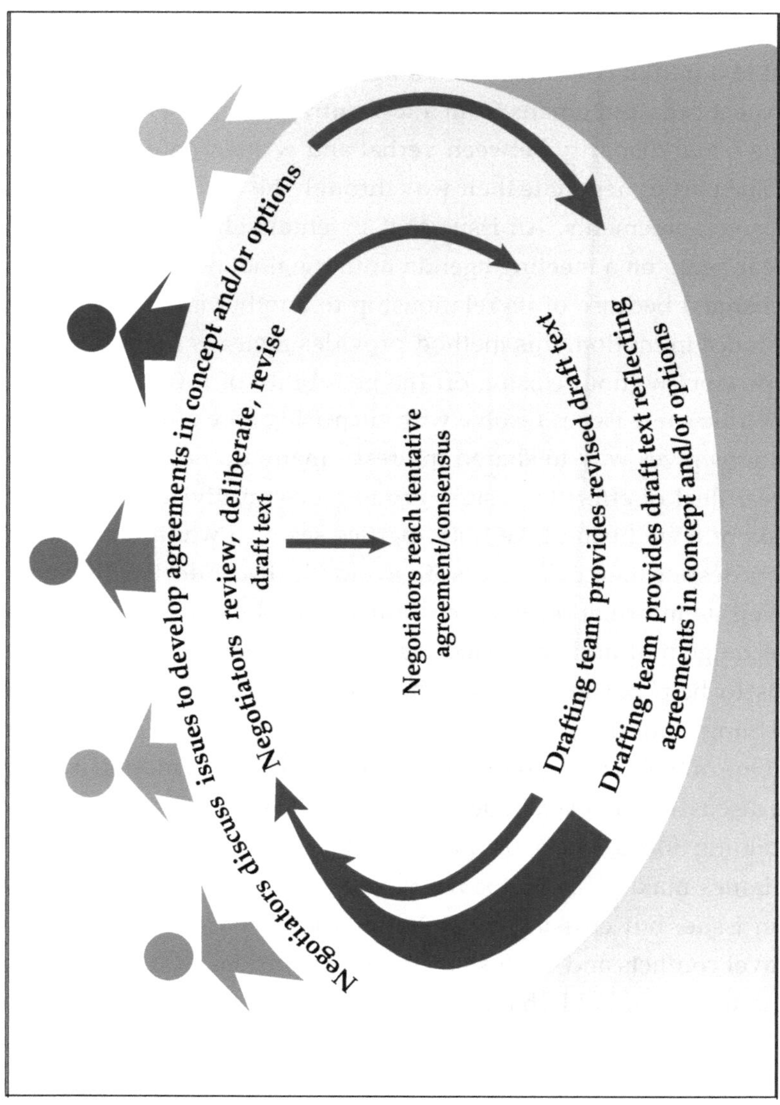

Figure 9.1
Dynamics of Substance in Motion

In managing people's negotiations, mediators track for any emergent, unifying nugget of substantive agreement on which to build. It's not unusual after a particularly feisty discussion for me to say something like, "If I heard you all correctly, I think you all agree on _______." Often there's a bit of a chuckle because I may have picked out the only unifying bit among a lot of disagreement, but if the group resonates with it, they will build on that nugget.

In pursuit of substantive closure, negotiations are a continuous search for options that satisfy the interests of the parties. The people around the table have the substantive knowledge to construct the solutions to each issue. If necessary, outside experts are tapped to fill any holes in their combined knowledge base. Throughout the negotiations, mediators work to draw out participants' best ideas and, if needed, help shape them into plausible options. Much time is spent generating, revising, and massaging various proposals into tentative agreements. With the text providing focus, mediators may also provide linguistic support to find the words that appropriately capture the nuances required to reach agreements.

Reaching tentative agreement often requires repeated efforts to peel back the layers of the broad-based conflict to clarify confusions from the actual dispute. The actual points in dispute turn out to be amazingly narrow compared to prior expectations!

For example, during the cranes assessment I repeatedly heard that operator qualifications would be a difficult issue. In early rounds of discussions, it seemed that the dispute centered on certifying or not certifying. After many hours of discussion, it turned out to be a dispute over who should be authorized to test crane operators.

As we worked to clarify the actual dispute, we reached tentative agreements on all the other subissues such as supervision, precertification supervision, the elements of qualifications, and the knowledge to be tested. What had initially looked like an overwhelming conflict boiled down to one subissue. It remained a difficult issue, which was only decided at the last meeting, but the narrowed disagreement was more manageable and enabled more focused discussions and proposals.

To keep the substance moving toward agreements, mediators need to frame questions with intent. For example, pointed questions may expose contradictions and reveal new understandings and possibilities. These are not open-ended questions. They are focused at particular points of confusion or conflict. Sometimes the questions require information from parties; sometimes they expose a lack of knowledge; and sometimes they are meant to trigger new thought. For example, when none of the crane negotiators could accurately explain the European standards for testing and verifying prototype cranes, it became clear that some of their previous arguments were misplaced.

Questions can also be used to elicit unifying and connective answers. For example, asking the abortion talk participants how the issue came to play such a central role in their lives revealed both reciprocal vulnerabilities and shared political astuteness.

Questions can also remind negotiators that no one can achieve his or her goals unless solutions are developed for achieving the group's common public goal. For example, a mediator may ask "What exactly do you need to satisfy your interests? What did you hear your colleague say he or she needs?"

The complexity of public policy disputes and their myriad gradations of nuance provide the possibility for solutions because there are so many ways to slice and dice a disagreement. In each round of talks, the issues in dispute become clearer. As we work the text, people propose word changes. Each rejected word provides greater insight into the dispute, as parties explain why a proposed word falls short. As we gain momentum by resolving many issues, for the sake of being able to reach a final agreement, people tend to suspend their own objections on issues they value less as they come to understand that others greatly value those issues.

The substantive negotiations are a continuous cycle of issue discussion, option generation, reflection on options, and massage of options to reach tentative agreements. Expert information is added to the mix, as needed.

Conceptualize Frameworks

Even as negotiations are centered on substantive specifics, sometimes it's necessary to look at an issue more broadly to conceptualize agreement frameworks that can provide the required flexibility. This is the case, for example, in implementing standards among different sectors of a regulated community or in allowing for future technological advances. Negotiators often get stuck in either/or patterns. They argue over whether the agreement should require this or that. In many instances, however, it's not a matter of this or that, or even this *and* that, but rather a reasoned construct responsive to the intricacies of the issue.

For example, in the cranes reg neg we spent almost an entire meeting discussing crane contact with electrical power lines, one of the greatest causes of death and serious injury related to crane accidents. During the first day, C-DAC members discussed a range of strategies for protecting workers operating near power lines, including how to eliminate the hazard, avoid the hazard, and protect against injury should contact occur. In addition, they discussed human, technical, and other causes of electrocution accidents as well as possible approaches for the standard. Although there was clear agreement on the need to eliminate hazards of contact with power lines, at many points in the discussions, negotiators tangled with demands for "musts" and "have-tos" and "alls."

During the discussion, an emerging realization of variations in danger levels came to be reflected in terms of red, yellow, and green zones. By the end of the meeting, the negotiators reached an agreement in concept on a framework that demarcated three risk zones, each correlating to particular hazards and required safety strategies. To accommodate different cranes and available and future technologies, the framework provided a menu of choices for complying with provisions for layered safety strategies. The one-size-fits-all mentality eventually gave way to flexibility under differing circumstances.

Passing on Issues

Before passing on an issue for discussions at a later date, it helps to bring the discussions to a head so the negotiators become aware of the actual conflicts. When discussions become repetitive and the group suffers a lack of creativity, mediators recap where things stand and then move the group to another issue. Even though they are passionately engaged on the issue, mediators make a determination that they are out of ideas and no new information can be expected to enter the system at that point. At the early stages of the negotiations, mediators may need to wrestle the negotiators onto another issue because some people hold tightly to their stance. With assurances that the group will return to the issue at a later meeting, they more willingly move onto the next issue on the agenda. These transitions usually become easier later in the process as negotiators find they are able to resolve issues during its second or third pass. Draft text on a passed issue is revised to reflect the latest discussions, and the document may include the options discussed as well as blank space to indicate the issue remains unresolved.

By the time they are passing on issues, the group has achieved a level of civic fusion that holds them together. Typically, the stuck issue stays on people's minds and group members rally with others offline to think of ways to move the issue forward. It's not unusual for these informal discussions to yield new ideas or perspectives. If needed, before the next meeting, there may be numerous offline telephone conversations and possibly, work groups to develop proposals for the team's review.

Final Consensus

After the negotiators reach tentative agreements on all issues, they review the entire product. The parties review the document on their own and with their constituents prior to the final meeting, and come to the last meeting prepared to identify items that require additional attention and possible revision. I ask them to let me know before the meeting which issues will need to be discussed.

At the final meeting, we walk through the document, page by page, and negotiators identify issues for review. Mostly, they clarify textual language based on questions raised, but sometimes they need to further negotiate specific issues.

When the negotiators have reaffirmed all their tentative agreements on all issues and there is no dissent on any part of the document as written, they have reached final consensus.

Good Faith Negotiations

Entering into a negotiation process doesn't guarantee success, but it does presuppose that everyone at the table will participate in good faith, that is, they are there to work hard to reach an agreement. From assessments, mediators expect to learn of the intent and commitment of the negotiators to work toward an agreement. However, mediators still need to be attuned to the possibility of bad faith negotiators working against agreements and therefore to possess strategies for exposing them.

People who engage in negotiations with the purposeful intent of frustrating efforts to reach an agreement can be said to be negotiating in bad faith. I have seen negotiators try to block agreements using three strategies: sowing confusion, disengaging, and coalition building with less sophisticated parties.

In one instance, intended bad faith negotiations became particularly obvious when the primary negotiator for one party stepped away from the table for a few hours to deal with a matter unrelated to the negotiations. He tasked his alternate with sowing confusion across substantive issues. Much less a master of this strategy than his boss, the alternate made clear their intent to work against an agreement. Throughout the process, the primary negotiator and I sparred over the focus of the discussions. Eventually, the negotiators reached tentative agreements on most issues. During the final negotiating session, we entertained a range of written proposals and counterproposals to narrow the differences on the outstanding issues. When it became clear that we wouldn't reach consensus on a central issue, the team agreed to reach final consensus on all its tentative agreements and leave it to the government to decide the outstanding issues.

After the meeting, the negotiator who seemed intent on undermining the process sent a letter to the government officials stating that he didn't know we were involved in negotiations. In my final report, I described the last meeting and included in an appendix the written proposals, counterproposals, and counter-counterproposals, many of which he had written. This gave the government enough evidence to publicly confirm that negotiations occurred. Ultimately, the federal agency promulgated the rule using the consensus text and the knowledge gained from intensive negotiations of the outstanding issues.

In another case, government negotiators failed to engage. Throughout the deliberations, other stakeholders demanded the government negotiators stop sitting at the table like "potted plants." The government negotiators' response was that they would go along with any consensus of the stakeholders. By the next-to-last meeting, we had reached tentative agreements on all issues, although they were conditioned on consultations with constituents. At the last meeting, the government negotiator stated its staff attorneys rejected a central element of the agreement. We spent the next three days renegotiating the affected issues and eventually reached final consensus on all issues. However, the government agency never published the agreement in the *Federal Register*, the first step to making it law, and the agreement was never implemented.

In a third case, during a negotiated rulemaking, one negotiator built a coalition, which she then led against a range of proposals. The politics of the situation made it impossible for her to block an agreement on her own. When my co-mediator and I realized her strategy, we met with the other members of her coalition and asked them to explain their interests relative to the proposals they opposed. With these clarifying discussions, they realized they had more to gain from an agreement than an impasse and broke from their coalition. Ultimately, the negotiators reached final consensus on all issues.

Negotiations won't always end in success. But if no agreement is reached, it should be because either there was no agreement to be had or the parties and mediators lacked the creativity to develop one. Mediators engaging large groups of stakeholders in complex negotiations need to keep alert for bad faith negotiators and respond with effective counterstrategies in pursuing closure.

CHAPTER 10

FROM CERTAINTY THROUGH NOT KNOWING TO CURIOSITY

Polarization of public issues is often sustained when long-held assumptions prevent parties from taking in new information related to the substance of issues and the intent of other parties. This makes them unable to consider alternative pathways out of the conflict.

Even a slight shift in assumptions can alter a polarizing configuration enough to enable new thoughts and ideas to emerge. The key is to trigger curiosity at the moment the person realizes she does not know something she was previously certain of.

In the hopes of enabling new ideas to surface, the mediator simultaneously acts to disturb the certainty of the parties by gently shaking their assumptions, creating space for not knowing, and then causing curiosity as a response to uncertainty. The need to cause such shifts exists throughout the negotiations.

Let's separately explore each part of the dynamic: certainty, not knowing, and curiosity even as we keep in mind that the movement occurs as a single action.

Certainty

Most parties enter into negotiations certain of their cause and the rightness of the positions they promote, but uncertain of their ability to negotiate a successful outcome. Thus, at the outset of a project, the dynamics support stagnation, impasse, and conflict, better known as polarization. Achieving civic fusion requires inverting the certainty–uncertainty dynamic.

Stakeholders often begin discussions feeling certain of the solutions to their situation, which typically satisfies their concerns but not those of their opponents. They may be frustrated by the inability of others to accept the validity and efficacy of their proposed solutions. Those in opposition may be perceived as ignorant, greedy, immoral, or simply misguided.

At the same time, given their failure to persuade others prior to the mediation process, they fear the uncertainty the deliberative process brings. They are aware of an inability to unilaterally control the outcome, and they may question their ability to succeed as negotiators. They may worry about failing to get what they want despite their belief in the validity of their positions. As representatives, they feel responsible to satisfy their constituents. Almost everyone holds in his or her mind a nightmare scenario of a feared, worst possible, perhaps even humiliating outcome.

For civic fusion to occur, the parties need to feel certain that they will succeed in satisfying their interests through the negotiations but uncertain of the configuration of the solution. The structure of the process, consensus decision rules, and the emergence of new and innovative ideas contribute to confidence in the process and reduce uncertainty stemming from fears of failing.

As early as the assessment interviews, mediators begin to develop relationships with the parties through questions that indicate an understanding of the situation and stakeholders' compelling interests. Negotiators enter the room with some sense that they have been heard. The process map indicates a clear plan for achieving the group's shared goal, and the ground rules provide procedures for managing negotiator interactions and clarify expectations. All combined these and other elements of the process structure contribute to creating a sense of safe space for the negotiations.

To assure negotiators that proposals they oppose will not become part of the product, I remind them of the group's consensus decision rule, which requires that either all, or in some cases, extraordinary majorities must agree to whatever goes into the product. Simply put, if a party vehemently opposes a proposal, it will not become part of the agreement. Multiple negotiators within each category of stakeholder provide this protection even when the consensus is defined as less than unanimity. To bring parties to this understanding, I often engage in some version of this conversation:

> *Me: What is your nightmare scenario?*
>
> *Negotiator describes.*
>
> *Me: Would you ever agree to that?*
>
> *Negotiator: Of course not.*
>
> *Me: Then how can that get into the agreement? We're working by consensus.*
>
> *Negotiator: [Breathes deeply, relaxes, and smiles.]*

Even as they develop the ground rules, the negotiators become familiar with the process of deliberative negotiations. As this orientation is brought to their substantive issues, people offer ideas that conform to the nuance of the situation, but have never before been considered. As tentative agreements emerge, participants begin to realize that the consensus decision rule protects them from their nightmare scenarios and that there actually are unforeseen possibilities. As confusions surface and clarify, and written draft agreements reflecting expressed interests and concerns are produced, confidence in the process builds.

As a result, the parties may become more comfortable and convinced that they will succeed in satisfying their interests.

The need to build confidence in the process to afford certainty of a satisfying product is one track among many that mediators continually attend to. In most projects, this track requires the greatest efforts early in the negotiations, eases as the parties move through the easy and moderately conflicting substantive issues, and reemerges during discussions of difficult issues.

As certainty about success in the process grows, assumed solutions and negative intent of others can more easily shift to a space of not knowing, which enables parties to explore old assumptions and embrace new information and ideas.

Create the Space of Not Knowing

As negotiators come to feel some certainty about their ability to succeed in the negotiations, and begin to question the efficacy of their rigid positions, the mediator acts to cause dissonance in long-held assumptions to create the space of not knowing.[1]

In policy disputes, people rarely occupy the space of not knowing. They rarely take in information that creates an acute awareness that their position or proposed solution does not reflect the complexity of the situation. Instead, parties often defend their positions and demand their solutions be adopted, often without actually understanding or giving credence to the concerns raised by others. Mediators slow down the conversation to enable people to experience the shortcomings of their assumed perspectives. At the moment of such awareness, one enters the space of not knowing. If he feels safe enough within that space, his mind may be open to and even create new ideas or thought patterns.

Socrates was thought to be the wisest man in Athens because he knew what he didn't know. As others came to discourse with him on subjects such as virtue and the good, he claimed he did not know what such things were, but he was willing to subject their knowledge to his

1. This idea is an extension of Z. D. Gurevitch, Z.D., "The Power of Not Understanding: The Meeting of Conflicting Identities," Journal of Applied Behavioral Science, Vol. 25, No. 2, 161–173 (1989).

understandings of what they were not. In Plato's *Dialogues,* Socrates repeatedly uncovers the fallacies of his interlocutors, who initially were certain of their knowledge.

Similarly in public policy mediation, most people come into the room thinking they know at least part of the solution to the situation. It's not necessarily that they are wrong, but rather, that their known solutions do not incorporate all the interests and concerns required for an actionable agreement. Most problematic, if someone is mistakenly certain of an answer to a question, that person cannot take in new information. For example, if I "know" that one plus one is three, there is little possibility that I will learn that the correct answer is two. My mind is closed to new information because for me the problem is already solved. There is no reason to explore a question I believe I've already correctly answered.

In the complexity of public policy negotiations, the "wrong" answers are not necessarily obvious. Often, they are rooted in assumptions that contribute to impasse and block creative thinking. To create the space of not knowing, the parties need to surface and slightly shift some of their long-held assumptions related to their perceptions of the situation while retaining commitments to their values and interests.

Surfacing and Shifting Assumptions

On political issues, assumptions generally fill in a lot of unknowns and crowd the space needed for new and more accurate information and understanding. Thus, to begin to reconfigure the existing state of affairs, the mediator must help people know what they do not know. Mediators help parties shift assumptions and perceptions to enable a new configuration to emerge that will be based on a closer approximation of the full reality of the situation, with its greater level of complexity and within the constraints of what is possible.

How many times have you tried to persuade another to your political position while they tried to persuade you to theirs? Most likely neither side learned from these conversations but more likely hardened their own positions. As you passionately argued your well-considered and logical argument, the other side articulated an alternative version, which made little sense to you. It wasn't the logic that was off, what may have frustrated you was that the other person didn't seem to even hear what you said. Your logical argument didn't enter into his mind except to stimulate the usual response that typically triggers in those arguments. You could probably be described as having a similar response. The lack of communication could be said to have resulted from the clashing assumptions on which your arguments were built.

In political conversations built atop unexpressed assumptions, we usually don't learn much. Perhaps we sharpen our debating skills, but we usually don't persuade or bring others into our fold. At some point, we stop having the conversations because we're frustrated that we don't get anywhere. We spend time with people we agree with, or we stay away from topics that may offend or lead to frustration. In the political arena, we negate positions of "the other." We may consider the other side to be morally bankrupt or simply ignorant—impervious to logical arguments. And then we gridlock. When this happens among political leaders, policy decisions don't get made. The issue sits or moves glacially, first right and then left, until the status quo is essentially frozen in time and space.

For example, where would you expect this conversation to go?

> Person A: "Life begins at conception."
>
> Person B: "A woman has a right to control her own body."

We know the conclusions drawn from these statements, but what are their embedded assumptions?

In the abortion dialogue, we discovered the need to surface embedded assumptions when the participants clashed over the use of contraception to reduce abortions. Without mutual understanding of their differing worldviews, the six women were unable to make progress on their mutual goal of understanding their similarities and differences.

Each side's worldviews described its working moral assumptions. The pro-life side began its worldview statement with:

We believe in one universal truth. We three, as Catholics, believe that each human life has its origin in the heart of God. This divine genesis of the human person calls us to protect and respect every human life from the moment of conception to natural death.

The pro-choice participants stated:

We recognize no single, universal truth that determines our moral decisions. On the contrary, we must consider a broad range of values whenever we seek to make wise, ethical, and compassionate choices. We respect a woman's moral capacity to make decisions regarding her health and welfare, including reproductive decisions.

With these worldviews surfaced and fully explained in the context of the talks, the participants experienced shifts in understandings—not in their positions on abortion issues—that resulted in deeper relationships and increased commitments to act to reduce the violence associated with abortion rhetoric. The pro-choice side came to understand that the pro-life women's stance on abortion was part of a broader constellation of issues associated with human sexuality. This explained what had seemed like a contradiction: why the pro-life women opposed abortion and also opposed contraception. Some on the pro-life side came to understand that the universal truth they believed in did not compel others to adopt it even when it was fully understood, and that although in conflict with theirs, the pro-choice women embraced a different moral system. Some considered the pro-choice moral construct reprehensible, but learned the individuals were not acting with evil intent.

In this case, these shifts occurred after a visible inability to communicate led the participants to consciously surface, express, and analyze their underlying assumptions. They embraced the space of not knowing because of a commitment to reduce the violent rhetoric used in the abortion debate, and to strengthen their relationships built by connecting across their deep divide—experience the bonds of civic fusion.

More typical to negotiations is the need to surface assumptions specific to substantive issues rather than to overall worldviews. As people enter into negotiations of a longstanding conflict, they usually have some strongly held and solidified opinions on the issues of great importance to them. They may not have had combative conversations with the individuals in the room, but they probably sense they know what many will say. In the past, things got stuck. Why should they expect it to be different this time?

In substantive disputes, people seem to operate from sets of unarticulated assumptions, which provide foundations for their logical arguments. We usually argue policy without considering its underlying assumptions. We don't even know to look for them! And we certainly don't respectfully explore the sources of our disputes. A willingness to explore for assumptions suggests a willing entry into the space of not knowing.

The following example provides an illustration of exploring technical assumptions that underlie a conflict. A number of years ago, I was hired by a regional government commission as it considered a proposed development with potentially substantial impact for the region. The developer submitted a traffic study, which detailed the expected traffic impacts that would result from the proposed development. A group of community abutters, opposed to the development, hired a different professional traffic engineering company to conduct its own traffic study. Not surprisingly, the developer's experts indicated fewer impacts than did the abutters'.

If left to the usual approach, the situation would probably have gotten stuck in a debate over the number of additional trips per day that would result from the proposed development. Neither side would likely accept the other side's estimates because each expert's numbers leaned in favor of the political decision favored by his client. Mitigation requirements would differ based on the expected increase in trips, which would then impact the profitability of the development. Eventually, each side would demand that the commission either grant or reject the permit. Still, the commission would need to make a legally justifiable decision.

During a meeting of the two traffic consultants and the commission's transportation planner, we discussed the assumptions each used to analyze the traffic impacts. First, we agreed that there was a reasonable range of assessment estimates, meaning that their expertise would not to be called into question.

The proposed development was a complex, mixed-use development including offices, apartments, condominiums, a hotel, and retail space as well as a water park, museum, and a park-and-ride lot for commuters. Trip generation analyses depend on land use codes associated with development types. Each part of the development fell under a different Institute of Transportation Engineers (ITE) land use. During the discussions, we identified the assumed land codes used by each traffic analyst, which clarified the causes of some of the discrepancies.

Next we looked at the assumed pass-by rates, diverted links, and internal trips. Pass-by rates are trips drawn from already existing trips and are, therefore, not counted as new trips. Diverted links are trips that are pulled from existing trips on surrounding roads. Internal trips are those from one part of the development to another. By delving into the assumptions that lay beneath the data, we were able to surface differences in how each expert calculated key variables. Some of these clarifications caused the traffic consultants to jettison incorrect technical assumptions. For those instances where their differing assumptions could both be considered valid, the clarity of those assumptions made it possible for the government officials to understand the possible range of additional trips per day and to choose which assumptions it would rely on for its decision.

In the abortion talks example, goodwill and motivation to connect encouraged the participants into the space of not knowing. In the traffic study example, technical expertise provided the safety for exploring technical assumptions.

In most public disputes, the space of not knowing is created through a less explicit surfacing and shifting of assumptions that are part technical and part worldview. Again, exploring assumptions is not undertaken to change anyone's values or beliefs, but rather to open up possibilities for creating and refining new ideas and proposals into actionable agreements to achieve shared public goals.

The need to intervene to pierce assumptions becomes apparent when the responses of some negotiators to others do not seem to make sense or connect, as with the pro-choice activist's response concerning contraception. Sometimes helping the negotiators go deeper and further into the minutiae of the substantive issues can penetrate past attitudes and cause people to think beyond their initial preferences. Prior judgments and attitudes often give way at the level of intricate detail because the subissues become too small to carry such passionate trappings.

To deconstruct substantive issues, the mediator poses a series of well-constructed piercing questions. In the same way that Socrates doesn't know what virtue is, but through intensive questioning, can help people discern what it is not, mediators do not know the solutions to substantive disputes but can help people know what is not a workable solution and possibly create the curiosity to construct what it could be.

Creating Curiosity

The move from uncertainty through not knowing to curiosity occurs as a single act although it rests on a process foundation built by the assessment, process design, ground rules, meeting design, and mediator strategy and technique. The curiosity component of the dynamic is sustained as each negotiator ponders this question: If I didn't know *that* about this situation, what else don't I know? As many negotiators discover what they don't know and become curious about their shared situation, they begin to work together to reconfigure the substantive issues to build a solution. They seek out and are able to take in new information and form new ideas as they move from their previously polarized debates into a joint problem-solving mode of negotiations. Learning—or as described by the abortion talks participants, being stretched—is an enriching experience that leads to a desire for fresh insights into old problems.

To create the possibility of curiosity, participants must feel secure and be at ease. With that security, substantive issues, misperceptions of people and entities, and limited expectations of the process provide opportunities for the surprises that can create curiosity. When your hope is to help people learn and you have no notion of what they will learn, you must operate with care.

A person at ease is better able to consider new opinions and information that may contradict strongly held opinions. In contrast, insecurities often cause people to hold tighter to the assumptions that make them feel rooted in the world. A person who feels discomfort is more likely to express negative emotions rather than bond in a paradoxical unity with people separated by deep value differences and substantive conflicts.

At the same time as the mediator helps to surface or analyze assumptions, he or she needs to tend to negotiators' emotional comfort. Mediators sometimes speak of an ability to "read people." To describe this capacity, Howard Bellman uses the metaphor of "having an ear," meaning an ability to hear the emotions and concerns behind the words. I think of it as *sensing energies* to ascertain, for example, perceptions of comfort and discomfort of the parties, power potentials, or ideas and concerns formulating in people's minds. This kind of information is useful for easing and harmonizing the energies of people to promote comfort and surface ideas that may help negotiators tackle difficult issues.

Throughout the negotiations, I find myself tracking the emotional state of each individual negotiator as well as of the room collectively. I may intervene to reduce unease, fear, anger, and disengagement, as well as to promote ease, security, and creative thinking. For example, if a person moves his chair back from the table and folds his arms across his chest, we all know he is closed to the discussions. During the negotiations, I may watch him for additional reactions to gain more information about what is bothering him and then frame a question in an attempt to break through that discomfort.

To sustain ease during negotiations, mediators must sometimes confront a negotiator to protect another. This may seem to contradict efforts to keep everyone in the room comfortable so they can become curious. However, when a party operates outside a group's established norms of mutual respect, mediators need to be visibly firm to promote productive negotiations. If someone launches an attack, the mediator may need to step in to stop the interaction to protect the individuals involved and reduce the discomfort among others that such attacks cause. In so doing, the mediator contributes to a sense of security among the negotiators who were either directly protected or who watched as others were.

I learned just how appreciated such interventions could be after I stepped into a feisty argument between a government official and the head of a trade association. The head of the trade association, a large and powerful man, was informing the group that he would not be available for the next scheduled meeting. The government official lashed out at him saying the negotiations should be his priority and everything else should be secondary. Just as they began going at each other, I jumped in. I told the government official to back off; they had agreed to appoint alternate negotiators for exactly such situations. As tempers cooled, the trade association head turned to me and jokingly asked, "Will you marry me?"

Of course he was able to take care of himself, but I took the opportunity to indicate my responsibility to ensure the security of all in the room. As a result of my actively protecting the deliberative space, the negotiators gave me increased margins to jostle them. It made me more able to ask piercing questions without causing anger.

In a safe environment, substantive issues, perceptions of people or entities, and expectations of the process offer opportunities for curiosity. During the assessment, the mediator often learns of inaccurate understandings of technical issues that are further complicated by assumptions of devious motivations and bad intent. To create curiosity, a mediator may strategically recommend expert panels or presentations to introduce alternative perspectives and provide negotiators with opportunities to ask questions to distill previously unknown credible information. Another strategy is to break broad issues into smaller and smaller component parts. Revealing unexpected nuances can also lead to unexpected learnings.

People often ascribe negative attributes[2] to those with whom they are in conflict. If their perceptions are challenged by a different, often more complex reality, curiosity may be triggered. Among the cranes negotiators were individuals whose contact with OSHA had been primarily in the context of inspections and enforcement actions. Few had met previously with officials responsible for crafting regulations. As the regulation drafting team showed an openness to learning about complex cranes issues and at the same time explained the characteristics of enforceable regulations as well as how to write regulations to focus inspectors' attention on priority safety issues, those individuals became somewhat curious about the demands and challenges of government. Their negative assumptions gave way to respect.

Skepticism of an actual role in crafting the product can also be an opportunity for creating curiosity. People who suspect their participation is merely political cover for decisions already made, can become quite surprised at their actual impact. I'll never forget the expression on the face of a man who saw his idea reflected in an emerging affordable

2. Daniel Heradsveit (1982), The Arab-Israeli Conflict: Psychological Barriers to Peace, Oslo: Universitetsforlaget (Second revised edition).

housing agreement. Having expected to have no influence, he became enormously curious about what other ideas he and others might contribute to the product.

Each experience of moving from certainty through not knowing to curiosity stretches people beyond their usual patterns of thought. It seems to be a satisfying experience as with each learning, people become more engaged in the process and seem more willing to reach for new thinking to innovate solutions. To initiate and sustain productive negotiations of substantive issues, negotiators must come close enough to each other to overcome their polarization to achieve civic fusion. To do so, they need to give up the certainty afforded by self-satisfying solutions, squelch fears of failing their constituents at the negotiating table, and slightly shift deeply held assumptions that maintain an impasse. Free to think more broadly, new thoughts and possibilities contribute binding energy that can create a chain reaction, as people around the table begin to rethink their assumptions and explore new possibilities together even as they maintain opposing core beliefs.

Self-interested inner voices and voices of constituents still ring in negotiators' ears, power differentials and resource limitations still exist, but there becomes a willingness to sort it out and to create and consider innovative solutions as a team. This is the essence of civic fusion.

CHAPTER 11

FOSTERING DELIBERATIVE NEGOTIATIONS[1]

To build actionable agreements, negotiators simultaneously consider the nuances of numerous perspectives and options within political and resource constraints. It's not an easy feat, and for most it's unfamiliar.

1. The term *deliberative negotiations* was coined by Jane Mansbridge in "Deliberative and Non-Deliberative Negotiations," *HKS Working Paper No. RWP09-010*, Harvard University—Harvard Kennedy School (HKS), April 6, 2009.
   In her paper, Mansbridge describes the deliberative ideal as meeting the following criteria: The deliberation should, ideally, be open to all those affected by a decision. The participants should have equal opportunity to influence the process, have equal resources, and be protected by basic rights. In the process of mutual justification, participants should treat one another with mutual respect. They should give reasons to one another that they think the others can comprehend and accept. They should aim at finding fair terms of cooperation among free and equal persons. They should speak truthfully. They should achieve their ends by a process of mutual justification, not try to change others' behavior through the exercise of coercive power.

To foster deliberative negotiations, mediators promote mutual respect even as parties bump up against the harsh realities of the situation. This, in turn, creates an enriched environment for sustained civic fusion.

Promote Mutual Respect

I often imagine a twelve-foot high, neon billboard sign that reads RESPECT. Unfortunately, seeing the word doesn't successfully enable people to be respectful. And yet, if there is a silver bullet to productive negotiations (even if there is not agreement to be had), it is mutual respect.

Mediators foster respectful deliberative negotiations, in part, by engaging people in their every idea, question, and proposal. With this purpose in mind, they manage the flow of the meeting and maintain a credible process to promote mutual respect and human dignity by protecting people from humiliation. Treating people with respect cascades into people acting respectfully toward one another.

No matter how far afield a statement or proposal may be, mediators assist the negotiators to fully discuss it with its originator. Whereas it may have caused snickers from some of the negotiators, the mediator must follow it until it builds into something useful or dissolves, as the person who offered it gains awareness of its value and limitations in the context of the negotiations. This looks similar to the teacher who weaves every question into his or her response so that even the student who offers remotely related comments or questions becomes a respected member of the classroom community.

If someone acts disrespectfully, mediators tend to respond rather than wait for the insulted person to defend him or herself. We've all seen people roll their eyes after a comment and then look around the room to connect with others who may be equally disdainful. However, if a comment is treated seriously and fully explored with the person who offered it, fewer people are likely to support the eye-rollers.

Consistency in this regard helps foster respect throughout the negotiations. Knowing they will not be made to feel ignorant, negotiators can feel safe enough to offer unusual and innovative proposals rather than self-edit for fear of sounding foolish. This is crucial to the process because otherwise parties might fail to offer the observations and ideas that may be key to building the unique agreement that helps to resolve the conflict. Knowing their comments will be fully vetted also seems to increase the quality of the comments.

Another necessity is to keep order throughout the deliberations. With a roomful of passionate people discussing issues they care a great deal about, you can imagine that each wants to immediately share his thoughts as soon as they are triggered by others' comments. If a mediator doesn't exert tight control, turmoil would likely occur with some frequency.

A method for sustaining a focused, productive conversation is to maintain a list of names as people indicate they have something to say, but to be flexible regarding the order in which people are recognized. Simply calling each name as it appears on the list risks a discussion of sequenced but disconnected comments.

Instead, if a mediator senses that a hand raised is relevant to a proposal then under discussion, she asks the person next on the list if he or she would mind holding his or her comment, if it relates to a new item, until we complete the discussion of the proposal currently on the table. If the mediator knows from previous conversations that a particular party will reject a proposal, to keep the negotiations efficient, he may call on that party to air his or her objections rather than wait until after multiple people have spoken in support of the proposal. In this way, the negotiations focus on either rejecting the idea or refining it to accommodate additional interests.

Transparency of the process is essential for fostering deliberative negotiations. In most policy mediations, discussions are open to the public, and no decisions are made behind closed doors. Although parties and the mediators may use caucuses and work groups to develop proposals, such proposals are presented during plenary sessions for analysis and discussion by the negotiating team and with opportunities for public comment. In addition, under open meetings laws all parties and the public have access to all the information distributed during the negotiations. Outside experts are brought in to fill the gaps, if needed, to explain complex issues or if there are fears of biases in the information provided. Negotiators are not asked to make decisions on issues or options without full understanding. The transparency of the process makes it difficult for people to sustain false assertions over time or to successfully manipulate the process to their benefit. Through questions and ever-deepening clarification, the balanced group of negotiators uncovers the core conflicts and dynamics within each issue. With every proposal vetted by twenty-plus stakeholder experts and the public, false claims and deceptive efforts are usually uncovered. Transparency also helps to affirm that the hard work of the negotiators will have actual impact on their situations.

Still, some information may be held in confidence and private caucuses may occur because parties may not be completely free to disclose all their interests or flexibilities publicly. Mediators and negotiators may want to explore particular ideas privately, and proposals and closing packages of proposals may be best built in caucuses. However, none are privately agreed upon; all proposals must be put before the full negotiating team for review before agreements can be reached.

By upholding dignity, the mediator increases the emotional comfort of negotiators, which enables them to take in new information, shift assumptions, and think creatively. In addition, as people act with respect toward others and are treated respectfully by others, they associate positive feelings with the negotiations—even in the face of conflict and constraints.

Promoting respect and personal dignity encourages people to express their best sides—the parts of us that make us feel good about ourselves. As this occurs, people attribute positive feelings to their time spent in negotiations and to the other people in the room because they become associated with their better selves. This group dynamic fosters the civil discourse required for deliberative negotiations.

As white light through a prism differentiates into many colors, one can think of human nature as passing through a prism to differentiate into the range of potential human behaviors. Just as when you move the prism, you can cause different colors to be more prominent within the spectrum, fostering deliberative negotiations is an effort to increase the likely expression of beneficent human behaviors.

Acknowledging Uncomfortable Realities

Complex policy negotiations occur within a context of conflict, power differentials, and human limitations. To sustain civic fusion, these sometimes uncomfortable realities must be acknowledged to become accepted aspects of deliberative negotiations.

Conflicts and an inability to control outcomes that we care passionately about can overwhelm our minds. Think about an emotional conflict you were in and how fully you experienced it as you told and retold its story. Our minds often flood with replays of angry events, fears of nightmare scenarios, and dreams of being able to assert absolute control. If we confuse these thoughts with the realities of a complex situation, we will negotiate in ways that contribute to gridlock.

To reduce their sting and promote productive negotiations, mediators contextualize these uncomfortable realities as usual and typical to policy disputes. As early as the assessment interviews, mediators ask questions to surface and display political realities, and describe them in formal assessment reports. Preliminary negotiation activities also help. For example, the consensus scope of the negotiations contextualizes the situation as a list of issues to be negotiated, which gives boundaries to a seemingly overwhelming conflict.

Still, during long-term negotiations, conflict, power differentials, and limitations often cause strong unsettling emotions that inhibit people's curiosity and willingness to explore new ideas. Reminding people that these uncomfortable realities are usual and typical to complex public policy situations, helps them become more able to sustain an open mind, even as conflict is passionately expressed, power is asserted, and limits on resources and the human ability to innovate solutions are reached. These constant reminders are an effort to normalize otherwise uncomfortable realities.

Deliberative negotiations, including its weighing and analysis of varying options, provide a means for resolving polarized conflict. All negotiators engaged in a civic fusion process are aware that conflicts exist, but may have varying levels of comfort with the expression of open conflict. Being in conflict with others is, for many, a state of discomfort. In fact, some cultures inhibit outright conflict so that explicit discussion of it is unusual. For others, argument is a normal mode of discourse—even when it gets loud.

Explicitly stating what is in disagreement and why particular proposals failed to resolve it helps to contextualize the reality of a conflict. To reduce discomfort among parties, mediators may engage an argumentative negotiator on behalf of other negotiators to draw out the actual issue in conflict and the proposals for resolution. Sometimes humor breaks the tensions of conflict.[2]

Power differentials always exist among negotiators involved with public policy conflicts. In a mediated setting, no one can act unilaterally, but some have more power than others. We know that power was likely asserted for the status quo to become unsustainable and that all the parties present embody enough power to have claimed a seat at the table.

Again, by making power differentials explicit, for example, through usual mediator reality testing strategies, negotiators are not taken by surprise when power is asserted. Clarifying the reality of power differentials may also encourage parties to analyze the limits of their own power and explore strategies for increasing their power in the negotiations, such as through coalitions or direct action.

During C-DAC's ground rules negotiations, the parties confronted the reality of OSHA's institutional power as the regulating agency. It became an accepted aspect of the negotiations.

In Chelsea, we included elected officials on the Charter preparation team because, although their institutional powers were suspended by the state, they still had personal power among their supporters and possessed the power that comes from knowing how to run a successful campaign. We knew there was to be a special election, and we respected the elected officials' power to sway that election.

In other cases, a party's access to and support from White House officials or members of Congress may indicate a power differential, which may be expressed as muscular reactions to particular proposals.

---

2. John Forester. (2004). "Responding to Critical Moments with Humor, Recognition, and Hope." *Negotiation Journal* 20: 221–237.

To normalize this reality, mediators may suggest that asserting power is not immoral but rather a usual aspect of the political process. The reality of negotiations is that if weaker parties cannot effectively project power to satisfy their interests, they have to consider what they can accomplish from the negotiations and from alternative forums.

In policy mediations, power is usually only asserted at particular junctures in the negotiations, most often during final discussions of difficult issues. Power typically does not come into play when the parties discuss the scope of issues, workshop those issues, and clarify confusions from interest-based conflicts.

What Should Be Versus What Is

Another form of denying unpopular realities is negotiating from a starting point of what should be rather than what is. Rather than looking at the complex issues, power relationships, conflicting interests, and historical dynamics, people sometimes posit a set of assumptions of the world as it should be, and then attempt to negotiate from that foundation. Mediators sometimes need to move people from a belief that good people should agree to what is "right and just" to a recognition of self interest and differing core values.

Ideas of what should be are often large, abstract concepts such as morality and justice. Although they may provide values that inform the negotiations, ideals must be translated into tangible issues and options to be negotiated. When demands are rooted in expectations of how the world should be, mediators try to help the party gain a more comprehensive understanding of the situational constraints.

Negotiating from a perspective of "what should be" indicates a strong form of being wrongly certain. It closes down one's ability to take in new information, to become curious, to respect the interests of others, to learn of or create innovative ideas, and to accept limitations. The world-as-it-should-be negotiators are often weaker parties that lack enough power to achieve their aspirations. They may inappropriately assume power equivalence among the negotiators and attribute negative intentions to those who would assert power.

Many years ago, Howard Bellman and I mediated negotiations for a regional affordable housing compact. Although all the negotiators accepted their legal obligations under the Fair Housing Act, many, especially those from rural and suburban towns, wanted to only minimally meet them. A participant from an urban community negotiated as though all in the room shared his deep commitment to providing affordable housing for all who needed it. It took great effort to introduce the unpleasant reality that they did not.

In fostering deliberative negotiations, mediators must respectfully introduce elements of the world-as-it-is to world-as-it-should-be negotiators or risk their blocking potential agreements that offer better alternatives than they may be able to accomplish in other forums.

CHAPTER 12

THE MARCH TO CLOSURE

Introduction

The act of participating in civic fusion has value in and of itself. People grow as a result of bonding with those they initially perceived as the "other side." But to reap its benefits—to achieve the common public goal—a negotiation must result in an actionable agreement. The final rounds of negotiations, those that take place during what I call the march to closure, are of great intensity. Getting closure on outstanding, tough issues is the most challenging and least forgiving phase of the negotiations.

From the first assessment interview to affirming final consensus, all elements of a civic fusion process contribute to a "pursuit of closure."[1] During that pursuit, 20 to 25 people sat around a hollow-square table—itself surrounded by members of the public—for months and months of meetings. They negotiated tentative agreements for all but a handful of issues, some of which may need to be tweaked just one more time. They repeatedly discussed and tabled the most difficult and still unresolved issues. By this time, there have probably been multiple work group sessions to develop proposals for those issues as well as numerous one-on-one conversations among and between the negotiators and mediators. A great many options were created and discussed, but the remaining issues continually defied resolution. Assuming good faith, everyone comes to the final meeting wanting success but not knowing if they will reach final consensus. There is palpable tension in the air.

During the march to closure, it becomes clear that a perfect solution is not attainable. The negotiators have thought about the outstanding issues every which way, and have generated creative options but they're out of ideas. They've understood the complexity, the limitations, the actual conflicts, and the perspectives of everyone in the room. They respect the interests everyone has raised during the negotiations. And so they learn that governing is complex. In the face of that complexity, citizen-representatives have the responsibility of making difficult choices.

By this time, everyone is well aware of the common public goal the negotiators seek to achieve. They want to make progress on their issues of greatest importance, and they know the status quo won't stand. They can't act unilaterally, and they want to assert some control over the way issues are resolved.

Over the course of the negotiations, parties have conferred on the mediator an authority to manage the process on their behalf, which he or she will likely need to assert during the march to closure. Like everyone else in the room, the mediator does not know if they will end the meeting with an actionable agreement. In these moments, like the parties, mediators want to succeed but can't focus on the abstraction

---

1. This phrase was coined by Howard Bellman, and is quoted in *When Talk Works: Profiles of Mediators,* edited by Deborah Kolb and Associates (San Francisco: Jossey-Bass Publishers, 1994).

of success or failure. They must focus on finding an agreement if there is one to be found, knowing full well that there may not be one. A focus on success would look like a baseball player missing an easy out because he was busy celebrating the double-play before he even caught the ball.

Closure Tactics

In pulling out all the stops to support the march to closure, mediators simultaneously utilize substantive, process-based, leveraging, and personal closure tactics. We'll look at each type and then see what they look like when combined.

Substantively, the parties need to clearly understand the outstanding issues, the associated options they've already considered, and how they might link the final issues to create a feasible package of agreements for closure. Process-based tactics use the previously established procedural ground rules to accommodate difference. Working within the rules of the game, the mediator works to sustain the individuals' comfort through the difficult choices and pressures of the march to closure. The mediator uses his or her accumulated leverage to turn up the pressure, sustain civic fusion, and ink the agreement.

Substantive Closure Tactics

Issue Clarity

On a substantive level, the mediator helps bring the outstanding issues into clearer focus: What exactly is in dispute once all the layers of excuses are shorn away? Sustaining clarity is often challenging. Parties tend to raise tangential and unrelated issues to avoid the discomfort of the actual conflict and their difficult choices.

For example, among the final C-DAC issues, the most difficult one to resolve was crane operator certification. This issue was considered absolutely central to increasing worker safety because to become certified, crane operators would need to get appropriate training to be able to pass comprehensive practical and written tests. After hours of discussions over many months, we discovered that the actual point of disagreement concerned authorizing other entities to certify crane operators, in addition to nationally accredited crane operator-certifying organizations.

Creating and Massaging Options

With greater clarity and intention, the negotiators reach deep into their knowledge base to create new options or massage existing options to meet the challenge of addressing all the concerns raised. Although the remaining issues have been discussed repeatedly, the pressure of a last meeting can result in a greater articulation of concerns. Greater clarity and nuance of a concern increases the opportunity to invent a mutually agreeable solution. In addition, at this point, the dissenters are challenged to weave their concerns into the proposals they reject. As explained during the ground rules discussion, I tell them, "It's not enough to reject an option, you need to try to construct one that you and everyone else can live with, or at the very least explain why you can't live with the proposal on the table."

At past C-DAC meetings, concerns had already been raised regarding employers' costs for training and testing employees for certification. During the last meeting, a proposal under consideration allowed employers to self-train their employees or to send them to training centers. Sustained controversy centered on the entities authorized to test and, thereby, certify crane operators.

During the final negotiations, some parties expressed concerns about employers paying to train and certify their employees, only to have competitors offer higher wages to their already certified crane operators. In addition, government entities with existing crane operator licensing programs wanted to retain authority for their programs. Still others were concerned about a limited national capacity for certifying crane operators. At the time of the negotiations, there was only one accredited entity for certifying crane operators in the United States: the National Commission for the Certification of Crane Operators (NCCCO).

In response to these concerns, the proposal was revised to allow employers to certify their crane operators under particular arrangements. For example, the employer's certifying program would be periodically audited to ensure that it used tests that met national psychometric standards and that they were administered in accordance with nationally recognized standards. The outside auditor would be certified to audit employer programs by a nationally accredited, crane operator certifying organization. In addition, government entities such as the U.S. military and state and city licensing agencies could certify crane operators as long as their programs met the new OSHA standards.

Certification from the employer and non-OSHA government programs was not transferable to other companies. The military certification was recognized only within the military, and the state or city licenses were recognized only within the geographic boundaries of the licensing entity.

A proposal to authorize already accredited educational institutions or programs, such as universities, to certify crane operators was rejected because the existing accreditations of such entities were not specific to crane operator certification. If such entities sought specific accreditation, they would fit into the category of nationally accredited crane operator certifying organizations, which were permitted under the proposal.

To address the concern of a limited national capacity for certifying crane operators, C-DAC members added a provision for a four-year phase-in of the certification requirement beginning on the effective date of the new standard. Many negotiators expected additional accredited crane operator certifying entities to be established to service the markets that were expected to result from the new regulations.

As you can see, generating options responsive to specific concerns required great clarity and focus on the actual subissues in dispute. Keep in mind that seemingly rational solutions are developed amid a great sea of emotion and flights into tangentially related issues. Negotiators' frustrations with their limited choices or by others' unwillingness to consent may make it more difficult to focus on building solutions. It takes some wrestling with people to sustain productive negotiations under pressure.

Linking Issues

As the negotiators work to clarify each of the remaining issues, some resolve early in the march to closure. For the remaining issues, the mediator may work with a subset of negotiators to develop packages that give everyone a little more. As integrative bargaining suggests, groups value issues differently, which enables a linking of issues to create packages that align differing interests. If parties can get what they want on their more important issues, they may be flexible on issues they value less, but which are highly valued by others.

Sometimes a final package can be created jointly at plenary sessions, and sometimes it is best assembled through sequential caucuses. Once a seemingly final package of proposals on all outstanding issues is developed, it may be introduced as a final proposal to be wholly accepted or rejected. The effort of constructing the package requires a great deal of persuasion and often requires parties to "cut as close to the bone" on outstanding issues as they can, to get the final deal. Thus, additional negotiations may sink the package.

Sometimes the mediator must be strategic in deciding who should introduce the package. For example, if the government negotiator introduces a proposed closer package, he or she may effectively couple it with statements about the consequences of not reaching an agreement. On the other hand, the package may be best received if a powerful or trusted negotiator or the mediator introduces it.

Although policy mediators try hard to prevent the negotiations from getting to such a point, there are times when there is only one issue left and people line up on different sides of it. It is more difficult to resolve a final issue if there is nothing left to link it to. Such a situation requires a combination of nonsubstantive closure tactics.

To avoid this situation, a mediator may occasionally suggest that a negotiator delay reaching a tentative agreement on a particular issue if it can be useful as part of an end-game package. More than once, I wished the site conditions issue had remained in play during the C-DAC negotiations. It might have been linked to operator certification during the march to closure as it had been a key issue for one of the dissenters. However, the mediator cannot prevent agreements from being reached.

To finalize agreements, substantive closure tactics always need to be combined with other types of closure tactics.

Process-Based Closure Tactics

The Common Public Goal

The common public goal, which helps trigger civic fusion, serves throughout the process as a means to wrap all the participants in a joint vision of a future that resolves their situation by balancing their combined concerns and interests. As an abstract unity, it provides occasional relief from the intensity of negotiating the final issues. As they struggle through the tough issues, the mediator may remind the parties that their efforts are focused on translating their common goal into tangible outcomes.

For example, the common goal for the Chelsea charter case read, "The charter preparation team will develop a charter document that has the future of Chelsea in mind, not just current issues, and reflects and wins the support of the people of Chelsea." Thus, as we spoke about district versus citywide candidacies for the school committee, I could remind the negotiators of both the feedback generated during the community meetings and their expectations of voter preferences in the special election.

Play the Ground Rules

The procedural ground rules developed early in the negotiations establish agreements regarding the process and the product. These norms, primarily designed to prevent process conflicts, may also provide opportunities for closing strategies. Sometimes closure is a matter of playing the previously established rules of the game. Among other things, the ground rules set out the decision rule and typically include a definition of consensus. If groups defined *consensus* as less than unanimous agreement, the ground rules may provide opportunities for closure tactics.

C-DAC defined final consensus as agreement of all but two nonfederal negotiators. They agreed that if final consensus was reached, no C-DAC members, including any dissenters, could submit formal negative comments on the proposed rule OSHA published in the *Federal Register*. However, a dissenter was permitted to submit a letter to OSHA outlining his organization's reasons for dissent and that letter would be included in the preamble of the proposed rule.

In making these decisions, C-DAC members were responsive to concerns about losing the benefits of their yearlong effort because a few members dissented on one issue. Because they decided to define consensus as "all but two nonfederal members," they also made provisions for enabling dissenters to voice their reasons formally for dissenting.

With unanimous consent on all issues except the entities that would be authorized to test crane operators, two nonfederal negotiators dissented on the final issue. Under the ground rules, this meant the team had reached final consensus. The two dissenters were invited to share their reasons for dissent with OSHA for inclusion in the preamble to the rule. Ultimately, one did.

In contrast, the Chelsea ground rules required unanimous consent on the entire charter but authorized the mediator to call for a vote on a specific issue if the group reached an impasse. Such an issue was considered tentatively agreed on if 80 percent of the negotiators present approved a proposal. School committee composition was the only issue subjected to a vote, and it enabled us to move forward on the issue. However, the definition for final consensus on the entire city charter required the attained unanimous consent.

Opportunity Outside the Consensus Product

The formal product constrains the scope of the discussions—a regulation and a city charter are legal documents. A consensus article by definition means that all agree with the written words. Sometimes achieving consensus requires finding opportunities for parties to express opinions outside the product.

For example, during the abortion dialogue, some participants were fearful of being labeled traitors by activists who might read the consensus article. This led some participants to urge that the article include clear statements of each camp's positions. In response, the consensus article was published with separate sidebar statements of the pro-life and pro-choice "worldviews." This provided each side the freedom to articulate its individual positions and to maintain consensus on all language of the jointly written article.

In negotiated rulemakings we often use the preamble, as with the C-DAC letters from dissenters, as a means for including statements outside the consensus product. Government officials write the preamble to the regulation after final consensus is reached. Although in some cases, negotiators are given the opportunity to review and comment on the preamble prior to publication, the government agency is not required to integrate suggested changes. Sometimes to get to closure, the government and all other parties agree to include particular preamble language to accommodate parties' requests concerning shared intent and meaning of specific sections of regulatory text.

Calling Breaks

With the right timing, breaks can be highly effective in dislodging substantive impasses. In discussing an outstanding issue, I may push for clarity while increasing the pressure in the room to cause people to work harder to find solutions to difficult issues. As an issue is discussed, I might also ask questions about the consequences of failure to reach an agreement and gently work a party into a corner by exposing the quandary of the issue including its existing options, constraints, and alternatives to a consensus agreement. When that party has nowhere left to go—he or she understands we have to find a solution to the issue, but can't propose one—I may call a fifteen-minute break. Inevitably, the leaders on various sides of the issue find their way to each other and continue the conversation. They are still bonded, and they want badly to succeed. They don't want to be the cause of failure. I sometimes stay away but watch the state of the conversation out of the corner of my eye. If it looks positive, I may let the break go longer. Sometimes I mediate the conversation. During these offline conversations, new ideas or refinements to options often emerge. Before the group reconvenes, I check in with the lead negotiators of the issue to learn the results of the conversation and to plan how to proceed regarding the introduction of new proposals or a decision to pass the issue until later in the meeting to create opportunities for additional offline conversations.

Leveraging Tactics

With little institutional power of their own, mediators must identify and exploit ways to leverage the group toward closure. Levers may be derived from the situational dynamics as well as from the authorities and powers of the participating organizations, including government. In addition, the mediator and individuals who played leadership roles throughout the process, often over time, gain personal authority derived from the respect and trust of the parties. The pulling and pushing of these levers must be done with sophistication and care. In civic fusion processes, inappropriately blunt force can break the bonds that unify the parties and result in chaotic dissolution.

Reality Testing

One of the most used mediator levers is reality testing the consequences of not reaching an agreement, or exploring their "best alternative to a negotiated agreement."[2] The art of mediation involves gently drawing out answers to reality-testing questions such as those below to elicit a reflective thought process. Timing and sequence are crucial and must be appropriately coupled with other aspects of a march to closure strategy.

Illustrative Questions

Overall:

- What happens if we fail to reach agreement today?
- What are your expectations for getting what you want?
- What dynamics have changed since we began this process?
- Do those changes make it easier or harder for you to get what you want?

On the outstanding issues:

- If we fail to agree, what do you expect will be the decision on the outstanding issue(s)?
- Who makes those decisions?
- What do you gain by dissenting?

---

2. Roger Fisher, William Ury, and Bruce Patton, *Getting to Yes: Negotiating Agreement Without Giving In* (New York: Penguin Books, 1991).

- What will you do to get what you want on that final issue if we fail to reach consensus today?
- What will it cost you? Will your organization actually do it? For example, will your organization engage in a lobbying campaign, letter or email campaign, or a direct action such as a strike or demonstration?
- Would a lawsuit prevent implementation of the option you dislike on the final issue?
- Given that we all understood at the outset that no party could unilaterally get their way or solve the problem, what is the likelihood your organization will ultimately prevent what it doesn't want on that one remaining issue?

On losing the gains achieved on tentatively agreed issues:

- What has your organization gained from the negotiations so far?
- What concessions have you derived from other parties?
- Do you expect to be able to sustain those gains?
- What will you lose if we fail to reach consensus?
- What do you gain by maintaining some control over the outcome?
- What do you want to avoid?
- To the government official: What do you expect will happen if we don't reach final consensus on all issues?

Given the national cynicism toward government generally in the United States, people usually fear that when left to make decisions on its own, government will cause undue bureaucratic red tape, unintended consequences, higher costs, and be less likely to achieve the public goal effectively. For mediators, these perceptions provide leverage for reaching closure. Framed in another way, the mediator may stress loss of control of the outcome. By reaching an agreement, parties have some level of control over decisions that directly affect them. If they fail to agree, they risk an outcome that may be worse than the final proposals considered during the negotiations.

The actuality of what happens if the group fails to reach agreement is hard to predict. For many government agencies, a negotiated consensus carries a great deal of weight internally. Without consensus, various offices within the initiating government agency are likely to pick apart the draft regulatory text. On the other hand, the consensus document provides the government negotiator with leverage inside his or her agency and during other government regulatory reviews to keep the regulation intact, as negotiated. Policymakers respect consensus products of balanced groups of relevant interested parties.

Press for the Difficult Choices of Civic Responsibility

The moments before closure present difficult decisions for the negotiators. And I respect that. At the same time, as leaders they have the civic responsibility to make those decisions. It is part of the national psyche to berate government for its decisions, but in discussions of outstanding issues, one learns how difficult the jobs of government officials are. Without the benefit of stakeholder negotiations, government makes decisions that balance its public policy goals with the diverse interests of those who will be affected by its decisions. In a civic fusion process, the affected parties have the opportunity to make those tough choices—or they leave it to government officials to do so.

I'm always impressed with how people avoid making tough decisions. In the face of clear focus on the choices before them, they effectively squirm. They seem unconsciously to do what they can to obscure the difficult choices before them. The individuals at the table often represent thousands, sometimes even millions of people; they are leaders. Mediators have to hold their feet to the fire to get them to make the tough choices from among the existing imperfect choices—and at the same time empathize with the constraints of reality and their future need to explain the negotiated outcomes to their constituents.

Wasted Effort

Civic fusion processes hold the promise of people influencing their laws and situations. The process is set up to result in a consensus solution that addresses their problems. By the last meeting, there is a great deal of momentum to realize the benefits of their strong commitment and long hours of work. Policy mediators often suggest that "it would be a shame to lose it all over one last issue" as a means to leverage them toward closure.

Contact Constituents or Superiors

It's not unusual for people to make a phone call at the last meeting. Throughout the negotiations, parties check in with constituents and higher-ups. For the outstanding issues, they may have been given specific directives prior to the last meeting. If those instructions prevent agreements, the mediator may recommend that parties contact those who may be able to provide them with increased flexibility after a refined assessment of the situation. It's important to make room for these calls to avoid the dynamics of the moment leading to an agreement only to have bosses or constituents reject it after the negotiations conclude.

Similarly, the federal negotiators often "go upstairs" to speak with their senior leadership to determine the limits of the government's positions on outstanding issues. Sometimes a final concession may be made if it will result in final consensus on all issues.

Power Differentials

Power differentials among the negotiators, inherent throughout the process, often surface toward the end of the negotiations, particularly during "reality-testing" discussions. Contrary to some, I do not believe it is possible for a public policy mediator to balance power among negotiators. I have no store of power in my pockets to distribute. Mediators ensure that all parties have equivalent opportunities to fully participate in the negotiations, but it's also part of their job to use the levers of power effectively to get closure. In fact, in the context of public policy mediation, if the product is to survive outside the confines of the room, it must be somewhat reflective of the power relations among the negotiators' constituents.

Mediators need to be cognizant of the power relationships and help the parties understand how they play into the final issues. Asserting power isn't a matter of fairness. All parties use the means at their disposal to further their interests.

During the march to closure, mediators sometimes must make clear that a proposal opposed by the government "at the highest levels" is simply not going to fly, nor is it likely to make its way into the product if there is no consensus agreement. In these situations, mediators can explain that unless a party has the means to force the option, the group needs to move on. Sometimes parties use political contacts to further their proposals. If a party has political power and the ability to use it to further his or her interests, it is a legitimate negotiation move. However, given the transparency of the process, such backdoor levers of power may eventually need to be justified publicly by officials. Efforts by powerful parties can backfire as occurred when a proposal was rejected after a senator's staffer pressured all parties to support it.

Occasionally, there are negotiators who have institutional power but have little interest or experience in asserting it. Sometimes, to reach final agreements on outstanding issues, they let the mediator "play their power" in that they allow her to advise them regarding when and how to make particular proposals during the negotiations when getting closure requires an assertion of those institutional powers.

Actions to Sustain Individuals

Maintain Awareness of Negotiators

Most of the focus during the march to closure is on the outstanding issues, but it is the individuals who make the difficult choices. As the pressure builds, the mediator needs to ensure their continued comfort amid discomfort and uncertainty. The parties must maintain their proximity to sustain civic fusion even as the pressure increases the potential for an explosive disintegration.

To do this, I maintain an awareness of the parties' emotional states and subtly check in with those in need of attention. My action may be something as simple as a smile in their direction, a conversation during a break, or providing an opportunity to share visibly brewing concerns they have. If negotiators hold back their thoughts, or if I sense constructive thought behind their eyes, I may call on them to speak. Often they share fresh thinking, which is helpful for clarifying their concerns and objections or for generating new ideas and options.

Fairness Factor

Throughout the negotiations, the parties generally maintain mutual respect and have equivalent opportunities to articulate their ideas and concerns. Each person has the opportunity to contribute. The process is transparent. During the march to closure, this dynamic must be sustained into the last moments. As the pressure builds, mediators continue to foster civil discourse and deliberative negotiations. Doing so should be invisible, meaning there is no appearance of active interventions unless a problem arises. The ongoing fairness and credibility of the process is something that all the parties need to be able to rely on, and even more, they should be able to take for granted.

Over the course of the process, people have seen me foster new ideas and press people when they have steadfastly stuck to an option that failed to account for all the interests expressed. Each negotiator has likely felt both supported and pressured, and they have seen the others in these same situations. As we tangle with the outstanding difficult issues, amid greater intensity, it is critical to sustain fair discussions in the midst of increasing pressure.

Reaching to the Limit

In some cases, parties incessantly push for an option already deemed unacceptable by some, and not necessarily because they absolutely need it to support the final agreement, but because they want to see how much they can get. In keeping with the norms of mutual respect, everyone continually engages their ideas. With the pressure building, it is not unusual for someone finally to call them out. Given the norms developed over the course of the process, they have probably already been pressed to consider the likelihood of successfully pursuing the option at the negotiating table and in other forums.

During the EPA brownfields reg neg, the final issue was the definition of an "environmental professional," which would determine who would be able to partake of the brownfields assessment business that would result from the rule. One party insisted on particular academic degrees. The negotiating team repeatedly entertained his proposals in plenary sessions, work groups, caucuses, and numerous one-on-one phone calls. At the last meeting, this negotiator asked for one more caucus with the government negotiators—and at that point, the government technical expert refused. She stated simply there was nothing new to be said. She'd been over it with him repeatedly. She had reached her limit. Ultimately, the agreement provided for a face-saving device to enable him to agree, and the parties reached final consensus on all issues.

Personal Choices

Although negotiators represent others, sometimes the only way to reach final agreements is when people make personal decisions based on their sense of what is right—even if that decision deviates from their organization's instructions. This may involve a decision that relates only to a particular issue or it may impact the overall outcome of the negotiations. Mediators generally work to encourage decisions to support final consensus.

In C-DAC, one of the parties was put in an odd situation. His organization instructed him to dissent on the operator certifying entity proposal because its board had not had time to discuss it prior to the final C-DAC meeting. Had he dissented, it would have been the third nonfederal dissent, and the proposal would have failed. Personally and professionally, he could not live with that result. Moreover, his boss, who was president of a highly respected crane company and a leader in worker safety issues, supported his consenting to the proposal. In this case, I learned about this only after the fact, when he asked that I note his situation in the meeting summary.

On the day of the final meeting in Chelsea, I was informed that a team member was planning to vote against the charter because of the decision on school committee composition. I called him and asked if we could meet. He said he was busy. When I told him I could be at his office in fifteen minutes, he agreed to meet with me. I learned that his wife, a member of the school committee, was furious about the proposed at-large school committee.

We talked at length about the elements of the charter for which he had successfully negotiated, that he considered his high-value issues apart from the school committee. For example, he had strongly urged an expanded city council and a public process for hiring the city manager and police chief. When I left, he agreed to think about his stance on the complete charter. Ultimately, he supported it.

Combining Tactics for Closure

Much of a long-term negotiation involves tedious discussions that literally may focus on the use of a comma versus a semicolon, but the march to closure is a time of high alert and focus. In the sections above, I've outlined closure tactics largely in isolation of each other. The system, as it really works, involves multiple tactics in play simultaneously, as when many instruments combine to express a symphonic sound.

Overall, mediators use many elements to dial up the pressure in the room: the deadline, the potential loss of gains made, the disappointment of failing to get what they had worked so hard to achieve. At the same time, they try to keep all at the negotiating table comfortable enough to be able to continue absorbing new information, generating new ideas, and understanding and accepting the uncomfortable realities of the situation and their place in it. The mediator also needs to keep his or her own focus amidst high energy and emotion to keep the process fair and the space available for deliberative negotiations.

One method for combining tactics is continuous questioning. Even mediator statements should have an upward inflection at their ends. At this point in the process, mediators avoid declarative statements because of the risk of being wrong. To help make negotiators cognizant of the situation, they may ask questions such as:

- What happens if we don't reach an agreement?
- What are your reasons for rejecting that proposal?
- Do you have an alternative? What would that alternative need to include?
- Do you have a way of incorporating Charlie's concern?

And so on. The questions integrate many of the substantive and leveraging tactics available to the mediator.

The combined strategies are both assertive and engaging. After clarifying the substantive disagreements through questions, the mediator may turn the discussion to the reality in which the negotiators find themselves. The parties sustain their focus on the issues and pull back from unrelated issues and fears. We parse concerns, interests, and absolutes to build solutions that match the nuances of the situation. We maintain norms of respect for people and their ideas and at the same time allow for some to get to their limit. I remind them of the goal we set out at the beginning, the deadline fast approaching, and the need to "not let the perfect be the enemy of the good."

Then I hold their feet to the fire to get them to make the tough decision. As they throw up all sorts of "buts," and "what ifs," and obfuscating facts, I remind them that the ball is in their court. I can't make it any better. They have to decide. In essence, they need to lead. The final discussions will not only settle the outstanding issues, but the vetting of each element of the issue will provide negotiators with a deeper understanding of the agreement that will help them make it sensible to their constituents. If they fail to reach an agreement, the government officials will have a clear sense of their choices and the consequences of each.

If you were in the room during the march to closure, you would see me continually scanning the table to sense the comfort level of each person and to find new thoughts. You would find me acting to put people at ease and pausing to make space for thought and reflection. You would feel tense but safe. You would want it to work.

I imagine these moments as a host of ideas with spaces between them. It looks like pieces that want to fit together but some aren't shaped quite right—yet. And it cannot come together if not enough pieces are included. A few more need to be refined or sculpted to settle the final issues.

Some cases end without agreements, but for those that do, when it becomes clear that all the pieces finally fit, I pose the question: Is there any dissent on reaching final consensus on all issues? In the silence that follows, people realize their success and break out into applause. I record the moment of closure for the final meeting summary.

CHAPTER 13

OWNING THE FUTURE

Introduction

Owning the product is an important part of making change stick. Civic fusion processes result in communal ownership of the product, which underpins a commitment to act on the agreement. Throughout the process, that sense of ownership builds as negotiators see tangible evidence of their influence on the product. As a mediator in such processes, I also feel a deep commitment to the successful implementation of the agreement.

It stands to reason that people will be committed to an agreement that they crafted to fit the unique characteristics and limitations of their situation. In contrast, decisions from government that do not make sense to the citizens who must abide by them will be begrudgingly implemented amid an all-out search for the loopholes that inevitably exist.

When the public goal is clear, when trade-offs are respectfully discussed and responsibly decided, and when common sense prevails, people are more likely to live according to the rules. More than that, those who had a role in creating such agreements are likely to champion them.

Building Product Ownership

Product ownership builds throughout the process as negotiators see their thumbprints on an emerging document that evolves into their consensus agreement. Their impact registers as their ideas, and even suggested word and punctuation choices, appear in the distributed draft text.

Most of us appreciate being taken seriously, and all the more so for those selected by their peers to serve as representative negotiators. Their sense of responsibility increases and mutual respect grows as people make progress in tackling complicated public policy dilemmas.

Previously we discussed creating an environment in which people can build relationships that foster their better sides during the process. The emerging agreement and growing trust tend to support this as well, and a sense of owning the future naturally follows. This is contrary to the results when decisions are imposed by others, particularly others without a deep understanding of the unique dynamics, history, and workings of the situation on the ground.

It also seems that the act of being intellectually and emotionally stretched contributes to feelings of ownership and commitment to action. As people learn things they didn't know, and as they jettison false assumptions about issues and people, they feel an even greater sense of responsibility to the product. They grasp complexities of the situation that are not known by those who sent them to engage directly in the negotiations.

Throughout the six, long years between completing the negotiations and enactment of the final rule, the C-DAC members' commitment to the final product was evident in its members' actions. They spoke at union halls and industry conferences, lobbied states to enact the C-DAC standard, and provided pressure to move the standards through federal bureaucratic bottlenecks.

As the consensus proposal made its way through the expected multiyear effort of required rulemaking procedures, including economic analysis reviews by the Advisory Committee on Construction Safety and Health, and a Small Business Regulatory Enforcement Fairness Act Panel, C-DAC members spoke at constituent, state, and OSHA conferences to educate colleagues of the proposed standards. With support from C-DAC, a number of states and cities adopted elements of the consensus agreement. North Carolina adopted it in its entirety![1]

With regard to the federal regulation, eventually our patience began to wear thin. As three years approached four, and we rounded toward a presidential election, fatal crane accidents around the country reminded us of the nation's continued lack of effective worker safety standards for construction cranes and the lives the revised standard was expected save. Some C-DAC members held a press conference in Washington, D.C., to demand immediate action on the draft regulations. In a letter to the Secretary of Labor, they stated: "The lack of progress on this important safety and health standard remains a disservice to the entire industry affected by this Standard. We strongly urge you ensure this Standard and its publication receive the immediate attention it requires."

A day after New York City's second fatal crane accident in three months, the *New York Times* published an article[2] describing a presidential directive—effective the next day—against publishing proposed rules for the balance of his administration, and I felt compelled to act.

In the past, I had seen new administrations toss out the work of predecessors. I thought about the C-DAC members' self-supported travel and countless hours—25 percent of a work year—that the negotiators and their organizations had contributed. I also thought about my past heart-rending case when a government agency responsible for fisheries failed to publish a consensus plan to reduce the incidental take of Atlantic pelagic marine mammals by commercial fishermen. Instead, it shut down two of the three fisheries that had been represented in what were extraordinarily tough negotiations, thereby making the consensus

---

1. North Carolina repealed its law after the revised crane and derricks standard became federal law.
2. Charlie Savage and Robert Pear, "Administration Moves to Avert a Late Rules Rush," *New York Times*, May 31, 2008.

plan moot. I still get a sharp pang when I remember the call I got from an affected fisherman-negotiator, who lost his boat as a result.

Fearing the potential for a repeat performance, I did what I could to prevent the product from falling into the abyss. Within a few days, the *New York Times* published an op-ed commentary I wrote stating that an industry-union consensus crane standard was stuck at OSHA. I suggested that the OSHA administrator request from the White House an extraordinary exemption from the no new rules policy.[3] Part of the delay, we later learned, was a result of time spent by OSHA in preparation of a rigorously comprehensive and very lengthy preamble meant to protect against future litigation concerning the standards.

Soon after C-DAC's activities, a congressional hearing, and editorials and op-eds in major newspapers across the country, OSHA sent the proposed standard to the Office of Management and Budget (OMB) for the final economic analysis hurdle before publication.

Concerned that OMB could act as a black hole for the standard, C-DAC members, Congress, and the media continued to press for action on national crane safety standards. C-DAC members met with OMB officials to express strong support and explain the benefits of their consensus agreement.

The *New York Times* piled on more pressure with an editorial that supported pushing the proposed standards out of OMB and onto the pages of the *Federal Register*. It stated: "Both the building industry and labor groups have pressed for new standards and helped draft rules for the Occupational Safety and Health Administration. That was four years ago. The rules are now parked at the Office of Management and Budget, where the White House seems content to let the clock run out without approving them."[4]

According to some, OMB reviewed the standard with surprising speed. The Notice of Proposed Rulemaking was published only months before the end of the Bush administration. During the formal public comment period that followed, and a requested public hearing, C-DAC

---

3. Years later, I learned that although the memo initially caused some alarm within OSHA, after internal discussions, OSHA determined the memo did not apply to the cranes rule.
4. "Long Overdue Crane Safety," New York Times, August 2, 2008.

members again kicked into gear to act, virtually all in support of their agreement. Many C-DAC members spoke in support of crane operator testing by an independent accredited organization. One member organization spoke against the provision because of ongoing concerns about cost.

Ultimately, C-DAC prevailed. After more than six years of patience and determination, with few changes, C-DAC 's consensus agreement became federal law.

Shifting Skepticism to Ownership and Commitment

Initial skepticism often colors the early negotiating sessions of a civic fusion process, particularly when most participants have limited or no experience with such proceedings. Many expect that government has already made the critical decisions and fear they are being used for political cover.

In most cases, this skepticism recedes as people see their impact on the emerging document. Because the government or someone else was not likely to have thought of the same idea and certainly not with the precise words, their prior assumptions are replaced with the knowledge that they are, in fact, building a unique solution to address their situation.

The Chelsea charter preparation team gradually claimed ownership of the charter and the charter process long before it was complete, despite its persistent skepticism. Team members spoke before the board of aldermen in response to charges that the charter had already been written—and in one case, a claim that it was being printed up at the State House.

With their intimate knowledge of the charter, the negotiators were able to ensure it was accurately implemented. In true Chelsea fashion, a man who won an at-large city council seat in the first election under the new charter, declined the position to maintain his seat on the Conservation Commission. (The charter explicitly stated that a person could not hold both appointments concurrently.) This left a vacancy, which, according to the charter, was to be filled by the next top vote-getter for the citywide council seats, a Hispanic woman, who was a former school committee member. A former alderman—a member of the "old guard"—trailed her in votes, but tried to claim the vacant seat.

In response, members of the charter preparation team weighed in and publicly explained the vacancy section of the charter. The former alderman backed down, and Chelsea-watchers expressed surprise and hope at the change in community conduct. Having discussed, deliberated, and decided every detail of the charter, members of the charter preparation team acted on their commitment to its fair and just implementation.

Commitment also emerges when the agreement reflects the unique characteristics of a complex situation. The hard work and integration of ideas and comments from thousands of Chelsea residents gave the charter a decidedly local flavor. For example, to protect against future corruption, the charter explicitly denies elective office to convicted felons.

The second election under the new charter also required action by engaged officials and citizens. A former police captain, who served a one-year prison term for a tax evasion conviction, which stemmed from corruption, won a district seat on the city council. By state law, Chelsea needed the attorney general to enforce the charter's antifelon provision.

The city manager, Guy Santagate, asked the attorney general to prevent the former police captain from serving on the council. When little action occurred, the city manager and charter team members held a news conference to bring public attention to the need for the attorney general, then a gubernatorial candidate, to seek an injunction to prevent the former police captain from being sworn into office.

The *Boston Globe* weighed in with an editorial that stated: "The members of the Charter Commission and the city manager saw this one coming. They deserve support from the court for their foresight."

Ultimately, at the request of the attorney general, the Massachusetts Supreme Judicial Court issued a preliminary injunction. Only hours before Chelsea's city council was to be sworn in, a state appeals court judge left in place the superior court injunction supporting the antifelonious city councilor charter provision. The community's ability to create a charter that fits its unique circumstances—in this case, a history of corruption—resulted in a strong commitment to act to preserve the integrity of the new charter among those who helped write and implement it.

Mediator Commitment to the Process and Product

Like the negotiators, I continue to feel part of the fused system even after the meetings conclude. My ongoing commitment to the process stems from my passion for involving people in self-governance as a means to strengthen the practice of democracy. When people participate wholeheartedly and responsibly and succeed in building a consensus agreement responsive to their stated public goal, I believe that product should be implemented. To do otherwise rightfully breeds political cynicism and popular anger toward government. I feel responsible to act if I can contribute to increasing the likelihood of implementing the consensus agreement.

In all three projects, the cranes reg neg, Chelsea, and the abortion talks, I found myself deeply committed to the consensus products. I continually supported efforts for promulgation of the C-DAC consensus. In Chelsea, I checked in regularly with officials through the special vote for the charter, elections for the first city council, and hiring the city manager. People on the ground had things under control and there was little for me to do. For the abortion talks, I participated in group presentations and media events, but more importantly, stayed in the lives of the participants. To this day, we continue to meet occasionally to support each other through challenging life events.

When civic fusion is achieved, the resulting actionable agreements engender a sense of ownership and commitment among the participating negotiators, which makes them likely to act to ensure implementation. As mediator, sometimes I also find myself committed to protect the process and preserve the consensus product even years after I have any formal relationship to the process.

CONCLUSION

It sure seems like the world is convulsing. In the Arab world, long time dictators have been toppled. Greece and other European countries have been rocked by riots and demonstrations against the austerity plans demanded by central bankers to avoid sovereign debt bankruptcy, and Russians have taken to the streets to protest alleged election fraud.

Here in the United States, we avoided an economic collapse only to descend into The Great Recession. Unemployment is high, foreclosures are widespread, and the U.S. credit rating was downgraded for the first time in history. As the Tea Party rallied against Obamacare, an Occupy movement put income inequality on the national agenda. In the usually level-headed Midwest, citizens took over the Wisconsin State House as its democratic legislators fled to Illinois to block a vote to limit the collective-bargaining rights of public workers and initiated recall elections of their governor and legislators. In newspapers, television reports, and across all social media, people and experts decry the state of polarization in our political arena.

And there is little confidence in our governing bodies to fix things. Only 17 percent of Americans approve of how Congress is doing its job, according to a June 2012 Gallup poll.[1] That we stand at the edge of a fiscal cliff because the Joint Select Committee on Deficit Reduction (the *Supercommittee*) failed to agree on strategies for reducing the national debt amid routine threats to shut down the federal government is further evidence of Congress' inability to effectively address our national challenges.

And yet, amidst this colossal mess, citizens worldwide still connect across boundaries. Most of us effectively work and play daily with people across different political persuasions. Some of us join forces to address community issues. In our day-to-day, we don't ask for political opinions before we send coordinating memos to work team members, and local chorus and theatre groups practice and perform, despite likely political differences members may not even know of. People with varied political opinions work together to build parks and community gardens, improve local schools, and help returning veterans. In Cairo, during the early days of protests in Tahrir Square, Ismael Abdul Latif observed, "A secular artist is having a political debate with a fully veiled lady and having a meaningful conversation. What's the world coming to?"[2]

Civic fusion naturally occurs in communities around the world. People surprisingly connect with and act in support of others they may have considered political polar opposites. They reach for common goals that enable them to transcend their differences to act on behalf of a greater good. But, like the nuclear fusion that occurs on the surface of the sun and the civic fusion of Tahrir Square, to address complex policy challenges, we need to achieve sustained fusion under conditions that enable us to harness its power for our benefit.

To do so, citizens and their leaders need to have a determined will to move beyond a failed status quo and build something new.

The Massachusetts leaders of the pro-choice and pro-life movements decided that killing born people over abortion policy disputes had to stop. The crane industry and unions decided that too many workers

---

1. Frank Newport, "Congress Approval at 17% in June" *Gallup*, June 11, 2012.
2. Sharon Otterman and J. David Goodman, "Hundreds of Thousands Protest Across Mideast," Sharon Otterman and J. David Goodman, *New York Times*, February 25, 2011.

were crushed in crane accidents. And the citizens of Chelsea demanded democracy with safeguards against corruption.

Civic fusion will happen naturally in pockets around the world. But those who can cause it to happen and sustain it long enough to address complicated public problems are likely to make gains in the global contest.

The United States has the advantage of vast experience in bridging across differences. As a nation, we value diversity, and our educational system promotes thought and creativity unlike the rote memorization of other systems.

But somehow we've gotten to a place where we express the worst sides of ourselves—from blatant disrespect for the Office of the President of the United States of America—our Commander-in-Chief, to the anonymous nastiness of cyberspace and everything in-between.

Government is not the enemy. It reflects us. Public employees in the United States work for us, the citizens. In my experience, I've found most are hardworking public servants committed to their agencies public missions. Government will play a critical role in initiating the processes needed to address our shared challenges, but it will need to do so in partnership with citizens and stakeholders. We need to reset our democracy from the top down and the bottom up.

The method I've described to initiate and sustain civic fusion to address complex public disputes is a tool for getting beyond our polarization. It won't solve every problem, but it can solve some.

We can create regulations that efficiently meet our shared public goals. To do so, we need to get the right people to the table to negotiate those rules in public sunshine. For value-based conflicts—like abortion—that we will likely never resolve, we need to work within the confines of our democratic system where we are invited to put our passions and wisdom to work to change laws. As we use our arguments and available levers of power to do so, we need to respect that those who disagree with us operate from a different set of assumptions and an equally passionate sense of right and wrong.

We need to have conversations about those assumptions rather than maintain ongoing attachments to presumed immorality on the part of those with whom we disagree.

To sustain civic fusion long enough to resolve a policy conflict requires carefully designed processes. Policy mediators identify and integrate situational dynamics and challenges into specifically tailored process designs. They can help identify who needs to participate to develop actionable agreements, what issues will need to be discussed, in what sequence, how to break issues down to component parts to clarify real conflicts from confusions, and sustain productive negotiations.

Conflict is integral to representative democracies in which laws evolve alongside societal values and priorities. The democratic system suggests that from a clash of interests beneficial solutions will emerge to address many public problems. But in today's political climate, when actual policy conflict has been replaced by personal attacks, we risk falling behind because of inaction. Perhaps policy makers and the public will practice civic fusion to solve complex public conflicts—groups of people will identify their common goals, find ways to respect their differences, and bond together to develop innovative solutions to their shared problems. And perhaps civic fusion will become a natural way of thinking so that the next time a secular artist has a meaningful political conversation with a veiled woman, it's a normal and usual interaction.

RECOMMENDED READING LIST

Bellman, Howard, "Improvisation, Mediation, and All That Jazz," *Negotiation Journal,* vol. 22, no. 3, July 2006.

Carpenter, Susan L., and W. J. D. Kennedy. *Managing Public Disputes: A Practical Guide for Professionals in Government, Business, and Citizen's Groups.* San Francisco: Jossey-Bass Publishers, 2001.

Dukes, E. Franklin. *Resolving Conflict: Transforming Community and Governance.* Manchester, UK: Manchester University Press, 1996.

Fisher, Roger, Ury, William, and Patton, Bruce, *Getting to Yes: Negotiating Agreement Without Giving In,* New York: Penguin Books (2nd Edition) 1991.

Forester, John. *Dealing with Differences.* New York: Oxford University Press, 2009.

Forester, John, "Responding to Critical Moments with Humor, Recognition, and Hope." *Negotiation Journal,* 20: 221–237, 2004.

Gurevitch, Z.D., "The Power of Not Understanding: The Meeting of Conflicting Identities,"" *Journal of Applied Behavioral Science,* Vol. 25, No. 2, 161–173, 1989.

Heradsveit, Daniel, The Arab-Israeli Conflict: Psychological Barriers to Peace, Oslo: Universitetsforlaget (Second revised edition), 1982.

Kolb, Deborah, and Associates, eds. *When Talk Works: Profiles of Mediators.* San Francisco: Jossey-Bass Publishers, 1994.

Mansbridge, Jane J. *Beyond Adversary Democracy.* Chicago: University of Chicago Press, 1980.

Mansbridge, Jane "Deliberative and Non-Deliberative Negotiations," *HKS Working Paper No. RWP09-010*, Harvard University—Harvard Kennedy School, April 6, 2009.

Plato, *The Republic.*

Riskin, Leonard, Further Beyond Reason: Emotions, The Core Concerns, and Mindfulness in Negotiation, Annual Saltzman Lecture, Nevada Law School 10 Nevada Legal Journal, 2010.

Riskin, Leonard, "Mindfulness: Foundational Training for Dispute Resolution," Journal of Legal Education, Vol. 54, pp. 79–91, 2004.

Schon, Donald, The Reflective Practitioner: How Professionals Think in Action, Basic Books, 1983.

Susskind, Lawrence, and Jeffery Cruikshank. *Breaking The Impasse: Consensual Approaches to Resolving Public Disputes.* New York: Basic Books, 1987.

Susskind, Lawrence, et al., eds. *The Consensus Building Handbook.* Thousand Oaks, CA: Sage Publications, 1999.

Appendix A
Talking with the Enemy, The *Boston Globe*

Talking with the Enemy

The Boston Globe

PROLIFE

Frances X. Hogan

Madeline McComish

Barbara Thorp

For nearly six years, leaders on both sides of the abortion debate have met in secret in an attempt to better understand each other. Now they are ready to share what they have learned.

By Anne Fowler, Nicki Nichols Gamble, Frances X. Hogan, Melissa Kogut, Madeline McComish, and Barbara Thorp

On the morning of Dec. 30, 1994, John Salvi walked into the Planned Parenthood clinic in Brookline and opened fire with a rifle. He seriously wounded three people and killed the receptionist, Shannon Lowney, as she spoke on the phone. He then ran to his car and drove two miles down Beacon Street to Preterm Health Services, where he began shooting again, injuring two and killing receptionist Lee Ann Nichols.

Salvi's 20-minute rampage shocked the nation. Prochoice advocates were grief-stricken, angry, and terrified. Prolife proponents were appalled as well as concerned that their cause would be connected with this horrifying act. Governor William F. Weld and Cardinal Bernard Law, among others, called for talks between prochoice and prolife leaders.

We are six leaders, three prochoice and three prolife, who answered this call. For nearly ½ years, we have met together privately for more than 150 hours–an experience that has astonished and enriched us. Now, six years after the shootings in Brookline and on the 28th anniversary of the US Supreme Court's landmark Roe v. Wade decision, we publicly disclose our meetings for the first time.

How did the six of us, activists from two embattled camps, ever find our way to the same table?

Abortion, Page F2

PROCHOICE

Melissa Kogut

Anne Fowler

Nicki Nichols Gamble

Getting it started

➤ **ABORTION**

Continued from F1

In the months following the shootings, the Public Conversations Project, a Boston-based national group that designs and conducts dialogues about divisive public issues, consulted many community leaders about the value of top-level talks about abortion.

Encouraged by these conversations, the project in July 1995 invited the six of us to meet together four times. The meetings would be confidential and we would attend as individuals, not as representatives of our organizations.

Since that first fear-filled meeting, we have experienced a paradox. While learning to treat each other with dignity and respect, we all have become firmer in our views about abortion.

Clockwise, starting with facilitators Laura Chasin and Susan Podziba, whose backs are to the camera, the Public Conversations group comprised Barbara Thorp, Melissa Kogut, Madeline McComish, Nicki Nichols Gamble, Fran Hogan, and Rev. Anne Fowler.

Our talks would not aim for common ground or compromise. Instead, the goals of our conversations would be to communicate openly with our opponents, away from the polarizing spotlight of media coverage; to build relationships of mutual respect and understanding; to help deescalate the rhetoric of the abortion controversy; and, of course, to reduce the risk of future shootings.

Still shaken by the murderous attacks in Brookline, we each agreed to participate.

As we approached the first meeting, we all were apprehensive.

Before the meeting, the prolife participants prayed together in a booth at a nearby Friendly's. Frances X. Hogan, a lawyer and president of Women Affirming Life and executive vice president of Massachusetts Citizens for Life, worried that a dialogue

Continued on next page

Who's doing the talking

The Rev. Anne Fowler is rector of St. John's Episcopal Church in Jamaica Plain and a past member of both the board of directors, Planned Parenthood League of Massachusetts, and the board of the Religious Coalition for Reproductive Choice.

Nicki Nichols Gamble served as president and CEO of the Planned Parenthood League of Massachusetts from 1974 to 1999. She is a director of the Center for Reproductive Law and Policy and of IPAS, an international women's reproductive health care organization, and volunteers for the Planned Parenthood Federation of America.

Frances X. Hogan, a partner at the law firm of Lyne, Woodworth & Evarts, is president of Women Affirming Life and consultant to the Pro-Life Committee of the National Conference of Catholic Bishops.

Melissa Kogut is executive director of Mass NARAL, state affiliate of the National Abortion and Reproductive Rights Action League.

Madeline McComish, a chemist, is past president of Massachusetts Citizens for Life, serves on its executive board, and is chairman of the North Suburban Chapter of Massachusetts Citizens for life.

Barbara Thorp has been director of the Pro-Life Office of the Archdiocese of Boston since 1985 and is on the executive boards of the National Office of Post-Abortion Reconciliation and Healing, the National Committee for a Human Life Amendment, and Women Affirming Life.

Continued from previous page

with pro-choice leaders might generate "a scandal if people thought I was treating abortion merely as a matter of opinion on which reasonable people could differ."

Madeline McComish, a chemist and president of Massachusetts Citizens for Life, had a "gut fear of sitting with people who were directly involved with taking life."

Barbara Thorp was "deeply anguished over the murders at the clinics." she feared that "if lines of direct communication between prolife and pro-choice leaders were not opened, polarization would only deepen." Despite misgivings, Thorp, a social worker and director of the ProLife Office of the Archdiocese of Boston, was "anxious to meet the other side."

The prochoice participants were also skeptical and concerned. As president and CEO of the Planned Parenthood League of Massachusetts, Nicki Nichols Gamble was directly affected by the shootings. Although

Prochoice advocates marked the first anniversary of the 1994 clinic shootings with a march that wound past the State House.

she felt that dialogue might help, she "wondered if the talks would divert my energies from co-ordinating my organization's response to the shootings and from assisting in the healing of my employees and their families."

Melissa Kogut, newly appointed executive director of Mass NARAL, the state affiliate of the National Abortion Rights Action League, wondered how she would "justify to my board and colleagues spending time on something that arguably could be futile."

The Rev. Anne Fowler, rector of St. John's Episcopal Church in Jamaica Plain, believed that her perspective as a Christian leader who is prochoice would be essential, but worried that her viewpoint might not be respected by either side. "However, as a priest, peacemaker, and activist, I had to accept this invitation."

The two facilitators who would moderate all the meetings were also anxious. Laura Chasin, director of the Public Conversations Project, "was afraid that talks might do more harm than good." Susan Podziba, an independent public policy mediator

Continued on next page

we have glimpsed a new possibility: a way in which people can disagree frankly and passionately, become clearer in heart and mind about their activism, and, at the same time, contribute to a more civil and compassionate society.

Prochoice

The prochoice members of the group describe their views this way:

We recognize no single, universal truth that determines our moral decisions. On the contrary, we must consider a broad range of values whenever we seek to make wise, ethical, and compassionate choices. We respect a woman's moral capacity to make decisions regarding her health and welfare, including reproductive decisions.

A woman's choices reflect how she weighs her various life circumstances: her important relationships, her economic, social, and emotional resources and obligations, her health, her religious or philosophical beliefs, and the wellbeing of others for whom she has responsibility.

We live out our destinies in a world of vast and profound complexity, where claims upon our compassion and our judgment compete and often conflict. A woman respects the preciousness of human life by acknowledging and honoring the intricate tapestry of her relationships and commitments; indeed, we believe that the complexity of human life can be a source of moral wisdom and courage.

Prolife forces rallied on Boston Common in October, days after the Food and Drug Administration approved RU-486 for prescribing to women seeking to abort pregnancies.

from Brookline, recalls, "The threat of violence was palpable. What if the wrong person found out about the dialogue?"

The first meeting took place at the project's office in Watertown on Sept. 5, 1995, a sweltering Tuesday evening. "I had wanted to wear my clerical collar, but it was too hot," recalls Fowler.

A growing trust opened a "hot line" channel of reliable communication between us. The prolife leaders alerted Gamble when there was a possibility of imminent physical danger.

That first discussion was grueling. We could not agree on what to call each other. All but one of us were willing to use each side's preferred designation, in virtual or actual quotation marks: "prolife" and "prochoice."

Our first of many clashes over language, this disagreement remains unresolved. To this day, Gamble still cannot call the other side prolife because "I believe my cause is also prolife," she says. This stand frustrates Thorp and her colleagues. "I have tolerated Nicki's refusal to call us prolife but, frankly, it angers me. I wasn't eager to call Nicki's side prochoice, but I did it because it seemed to be necessary for showing respect and for moving the conversation forward," Thorp says.

Kogut questioned her own willingness to agree to these terms, "but I came to two conclusions," Kogut says. 'To proceed with a civil dialogue, we needed to call each other what we each wanted to be called. Second, over time, I began to see 'prolife' as descriptive of the others' beliefs—that life itself, more important than the quality of life, was their preeminent value."

We also struggled over how to refer to what grows and develops in a pregnant woman's womb. The

PROLIFE

The prolife members of the group describe their views this way:

We believe in one universal truth. We three, as Catholics, believe that each human life has its origin in the heart of God. This divine genesis of the human person calls us to protect and respect every human life from the moment of conception to natural death.

The truth regarding the intrinsic dignity of the human person can also be understood through reason and scientific principles of human reproduction and genetics. Indeed, faith and reason resonate, both affirming the inviolable truth that every human life is inherently sacred.

Abortion kills the most vulnerable member of the human family: the unborn child. The right to be bom is the most basic of human rights. If it is not protected then all other rights are threatened.

Prolife forces rallied on Boston Common in October, days after the Food and Drug Administration approved RU-486 for prescribing to women seeking to abort pregnancies.

We understand, all too well, the often desperate and overwhelming circumstances that some pregnant women face. We remain committed to creating an environment in which no pregnant woman feels that she must choose between her own well-being and the life of her child. It is an utter failure of love and community for a pregnant woman to feel that abortion is her only choice.

prochoice women found "unborn baby" unacceptable and the prolife women would not agree to "fetus." For the sake of proceeding, we all assented, uneasily, to the term "human fetus."

These opening exchanges brought us to the heart of our differences, Nerves frayed. The chasm between us seemed huge.

To help us listen and speak across this divide, ground rules were critical. We would seek to use terms acceptable (or at least tolerable) to all participants. We would not interrupt, grandstand, or make personal attacks. We would speak for ourselves, not as representatives of organizations. Most important, the meetings would be completely confidential unless all of us could agree upon a way to go public.

We also made a commitment that some of us still find agonizingly difficult: to shift our focus away from arguing for our cause. This agreement was designed to prevent rancorous debates.

And indeed, we believe this ground rule has been essential to the long life of our dialogue. Knowing that our ideas would be challenged, but not attacked, we have been able to listen openly and speak candidly.

But it has not been easy.

"From the beginning, I have felt an enormous tension, Hogan says, "between honoring the agreement to not argue for our position and my deep hope—which I still feel—that these women for whom I have such great respect will change their minds about abortion."

Our ground rules also required us to refrain from polarizing rhetoric. In one early session, we generated a list of "hot buttons"—words and phrases that make it almost impossible for some of us to think clearly, listen carefully, or respond constructively.

Prochoice members are inflamed when called "murderers" or when abortions are likened to the Holocaust or to "genocide." Prolife participants are incensed by dehumanizing phrases such as "products of conception" and "termination of pregnancy" that obscure their belief that abortion is killing.

We also discussed stereotypes we thought were applied to us by people "on the other side."

we have glimpsed a new possibility: a way in which people can disagree frankly and passionately, become clearer in heart and mind about their activism, and, at the same time, contribute to a more civil and compassionate society.

Prolife participants feel maligned when characterized as religious fanatics taking orders from men, or as uneducated, prudish individuals, indifferent to women in crisis and to children after they are bom. Prochoice members are offended by labels such as antichild, anti-men, anti-family, elitist, frivolous, self-centered, and immoral.

Despite the strains of these early meetings, we grew closer to each other. At one session, each of us told the group why she had devoted so much of her time, energy, and talents to the abortion issue. These accounts—all deeply personal—enlightened and moved us.

After the fourth meeting, we agreed to extend our sessions through the one-yer anniversary of the shootings—an occasion, we feared, when tensions over abortion might ignite in Boston.

On the evening of Dec. 30, 1995, about 700 people gathered at Temple Ohabei Shalom in Brookline to honor the memory of Lowney and Nichols. All our pro- choice participants attended the service. Fowler and Gamble officiated. In the solemn crowd were Pod- ziba, one of our facilitators, and two of our prolife members, Hogan and Thorp, accompanied by David Thorp, her husband.

"Seeing the other members of the group walk in was one of the most meaningful moments of the service for me," Fowler recalls.

In her remarks, Gamble expressed gratitude "for the prayers of those who agree with us and the prayers of those who disagree."

Fowler, in her sermon, reminded us of the "God who calls out to all who love peace." She drew from the words of the Hebrew prophet Isaiah, saying "and new things have sprung forth in the year since Lee Ann's and Shannon's deaths. Much has been transformed, and much will be."

Indeed, to those of us involved in the confidential dialogues, much had been transformed. By the time of this sad anniversary, each one of us had come to think differently about those "on the other side."

While we struggled over profound issues, we also kept track of personal events in one another's lives, celebrating good times and sharing sorrows. As our mutual understanding increased, our respect and affection for one another grew.

This increased understanding affected how we spoke as leaders of our respective movements. The news media, unaware that we were meeting, began noting differences in our public statements.

In an article after the first-year anniversary of the shootings, Globe reporter Don Aucoin wrote, "Has the past year brought the lowering of voices... called for by Cardinal Law, Governor William Weld and others? The answer seems to be a qualified yes, at least among some activists."

The article quoted Gamble as saying, "There are numbers of people on both sides of this question who have tried to be thoughtful about the rhetoric they use." Gamble added that she was hearing fewer uses of such labels as "baby-killer, murderer, Nazi."

In the same article, Hogan is quoted as saying she uses "prochoice because that is what they want to be called. I have a basic respect for the person, even though I don't agree with or respect the position."

Thorp, too, was quoted. "This call for a lowering of voices sent a signal that we really needed to listen to each other with care and respect. I'm more mindful now than I've ever been of speaking in love, speaking in peace, and speaking in respect to anyone, no matter how wide the differences are."

Massachusetts Citizens for Life, Inc.

January 25, 1996

Reverend Donald Spitz
Pro-Life Virginia
P.O. Box 2876
Chesapeake, VA 23327

Dear Reverend Spitz:

We have been informed that you are intending to come to Massachusetts for the John Salvi trial. Your public statements on the acceptability of violence do not represent the views of the pro-life movement - rather they are counter to everything that the pro-life movement represents.

At this very difficult time, you are not welcome in Massachusetts.

Very truly yours,

Madeline McComish
Madeline McComish
President, Massachusetts Citizens For Life

The undersigned leaders of pro-life organizations in the Commonwealth of Massachusetts support this request.

Barbara S. Thorp
Barbara S. Thorp, Director
Pro-Life Office of the Archdiocese of Boston

Marianne Rea-Luthin
Mariann Rea-Luthin, President
Value of Life Committee

Frances X. Hogan
Frances X. Hogan, President
Women Affirming Life

Schrafft Center, 529 Main Street, Boston, MA 02129-1101 • (617) 242-4199
109 Centre Street, P.O. Box 96, Ludlow, MA 01056 • (413) 583-5034
24 hr Pro-Life News Service 242-4589

One result of the conversation: a redoubled commitment to stop the violence.

In a National Public Radio interview about the anniversary, Hogan explained that while she believed that abortion is killing, she did not call it murder. Hogan also said, "Toning down the rhetoric is critical. It's not just better manners, but it turns out it's also better politics. ... We reach people we may never otherwise have reached with the message."

Kogut felt and acted differently when she appeared with prolife spokespeople on news shows and at speaking engagements. Kogut recalls, "I was struck by the media's desire for conflict. One host of a radio talk show actually encouraged me to attack my opponent personally."

In early 1996, we continued to meet, anticipating that the up-coming Salvi trial would present new challenges to protect activists and the public from danger.

At one point, prolife advocates acted to keep proponents of violence away from Massachusetts. In February 1996, the Rev. Donald Spitz, head of ProLife Virginia, made it known that he was planning to come to Boston to show support for what he had called, according to the Globe, Salvi's "righteous deed."

McComish wrote a letter to Spitz, signed also by Hogan and Thorp. 'Your public statements on the acceptability of violence ... are counter to everything that the prolife movement represents," McComish wrote. "At this very difficult time, you are not welcome in Massachusetts."

Spitz and several of his allies objected to McComish's charge. They suggested that she was betraying the cause. But he did not come.

A growing trust opened a "hot line" channel of reliable communication between us. The prolife leaders alerted Gamble when there was a possibility of imminent physical danger. "It lowered my anxiety—and moved me deeply—to know that there were people on the other side who were concerned about my safety," Gamble says.

Throughout these 5½ years, though external events claimed much of our attention, we managed to explore many aspects of the abortion controversy, such as when life begins, the rights of women, the rights of the unborn, why women get abortions, and the aftermath of abortion.

We spent especially tense hours discussing the issue that prochoice members describe as "bans on certain abortion procedures" and that prolife participants call "partial- birth abortions." We also probed a host of other complex and challenging subjects: feminism, sex education, euthanasia, suicide, the death penalty, the role of law in society, and individual responsibility.

When addressing divisive topics, we expected to disagree. But at times, conflicts caught us by surprise—flaring when one side unwittingly used certain words in a way that struck the other as presumptuous or offensive.

One provocative word has been "violence." While the prochoice leaders use it to refer to shootings and other attacks on clinics, doctors, and staff, the prolife activists believe that abortion also is a violent act.

In writing this article, we came to an impasse when one side mentioned the Declaration of Independence. The prolife participants wished to cite the Declaration as a presentation of their core belief that the right to life is inalienable and self-evident. The prochoice members passionately objected to what they saw as an appropriation of a document that they also cherish. To them, the Declaration affirms every person's right to life and liberty.

when we face our opponent, we see her dignity and goodness.

In these and all of our discussions of differences, we strained to reach those on the other side who could not accept—or at times comprehend—our beliefs. We challenged each other to dig deeply, defining exactly what we believe, why we believe it, and what we still do not understand.

These conversations revealed a deep divide. We saw that our differences on abortion reflect two world views that are irreconcilable.

If this is true, then why do we continue to meet?

First, because when we face our opponent, we see her dignity and goodness. Embracing this apparent contradiction stretches us spiritually. We've experienced something radical and life-altering that we describe in nonpolitical terms: "the mystery of love," "holy ground," or simply, "mysterious."

We continue because we are stretched intellectually, as well. This has been a rare opportunity to engage in sustained, candid conversations about serious moral disagreements. It has made our thinking sharper and our language more precise.

We hope, too, that we have become wiser and more effective leaders. We are more knowledgeable about our political opponents. We have learned to avoid being overreactive and disparaging to the other side and to focus instead on affirming our respective causes.

Since that first fear-filled meeting, we have experienced a paradox. While learning to treat each other with dignity and respect, we all have become firmer in our views about abortion.

We hope this account of our experience will encourage people everywhere to consider engaging in dialogues about abortion and other protracted disputes. In this world of polarizing conflicts, we have glimpsed a new possibility: a way in which people can disagree frankly and passionately, become clearer in heart and mind about their activism, and, at the same time, contribute to a more civil and compassionate society.

Editor's note: Although the Globe's stylebook does not allow the use of "prochoice" and "prolife" (preferring instead such terms as "abortion rights advocates" or "abortion foes"), an exception was made in this article to better reflect the views of the authors.

Appendix B
C-DAC Federal Register Notices

Notice of Intent to Establish a Reg Neg Committee July 16, 2002

DEPARTMENT OF LABOR

Occupational Safety and Health Administration

29 CFR Part 1926

[Docket No. S–030]

RIN 1218–AC01

Safety Standards for Cranes and Derricks

AGENCY: Occupational Safety and Health Administration (OSHA), Department of Labor.

ACTION: Notice of intent to establish Negotiated Rulemaking Committee; request for nominees and comments.

SUMMARY: The Occupational Safety and Health Administration is announcing its intent to establish a Cranes and Derricks Negotiated Rulemaking Advisory Committee (C–DAC) under the Negotiated Rulemaking Act (NRA) and the Federal Advisory Committee Act (FACA). The Committee will negotiate issues associated with the development of a proposed revision of the existing construction safety standards for the cranes and derricks portion ("1926.550) of 29 CFR part 1926 Subpart N-Cranes, Derricks, Hoists, Elevators, and Conveyors. The Committee will include representatives of parties who would be significantly affected by the final rule. OSHA solicits comments on the initiative and requests interested parties to nominate representatives for membership on C–DAC.

DATES: Written comments and requests for membership must be submitted by September 16, 2002. Comments and requests for membership submitted by mail must be postmarked not later than September 16, 2002. E mailed or faxed comments or requests for nomination must be received by September 16, 2002.

ADDRESSES: Written comments, including nominations for membership, may be submitted in any of three ways: by mail, by fax, or by e-mail. Please include "Docket No. S–030" on all submissions. By mail, the address is: OSHA Docket Office, Docket No. S–030, U.S. Department of Labor, 200 Constitution Avenue, NW., Room N–2625, Washington, DC 20210, telephone (202) 693–2350. Note that receipt of comments submitted by mail may be delayed by several weeks. By fax, written comments and nominations for membership that are 10 pages or fewer, may be transmitted to the OSHA Docket Office at telephone number (202) 693–1648. By email, comments and nominations may be submitted through OSHA's Homepage at *ecomments.osha.gov.* Please note that you may not attach materials such as studies or journal articles to your electronic comments. If you wish to include such materials, you must submit three copies to the OSHA Docket Office at the address listed above. When submitting such materials to the OSHA Docket Office, clearly identify your electronic comments by name, date, subject, and Docket Number, so that we can attach the materials to your electronic comments.

FOR FURTHER INFORMATION CONTACT: Nancy Ford, Office of Construction Standards and Compliance Assistance, Occupational Safety and Health Administration, U.S. Department of Labor, Room NB3468, 200 Constitution Avenue, NW., Washington, DC 20210; Telephone: (202) 693–2345.

SUPPLEMENTARY INFORMATION:

I. Background

The existing rule for cranes and derricks in construction, codified in volume 29 of the Code of Federal Regulations (CFR), § 1926.550, which dates back to 1971, is based in part on industry consensus standards from 1967 to 1969. Since 1971, that section of subpart N has undergone only two amendments:

(1) In 1988, § 1926.550 was amended by adding a new paragraph (g) to establish clearly the conditions under which employees on personnel platforms may be hoisted by cranes or derricks (see volume 53 of the **Federal Register**, pages 29116 to 29141).

(2) In 1993, § 1926.550 was amended by adding a new (a)(19), which states that *all employees shall be kept clear of loads about to be lifted and of suspended loads* (58 FR 35183).

There have been considerable technological changes since the consensus standards upon which the 1971 OSHA standard is based were developed. For example, hydraulic cranes were rare at that time but are now prevalent. The existing OSHA standard does not specifically address hydraulic cranes. In contrast, industry consensus standards for derricks were updated in 1995 and crawler, truck and locomotive cranes were updated as recently as 2000.

A cross-section of industry stakeholders has asked the Agency to update Subpart N's crane and derrick requirements. They have indicated that over the past 30 years, the considerable changes in both work processes and crane technology have made much of Subpart N obsolete.

For the past two years, a number of industry representatives have been working with a cranes workgroup of the Advisory Committee for Construction Safety and Health (ACCSH). That workgroup has been developing recommended changes to Subpart N with respect to the requirements for cranes.

Based on the Agency's review of the issues, the progress made by the ACCSH cranes workgroup, and the continued interest in using negotiated rulemaking for this standard, OSHA proposes to use the negotiated rulemaking process to develop a proposed revision of the requirements in Subpart N for cranes and derricks.

The negotiated rulemaking effort described in this notice will be conducted in accordance with the Negotiated Rulemaking Act, 5 U.S.C. 561 *et seq.*, and the Department of Labor's policy on negotiated rulemaking. Further detail on the Department's negotiated rulemaking policy is in the "Notice of Policy on Use of Negotiated Rulemaking Procedures by Agencies of the Department of Labor" (57 FR 61860).

A. The Concept of Negotiated Rulemaking

Usually, OSHA develops a proposed rule using staff and consultant resources. The concerns of affected parties are often identified through stakeholder meetings and an advance notice of proposed rulemaking (ANPR) published in the **Federal Register**. This is followed by formal consultation with ACCSH (under the Construction Safety Act, OSHA is required to consult with ACCSH on all proposed construction standards). Affected parties do not generally have an opportunity to submit arguments and data supporting their positions until the proposed rule is published. In contrast, in a negotiated rulemaking, there is greater opportunity for face-to-face, back-and-forth communications during the process among parties representing different interests and with agency officials.

Many times, effective regulations have resulted from traditional rulemaking. However, as Congress noted in the Negotiated Rulemaking Act (5 U.S.C. 561), current rulemaking procedures Amay discourage the affected parties from meeting and communicating with each other, and may cause parties with different interests to assume conflicting and antagonistic positions * * *'' (Sec. 2(2)). Congress also stated that ''adversarial rulemaking deprives the affected parties and the public of the benefits of face-to-face negotiations and cooperation in developing and reaching agreement on a rule. It deprives them of the benefits of shared information, knowledge, expertise, and technical abilities possessed by the affected parties.'' (Sec. 2(3)).

In negotiated rulemaking, a proposed rule is developed by a committee composed of representatives of government and the interests that will be significantly affected by the rule. Decisions are made by consensus. As defined in 5 U.S.C. 562 (2)(a)(b), 'consensus' means unanimous concurrence among the interests represented on a negotiated rulemaking committee established under this subchapter, unless such committee agrees to define such term to mean a general but not unanimous concurrence or agrees upon another specified definition.

The process is started by the Agency's careful identification of all interests potentially affected by the rulemaking under consideration. To help in this identification process, the Agency publishes a document such as this one in the **Federal Register**, which identifies a preliminary list of interests and requests public comment on that list.

Following receipt of the comments, the Agency establishes an advisory committee representing these various interests to negotiate a consensus on the provisions of a proposed rule. Representation on the committee may be direct, that is each member represents a specific interest, or indirect, through coalitions of parties formed to represent a specific sphere of interest. The Agency is a member of the committee representing the Federal government's statutory mission.

The negotiated rulemaking advisory committee is chaired by a trained facilitator, who applies proven consensus building techniques to help the advisory committee work towards a consensus. The many functions that he or she will perform are discussed below.

Once the committee reaches consensus on the provisions of a proposed rule, the Agency, consistent with its legal obligations, uses that consensus as the basis for its proposed rule, to be published in the **Federal Register**. This provides the required public notice and allows for a public comment period. Members, other participants and other interested parties retain their rights under section 6(b) of the OSH Act to submit written comments and participate in an informal hearing (if requested). OSHA will then publish a final rule based on the record as a whole—the information that was received in the course of developing the proposed rule, together with the comments and information submitted after the proposal is published. OSHA anticipates that the pre-proposal consensus agreed upon by this Committee will effectively narrow the issues in the subsequent rulemaking and reduce the likelihood of litigation.

B. Selecting Part of Subpart N as a Candidate for Negotiated Rulemaking

The Agency may establish a negotiated rulemaking committee if it has determined that the use of the negotiated rulemaking procedure is in the public interest. As discussed above, OSHA has made that determination in this case.

The Agency bases this determination on prior experience with the negotiated rulemaking process. Even before the NRA was enacted, OSHA conducted negotiated rulemaking for its complex health standards for Methylenedianiline (MDA). This committee met seven times over a 10-month period (24 meeting days) and successfully negotiated standards for both general industry and construction. The final standards were ultimately based on the recommended proposed standards, and no litigation followed the standards' promulgation.

Also, the new Steel Erection Standard (29 CFR part 1926 subpart R) was based on a proposal that was developed by the Steel Erection Negotiated Rulemaking Advisory Committee (SENRAC). The new final rule was published on January 18, 2001, and became effective January 18, 2002. The standard addresses the hazards that have been identified as the major causes of injuries and fatalities in the steel erection industry.

OSHA believes that the cranes and derricks portion of subpart N is an appropriate subject for negotiated rulemaking. In 1998, the Advisory Committee on Construction Safety and Health (ACCSH) formed a workgroup to review subpart N. In December 1999, ACCSH passed a motion submitted by the workgroup, recommending that OSHA consider negotiated rulemaking as the mechanism to revise/update subpart N. The workgroup has made considerable progress in identifying and prioritizing areas in the current standard that should be updated to reflect modern safety procedures.

The Agency believes that the selection criteria listed in the NRA (5 U.S.C. 563(a)) have been met. Interests that will be affected by a revised subpart N are known, are limited in number, and to a significant degree are already organized in interest-based coalitions. There appears to be a good possibility of reaching consensus on a proposed rule. In addition, OSHA expects that persons likely to be significantly affected by such a rule will negotiate in good faith. The need for updating provisions is acknowledged by all known interests. As progress has already been made through the efforts of the ACCSH workgroup, OSHA believes that the negotiated rulemaking process will not unreasonably delay the proposal or issuance of a final rule.

C. Agency Commitment

In initiating this negotiated rulemaking process, OSHA is making a commitment on behalf of the Department of Labor that OSHA and all other participants within the Department will provide resources to ensure timely and successful completion of the process. This commitment includes making the negotiations a priority activity for all officials of the Department who need to be involved.

OSHA will take steps to ensure that the negotiated rulemaking committee has sufficient resources to complete itsbwork in a timely fashion. These include the provision or procurement of such support services as: adequate and properly equipped space; logistical support and timely payment of participant travel and expenses where necessary as provided for under the NRA; word processing, communications and other information handling services required by the committee; the services of a facilitator; and such additional statistical, economic, safety, legal, or other technical assistance as may be necessary.

OSHA, to the maximum extent possible consistent with its statutory mission and the legal obligations of the agency, will use the consensus of the committee as the basis for the rule proposed by the Agency for public notice and comment. The Agency believes that by updating the existing standard, it can limit or reduce the number of deaths and injuries to employees associated with cranes and derricks used in construction. The Agency, therefore, is committed to publishing a consensus proposal that is consistent with OSHA's legal mandates.

D. Negotiating Consensus

An important benefit of negotiated rulemaking is that it necessarily involves a mutual education of the parties on the practical concerns about the effect of different approaches to various issues. This stems from the fact that in negotiated rulemaking, agreement is by consensus of the interests. As noted above, the NRA defines consensus as the "unanimous concurrence among interests represented on a negotiated rulemaking committee * * * unless such committee agrees to (a different definition)." In addition, experience has demonstrated that using a trained facilitator to work with the Committee will assist alln parties, including OSHA, to identify their real interests in the rule, and will enable them to reevaluate previously stated positions on issues involved in this rulemaking effort.

E. Some Key Issues for Negotiation

OSHA expects that the key issues to be addressed as part of these negotiations will include:

1. The identification/description of what constitutes "cranes and derricks" for purposes of determining the equipment that will be covered by the proposed rule.
2. Qualifications of individuals who operate, maintain, repair, assemble, and disassemble cranes and derricks.
3. Work zone control.
4. Crane operations near electric power lines.
5. Qualifications of signal-persons and communication systems and requirements.
6. Load capacity and control procedures.
7. Wire rope criteria.
8. Crane inspection/certification records.
9. Rigging procedures.
10. Requirements for fail-safe, warning, and other safety-related devices/technologies.
11. Verification criteria for the structural adequacy of crane components.
12. Stability testing requirements.
13. Blind pick procedures.

II. Proposed Negotiation Procedures

OSHA is proposing to use the following procedures and guidelines for this negotiated rulemaking. The Agency may modify them in response to comments received on this document or during the negotiation process.

A. Committee Formation

This Committee will be formed and operated in full compliance with the requirements of the Federal Advisory Committee Act (FACA) and the NRA, in a manner consistent with the standards setting requirements of the OSH Act.

B. Interests Involved

The Agency intends to ensure full and adequate representation of those interests that are expected to be significantly affected by the proposed rule. Section 562 of the NRA defines theterm "interest" as follows:

(5) "interest" means, with respect to an issue or matter, multiple parties which have a similar

point of view or which are likely to be affected in a similar manner.

The following interests have been tentatively identified as "significantly affected" by this rulemaking:

— Crane and derrick manufacturers, suppliers, and distributors
— Companies that repair and maintain cranes and derricks
— Crane and derrick leasing companies
— Owners of cranes and derricks
— Construction companies that use leased cranes and derricks
— General contractors
— Labor organizations representing construction employees who operate cranes and derricks and who work in conjunction with cranes and derricks
— Owners of electric power distribution lines
— Civil, structural and architectural engineering firms and engineering consultants involved with the use of cranes and derricks in construction
— Training organizations
— Crane and derrick operator testing organizations
— Insurance and safety organizations, and public interest groups
— Trade associations
— Government entities involved with construction safety and with construction operations involving cranes and derricks.

This list of potential interests is not presented as a complete or exclusive list from which committee members will be selected. The list merely indicates interests that OSHA has tentatively identified as being significantly affected by the outcome of the Subpart N negotiated rulemaking process. One purpose of this document is to obtain public comment about whether an updated crane standard would significantly affect interests that are not listed above. OSHA invites comment and suggestions on this list of "significantly affected" interests.

C. Members

The negotiating group should not exceed 25 members, and 15 would be preferable. The Agency believes that the more members there are over 15, the more difficult it is to conduct effective negotiations.

OSHA is aware that there may be more interests, whether they are listed here or not, than membership slots on the Committee. In order to have a successful negotiation, it is important for interested parties to identify and form coalitions that adequately represent significantly affected interests. To provide adequate representation, these coalitions must agree to support, both financially and technically, a member on the Committee whom they will choose to represent their interest.

It is important to recognize that interested parties who are not selected to membership on the Committee can make valuable contributions to a negotiated rulemaking in any of several ways:

- Asking to be placed on the Committee mailing list and making written comments;
- Attending the Committee meetings, which are open to the public, caucusing with his or her interest's member on the Committee, or even addressing the Committee (often allowed at the end of an issue's discussion or the end of the session, as time permits); and/or
- Assisting in the work of a Committee workgroup.

Informal workgroups are usually established by an advisory committee to help it address technical issues or other particular matters. They might also help analyze costs and compliance data, help draft regulatory text, or initially address novel issues that arise during negotiations. Workgroup members usually have expertise or a particular interest in the technical matter(s) being studied. Because of the importance of this work on technical details, OSHA will also provide appropriate technical expertise for such workgroups, as needed.

D. Request for Nominations

OSHA solicits requests for appointment to membership on the Committee. Members can be individuals or representatives of organizations. However, an organization that requests membership should identify the individual who will be its representative. If the negotiation is to be successful, members must be able to fully and adequately represent the viewpoints of their respective interests. Those individuals or representatives of organizations who wish to be appointed as members of the Committee should submit a request to OSHA, in accordance with the "Public Participation" part of this document.This document gives notice of the selection process to all potential participants and affords them an opportunity to request representation in the negotiations. The procedure for requesting such representation is set out under the Public Participation part of this document, below.

E. Good Faith Negotiation

Committee members need to have authorization to negotiate on behalf of their interests and be willing to negotiate in good faith. First, each member needs to have good communications with his or her constituencies. An "intra-interest" network of communication should be established to channel information between the member and his/her organization and interest coalition. Second, in nominating a member to represent it, each organization or coalition should designate a person with credibility and authority to insure that information is shared and decisions are made in a timely manner. Negotiated rulemaking efforts can require a very significant contribution of time by the appointed members, which must be sustained for a year or more.

Certain considerations are central to negotiating in good faith. One is the willingness to bring all issues to the table in an attempt to reach a consensus, instead of keeping key issues in reserve. The second is a willingness to keep the issues at the table and not take them to other forums. Finally, good faith includes a willingness to move away from the type of adversarial positions often taken in rulemaking proceedings, and instead to explore openly with other parties all relevant and productive ideas that may emerge from the discussions of the committee.

F. Facilitator

The facilitator will not be a party to the substantive development of the standard. Rather, the facilitator's role will generally include:

(1) Chairing the meeting of the committee in an impartial manner;

(2) Impartially assisting the members of the committee in conducting discussions and negotiations, and

(3) Supervising the taking of minutes and keeping of records and other relevant responsibilities.

G. OSHA Representative

The OSHA representative, as a full member of the Committee, will participate fully with the other members in the negotiations. The OSHA representative will meet regularly with various senior OSHA officials, briefing them on the negotiations and receiving their suggestions and advice, in order to effectively represent the Agency's views regarding the issues before the Committee. OSHA's representative will also inform the Office of Management and Budget of the status of the negotiations. OSHA's representative will also communicate with ACCSH on a regular basis, informing it of the status and content of the negotiations.

In addition, the OSHA representative will present the negotiators with the available evidence that the Agency has gathered on an issue-by-issue basis for their consideration. The Committee may also consult OSHA's representative to obtain technical information, and to discuss issues associated with setting and administering standards (such as jurisdiction, scope, enforceability, costs and feasibility concerns, and paperworkn burden issues). The OSHA representative, together with the Facilitator, will also be responsible for coordinating the administrative and committee support functions to be performed by OSHA's support team.

H. Plain Language

OSHA intends to write its standards in plain language. This means that the provisions must be clear, logically organized, and written with a minimum of industry jargon. It is important to avoid the use of ambiguous regulatory language. It often takes significant effort to express complex and technical concepts in language that can be understood by non-experts. Agency staff will assist the Committee in its drafting efforts.

I. Additional Members

During the course of the Committee's negotiations, an unanticipated issue significantly affecting one or more unanticipated, unrepresented interests may arise. The Committee may decide that it is necessary for that issue to be addressed in the proposed rule. If so, the Agency will publish in the **Federal Register** a request for additional nominations to represent such interests. The Secretary may then select one or more additional representatives, who will be added as Committee members. The additional members will not beentitled to revisit any issue that has already been negotiated, unless the Committee agrees by consensus to do so.

J. Replacement Members

In the event an appointed member becomes unavailable or otherwise unable to serve, the Secretary will select a replacement member to represent the interest the original member had represented.

K. Tentative Schedule

When OSHA publishes a notice establishing the Committee and appointing its members, the Agency will include a proposed schedule of committee meetings. The first meeting will focus largely on procedural matters, including the proposed ground rules. The Committee will agree on dates, times, and locations of future meetings, and will identify and determine how best to address principal issues for resolution.

To prevent delays that might postpone timely issuance of the proposal, OSHA intends to terminate the Committee's activities if it does not reach consensus on a proposed rule within 18 months of the first meeting. The process may end earlier if the Facilitator or the committee itself so recommends.

L. Record of Meetings

In accordance with FACA's requirements, the Facilitator will supervise the keeping of minutes and a record of all committee meetings. These materials will be placed in the public docket No. S–030. Committee meetings will be announced in the **Federal Register** and will be open to the public.

M. Agency Action

As set forth in the NRA, "the Agency, to the maximum extent possible consistent with the legal obligations of the agency, will use the consensus of the committee with respect to the proposed rule as the basis for the rule proposed by the agency for notice and comment."

N. Committee Procedures Under the general guidance and direction of the Facilitator, and subject to any applicable legal requirements, appropriate detailed procedures for committee meetings will be established.

III. Public Participation

In a negotiated rulemaking, there are many opportunities for an individual who is interested in the outcome of the rule to participate. As a first step in response to this notice of intent to negotiate, OSHA recommends that potential participants take a close look at the list of significantly affected interests. They should analyze the list for completeness or over- or underinclusiveness, and for the purpose of coalition-building. Parties should try to identify others who share a similar viewpoint and who would be affected in a similar way by the rule. They should then communicate with these parties of similar interest and begin organizing coalitions to support their shared interests. Once the coalitions are formed, the parties can discuss which individuals should represent their interests and in what capacities.

As indicated above, not every interested party will be able to serve as a member of the Committee. However, an interested party may participate in a variety of other ways. These include working within the interest coalitions (promoting communication, providing expert support in a workgroup or otherwise helping to develop internal ranges of acceptable alternatives, etc.), attending committee meetings in order to caucus with the interest's member, or submitting written comments or materials to the Committee or workgroups.

Persons who will be significantly affected by the revision in the crane and derricks portion of Subpart N, whether or not their interest is listed above in this document, may apply for or nominate another person for membership on the committee to represent such interests. Such requests must be received by the Docket Office (see instructions under **ADDRESSES** near the beginning of this Notice), no later than September 16, 2002. In general, under the NRA, members of the negotiated rulemaking committee shall be responsible for their own expenses, except in certain limited circumstances (see 5 U.S.C. Section 588). Each application or nomination must include:

(1) The name of the applicant or nominee and a description of the interest(s) such person will represent;

(2) evidence that the applicant or nominee is authorized to represent those interests that the person proposes to represent, and (3) a description of the person's qualifications and expertise regarding those interests. Each applicant must submit a written commitment to actively participate in good faith in the development of the rule.

All written comments, including comments on the appropriateness of using negotiated rulemaking to develop a proposed cranes and derricks standard, and the topics to be covered regarding cranes and derricks, should be directed to Docket No. S–030, and sent to the OSHA Docket Office (see instructions under **ADDRESSES** near the beginning of this Notice).

IV. Authority

This document was prepared under the direction of John L. Henshaw, Assistant Secretary of Labor for Occupational Safety and Health, U.S. Department of Labor, 200 Constitution Avenue, NW, Washington, DC 20210, pursuant to section 3 of the Negotiated Rulemaking Act of 1990, (5 U.S.C. 561 *et seq.*), FACA (5 U.S.C. Appendix 2), the Occupational Safety and Health Act of 1970 (29 U.S.C. 651 *et seq.*), and Secretary of Labor's Order No. 3–2000 (65 FR 50017, Aug. 16, 2000).

Signed at Washington, DC, this 10th day of July, 2002.

John L. Henshaw,

Assistant Secretary of Labor for Occupational Safety and Health.

[FR Doc. 02–17768 Filed 7–15–02; 8:45 am]

BILLING CODE 4510–26–P

Notice of Establishment of Committee and Proposed Members Jun 12, 2003

DEPARTMENT OF LABOR

Occupational Safety and Health Administration

29 CFR Part 1926

[Docket No. S–030]

RIN 1218–AC01

Safety Standards for Cranes and Derricks

AGENCY: Occupational Safety and Health Administration (OSHA), Department of Labor.

ACTION: Notice of Establishment of Negotiated Rulemaking Advisory Committee.

SUMMARY: The Occupational Safety and Health Administration (OSHA) is announcing its decision to establish a Crane and Derrick Negotiated Rulemaking Advisory Committee under the Negotiated Rulemaking Act (NRA), the Occupational Safety and Health Act (OSH Act) and the Federal Advisory Committee Act (FACA).

DATES: The Charter will be filed on June 27, 2003.

FOR FURTHER INFORMATION CONTACT: Michael Buchet, Office of Construction Standards and Guidance, Occupational Safety and Health Administration, U.S. Department of Labor, Room N–3468, 200 Constitution Avenue, NW., Washington, DC 20210; Telephone: (202) 693–2345.

SUPPLEMENTARY INFORMATION: In accordance with the Federal Advisory Committee Act (5 U.S.C. App. I), the Occupational Safety and Health Act (29 U.S.C. 651 *et seq.*) and the Negotiated Rulemaking Act of 1990, (5 U.S.C. 561 *et seq.*) and after consultation with the General Services Administration (GSA), the Secretary of Labor has determined that the establishment of the Crane and Derrick Negotiated Rulemaking Advisory Committee is in the public interest in connection with the performance of duties imposed on the Department by the Occupational Safety and Health Act.

The Committee will function as a part of the Department's rulemaking on revising safety standards for cranes and derricks in construction. It will attempt, using face-to-face negotiations, to reach consensus on the coverage and the substance of these rules, which can be used as the basis of a Notice of Proposed Rulemaking. The Committee is responsible for identifying the key issues, gauging their importance, analyzing the information necessary to resolve the issues, attempting to arrive at a consensus, and submitting to the Secretary of Labor proposed regulatoryb text for an occupational safety standard governing worker safety for crane and derrick work in construction.

Meetings shall be held as necessary, however, no fewer than eight meetings shall be held over a two-year period. The Committee will terminate two years from the date of this charter or upon the publication of a proposed crane and derricks in construction rule, whichever is earlier.

The committee will be composed of no more than 25 members and a facilitator, appointed by the Secretary of Labor. Members may represent the following interests in appropriate balance: Crane and derrick manufacturers, suppliers, and distributors; companies that repair and maintain cranes and derricks; crane and derrick leasing companies; owners of cranes and derricks; construction companies that use leased cranes and derricks; general contractors; labor organizations representing construction employees who operate cranes and derricks and who work in conjunction with cranes and derricks; owners of electric power distribution lines; civil, structural and architectural engineering firms and engineering consultants involved with the use of cranes and derricks in construction; training organizations; crane and derrick operator testing organizations; insurance and safety organizations, and public interest groups; trade associations; government entities involved with construction safety and with construction operations involving cranes and derricks, and other companies, organizations, and trade associations whose interests are affected by an occupational safety standard governing worker safety for crane and derrick work in construction. Also, the Agency is a member of this committee.

The Committee will report to the Assistant Secretary for Occupational Safety and Health in compliance with the applicable provisions of the FACA and the NRA. Its Charter will be filed under the FACA fifteen (15) days from the date of this publication.

OSHA published a **Federal Register** Notice requesting comments on the advisability of establishing this Negotiated Rulemaking Committee (67 FR 46612, July 16, 2002). Virtually all commenters agreed with the need to establish this committee.

Authority: This document was prepared under the direction of Elaine L. Chao,n Secretary of Labor, U.S. Department of Labor, 200 Constitution Avenue, NW., Washington, DC 20210, pursuant to section 6 and 7 of the Occupational Safety and Health Act (29 U.S.C. 655 and 656); the Negotiated Rulemaking Act of 1990 (5 U.S.C. 561 *et seq.*); the Federal Advisory Committee Act (5 U.S.C. Appendix 1); 41 FR parts 101–6 and 102–3 and 29 CFR part 1911.

Signed at Washington, DC, this 6th day of June 2003.

Elaine L. Chao,

Secretary of Labor.

[FR Doc. 03–14856 Filed 6–11–03; 8:45 am]

BILLING CODE 4510–26–U

Notice of Final Committee Membership
July 3, 2003

DEPARTMENT OF LABOR

Occupational Safety and Health Administration

29 CFR Part 1926

[Docket No. S–030]

RIN 1218–AC01

Safety Standards for Cranes and Derricks

AGENCY: Occupational Safety and Health Administration (OSHA), U.S. Department of Labor.

ACTION: Notice of first meeting of Negotiated Rulemaking Committee.

SUMMARY: The Occupational Safety and Health Administration (OSHA) announces the first meeting of the Crane and Derrick Negotiated Rulemaking Advisory Committee (C–DAC). Members will be sworn in; the committee will be charged with its duties and will address certain procedural matters and substantive issues. The meeting will be open to the public.

DATES: The meeting will be on July 30, 31, and August 1, 2003. It will begin each day at 8:30 a.m.

ADDRESSES: The meeting will be held at The U.S. Department of Labor, 200 Constitution Avenue, NW., Washington, DC 20210 in conference room N3437 A, B and C.

Written comments to the committee may be submitted in any of three ways: by mail, by fax, or by email. Please include "Docket No. S–030" on all submissions.

By mail, the address is: OSHA Docket Office, Docket No. S–030, U.S. Department of Labor, 200 Constitution Avenue, NW., Room N–2625, Washington, DC 20210, telephone (202) 693–2350. Note that receipt of comments submitted by mail may be delayed by several weeks.

By fax, written comments that are 10 pages or fewer may be transmitted to the OSHA Docket Office at telephone number (202) 693–1648. Electronically, comments may be submitted through OSHA's Webpage at *http://ecomments.osha.gov*. Please note that you may not attach materials such as studies or journal articles to your electronic comments. If you wish to include such materials, you must submit three copies to the OSHA Docket Office at the address listed above. When submitting such materials to the OSHA Docket Office, clearly identify your electronic comments by name, date, subject, and Docket Number, so that we can attach the materials to your electronic comments.

FOR FURTHER INFORMATION CONTACT:

Michael Buchet, Office of Construction Standards and Guidance, Occupational Safety and Health Administration, U.S. Department of Labor, Room N–3468, 200 Constitution Avenue, NW., Washington, DC 20210; Telephone: (202) 693–2345.

Table of Contents

V. Authority

I. Background

On July 16, 2002, OSHA published a notice of intent to establish a negotiated rulemaking committee (Volume 67 of the **Federal Register**, page 46612). The notice requested nominations for membership on the C–DAC and comments on the appropriateness of using negotiated rulemaking to develop a proposed rule for cranes and derricks used in construction. In addition, the notice described the negotiated rulemaking process and identified some key issues anticipated to be addressed in the negotiation. Fifty-five nominations for membership on the Committee and several comments were received during the comment period. There was broad support for using negotiated rulemaking to update the standard and OSHA decided to go forward with the negotiated rulemaking process. On June 12, 2003 the Department of Labor published a notice establishing the Committee (Volume 68 of the **Federal Register**, page 35172).

II. Agenda

Following registration, assembly and a welcome by the Agency, the Facilitator will offer a brief overview of negotiated rulemaking and then address the matters that must be resolved by the Committee at its first meeting, including adoption of ground rules. These are the procedural rules that the Committee will use for conducting the meetings. In addition there will be discussion of a tentative list of C–DAC workgroups. The Facilitator will initiate discussions on identifying the substantive issues to be addressed by C– DAC. OSHA requests that committee members and all interested parties bring their calendars to facilitate the development of a tentative schedule of committee and workgroup meetings.

III. Anticipated Key Issues for Negotiation

OSHA anticipates that key issues to be addressed as part of these negotiations will include:

1. The identification/description of what constitutes "cranes and derricks" for purposes of determining the equipment that will be covered by the proposed rule.
2. Qualifications of individuals who operate, maintain, repair, assemble, and disassemble cranes and derricks.
3. Work zone control.
4. Crane operations near electric power lines.
5. Qualifications of signal-persons and communication systems and requirements.
6. Load capacity and control procedures.
7. Wire rope criteria.
8. Crane inspection/certification records.
9. Rigging procedures.
10. Requirements for fail-safe, warning, and other safety-related devices/technologies.
11. Verification criteria for the structural adequacy of crane components.
12. Stability testing requirements.
13. Blind pick procedures.

IV. Public Participation

All interested parties are invited to attend this public meeting at the time and place indicated above. No advanced

Appendix C
Ground Rules

Occupational Safety and Health Administration U.S. Department of Labor Crane and Derrick Negotiated Rulemaking Advisory Committee

Ground Rules

I. Mission Statement

The Occupational Safety and Health Administration of the U.S. Department of Labor (OSHA) has established the Crane and Derrick Negotiated Rulemaking Advisory Committee (C-DAC) to develop a proposed rule to increase employee protection by improving safety standards for cranes and derricks in construction (Subpart N 29 CFR 1926.550).

Every effort will be made to complete proposed regulatory language by July 31, 2004.

II. Participation

A. The Committee consists of the following members:
  - Stephen Brown, International Union of Operating Engineers
  - Michael Brunet, Manitowoc Cranes, Inc., Crane Manufacturers (AEM/CIMA)
  - Stephen P. Charman, Viacom Outdoor, Inc., Outdoor Advertising Association of America (OAAA)
  - Joseph Collins, Zachry Construction Corporation, American Road and Transportation Builders (ARTBA)
  - Noah Connell, U.S. Department of Labor/OSHA
  - Michael Hyland, American Public Power Association
  - Peter Juhren, Morrow Equipment Company, L.L.C.

Bernie McGrew, Link-Belt Construction Equipment Co.
Larry Means, Wire Rope Technical Board
Frank Migliaccio, International Association of Bridge, Structural, Ornamental and Reinforcing Iron Workers
Brian Murphy, Sundt Construction, Associated General Contractors (AGC)
George R. "Chip" Pocock, C.P. Buckner Steel Erection, Steel Erectors Association of America
David Ritchie, The St. Paul Companies, Training and Testing
Emmett Russell, International Union of Operating Engineers
Dale Shoemaker, Carpenters International Training Center
William Smith, Maxim Crane Works
Craig Steele, Schuck & Sons Construction Company, Inc., National Association of Home Builders (NAHB)
Darlaine Taylor, Century Steel Erectors, Co., Association of Union Constructors
William J. "Doc" Weaver, National Electrical Contractors Association, Inc.
Robert Weiss, Cranes Inc. and A.J. McNulty & Company, Inc., Allied Building Metal Industries
Doug Williams, Buckner Heavylift Cranes, Specialized Carriers and Rigging Association
Stephen Wiltshire, Turner Construction Company, Associated Builders and Contractors
Charles Yorio, Acordia

B. C-DAC may, by consensus, recommend that OSHA add members if it determines that there are unrepresented interests relative to the issues to be addressed in the proposed rule. If so, OSHA will publish a request for additional nominations to represent such interests in the Federal Register. The Secretary or her designee may then select one or more additional representatives, who will be added as C-DAC members. The additional members will not be entitled to revisit any issue that has already been negotiated, unless the C-DAC members agree by consensus to do so.

C. If a C-DAC member becomes unavailable or otherwise unable to serve, the Secretary or her designee will select a replacement member to represent the interest represented by the original member.

D. C-DAC may, by consensus, invite experts to address the Committee, as appropriate.

III. Decision Making

A. C-DAC will make every effort to reach unanimity on all issues related to the proposed regulatory text, meaning that there is no dissent by any member. However, if the facilitator determines that additional discussions are not likely to lead to unanimous consent, C-DAC will consider consensus to have been reached when there is no dissent by more than two non-federal C-DAC members. Agreement will not be considered to have been reached if there is dissent by OSHA. If OSHA is the sole dissenter on an issue, OSHA will publish the regulatory text on that issue, as endorsed by the other C-DAC members, in the preamble to the proposed rule as an alternative approach, and ask the public to comment on that alternative. A member must be present to dissent.

B. Upon the request of a dissenter to an agreement, OSHA will include the dissenter's reasons for dissenting in the preamble of the proposed rule.

C. Work groups may be designated by C-DAC to address specific issues. Work groups are not authorized to make decisions for the full committee.

IV. Agreement

A. The goal of C-DAC is to develop a proposed standard that improves worker protection and that reflects a final consensus of the Committee.

B. If C-DAC reaches a **final** consensus agreement on all issues, OSHA agrees to use the consensus-based language as its proposed standard, and C-DAC members will refrain from providing formal written negative comments on the consensus-based regulatory language published in the Federal Register, except as provided in paragraph IV E.

C. If the C-DAC reaches a **final** consensus agreement on some but not all issues, OSHA will include the consensus-based language in its proposed standard, and C-DAC members agree to refrain from providing formal written negative comments on the consensus-based language published in the Federal Register, except as provided in paragraph IV E.

D. During the course of the negotiations, C-DAC will provide reasons for the proposed regulatory text. The preamble to the proposed rule will not be subjected to C-DAC negotiations, but OSHA will provide the draft preamble to C-DAC members prior to publication of the proposed standard.

E. Once C-DAC has reached a final consensus agreement on a completed document, OSHA will use the C-DAC regulatory language in its proposed standard without altering the consensus-based regulatory text unless OSHA reopens the negotiated rulemaking process or provides to C-DAC members a detailed statement of the reasons for altering the consensus-based language. This written explanation will be provided to C-DAC members sufficiently in advance of publication of the proposed standard so as to provide C-DAC members with an opportunity to express their concerns to OSHA. If OSHA alters consensus-based language, it will identify such changes in the preamble to the proposed standard, and C-DAC members may provide formal written negative or positive comments on those changes and on other parts of the proposed standard to which that issue was "linked."

V. Committee Meetings

A. The facilitator will draft meeting summaries to maintain a clear and reliable record of tentative and final agreements reached during the negotiation process. After review and approval by the committee, meeting summaries will be certified by the designated federal official and made available to the public.

B. To the extent practicable, OSHA will distribute documents for discussion at C-DAC meetings at least seven days in advance of the meetings.

C. C-DAC members will communicate their interests and concerns to each other. They will present proposals and counter proposals in an effort to address those interests and concerns.

D. A C-DAC member may request a caucus (a private meeting of a subset of C-DAC) for consultation at any time.

E. The facilitator will be responsible for preparing the agenda for each meeting in consultation with C-DAC members.

F. All C-DAC meetings, but not caucuses, will be open to the public.

VI. Safeguards for Members

A. Any member may withdraw from the negotiations at any time by notifying OSHA in writing.

B. All members shall act in good faith in all aspects of these negotiations.

C. Members will maintain contact with constituencies throughout the negotiations to obtain feedback on proposals and to provide information about tentative agreements reached.

D. Contact with the media should generally be limited to discussion of the overall objectives and progress of the negotiations. C-DAC members should refrain from characterizing or commenting to the media on positions taken by other C-DAC members and from commenting negatively on agreed upon regulatory text. If an article appears that misquotes or inaccurately represents an individual's position, that individual should inform the C-DAC members of it.

VII. Meeting Facilitation

A. Facilitation services will be provided by Susan Podziba & Associates. The facilitator will support the deliberative process of C-DAC and will be responsible for helping to ensure that the process runs smoothly, developing meeting agendas, preparing and distributing meeting summaries, which will provide a record of agreements, and helping the parties resolve their differences and achieve consensus on the issues to be addressed by C-DAC.

B. The facilitator will be available to facilitate all meetings of the full C-DAC and may assist with caucuses and work groups.

C. The facilitator is obligated to keep verbal communications confidential if requested by a C-DAC member to do so.

CHARTER '94: The New Chelsea Making History Together Charter Preparation Team

GROUND RULES

1. MISSION STATEMENT

The Charter Preparation Team (Team) will develop a charter document that has the future of Chelsea in mind, not just current issues, and reflects and wins the support of the people of Chelsea.

To accomplish this mission, the Team will work together as a team; generate ideas; evaluate alternatives from existing charters; meet with people who work in different forms of government; think of additional ways to generate community input; and incorporate community input from all the meetings that are held.

Every effort will be made to complete a draft of the charter by May 1st and the final Charter by June 14, 1994.

2. PARTICIPATION

The Team is comprised of elected officials, a representative of the Receiver's office, and citizens, who were selected based on the following criteria:

- Commitment to securing the best form of government for the City of Chelsea
- Willingness and ability to learn and discuss issues of governance
- Willingness to learn and operate by consensus
- Available and willing to commit to attend at least 2 meetings per month between February and June

- The team as a whole should represent the various perspectives of the city.

Alternates are expected to attend meetings to keep themselves informed of the deliberations should they need to sit in for the official who is unable to attend.

Observers will attend meetings to listen, but will not actively participate in the discussions.

To add members to the Team, names will be forwarded to the committee that selected the team members, who will decide whether or not to add members. Members may be added until March 1, 1994.

Team meetings will be open to the public. Interested individuals, who are not team members may sign up to speak during the first 10 minutes of a meeting. The ten minutes will be divided equally among those who signed up to offer comments. Meetings will start promptly at 7pm.

3. DECISION-MAKING

The Team will operate by consensus, meaning that decisions will be made only if there is no dissent by any member of the Team. Absence will be equivalent to not dissenting.

If a timely decision needs to be made and it is impossible to reach consensus, the mediator may acknowledge an impasse and will call for a vote. Proposals voted on will require 80% of the Team members present for passage.

Smaller working groups may be designated by the Team to address specific issues or to make recommendations to the full Team. Work group meetings will be open to team members and other members of the community. Work groups are not authorized to make decisions for the Team as a whole.

Decision-making authority rests with the Team members. Other individuals present at Team meetings will not have the right to dissent or vote.

4. ATTENDANCE

Attendance at all meetings is mandatory. If a Team member is unable to attend a meeting, s/he will call the mediator. Beginning March 1st, if a member misses two meetings, s/he will be contacted. If s/he misses a third meeting, s/he will be dropped from the Team. A person dropped from the Team may petition the Team, and by consensus, be reinstated.

5. MEDIA

Team members are free to make statements to the press regarding their own opinions, but will not attribute statements to others present at the meetings. Contact with the media should generally be about the overall objectives and progress of the Team. Team members should refrain from characterizing or commenting publicly on positions taken by other members of the Team. If an article appears that misquotes or inaccurately represents an individual, that individual will inform the group of it.

The mediator will discuss only points of process with the media. Press releases will be prepared for review by the Team prior to release.

6. OBLIGATIONS OF TEAM MEMBERS

Team members will communicate their interests and concerns to each other and be accountable for points of disagreement. They will present proposals and counter proposals which will be designed to address those concerns. Members will not block consensus unless they have serious reservations with the approach or solution proposed for consensus.

Team members will attend regularly scheduled monthly meetings and read and think about the materials provided to them prior to meetings. They will work on tasks between meetings as agreed to at Team meetings.

Team members will participate with the long term interests of the City of Chelsea in mind.

7. MEETING FACILITATION

The mediator will help to: 1) establish agenda; 2) identify points of agreement and disagreement; 3) remain neutral with respect to outcomes; 4) facilitate Team meetings; and 5) prepare documents outlining input received from the community. The mediator is obligated to keep information confidential if requested to do so.

8. MEETINGS

Regular meetings will be held every other Tuesday, beginning February 15, 1994. Work group meetings will meet between regular meetings on an as needed basis. Additional meetings may be added, if necessary. On March 1st, the Team will decide whether or not to hold meetings every week rather than every other week.

9. RECORD OF THE SESSIONS

Following each regular meeting, the mediator will write and distribute a meeting summary to the members of the Team. It will not attribute statements to any individual. The meeting summary will be made available to the public.

Following each meeting, the charter drafter will draft the elements of the charter that were decided on. The team will review all elements of the draft and suggest revisions, as necessary.

Appendix D
Assessment Reports

FINAL Convening Assessment Report on the Feasibility of a Negotiated Rulemaking Process to Develop the All Appropriate Inquiry Standard Required under the Small Business Liability Relief and Brownfields Revitalization Act (Public Law No. 107-118)

U.S. Environmental Protection Agency
Office of Solid Waste and Emergency Response
Office of Brownfields Cleanup and Redevelopment

Submitted by
Susan L. Podziba
Susan Podziba & Associates
21 Orchard Road
Brookline, MA 02445

under subcontract to
Marasco Newton Group
Alexandria, VA

December 17, 2002

Convening Assessment Report on the Feasibility of a Negotiated Rulemaking Process to Develop the All Appropriate Inquiry Standard Required under the Small Business Liability Relief and Brownfields Revitalization Act (Public Law No. 107-118)

Table of Contents

Convening Assessment Report on the Feasibility of a Negotiated Rulemaking Process to Develop the All Appropriate Inquiry Standard Required under the Small Business Liability Relief and Brownfields Revitalization Act (Public Law No. 107-118)

INTRODUCTION

In accordance with the Negotiated Rulemaking Act of 1996, this report describes the findings and recommendations of Susan Podziba, the neutral convener, regarding the feasibility of a negotiated rulemaking process to develop the All Appropriate Inquiry Standard (CERCLA §101(35)(B)), which the U.S. Environmental Protection Agency (EPA) is required to promulgate under the Small Business Liability Relief and Brownfields Revitalization Act (Public Law No. 107-118).

Negotiated rulemaking is a process whereby a committee composed of representatives of stakeholder groups, which will be significantly affected by a proposed rule, is charged with the goal of reaching consensus on the text of the proposed rule. The federal agency responsible for the regulation, "to the maximum extent possible consistent with the legal obligations of the agency, will use the consensus of the committee with respect to the proposed rule as the basis for the rule proposed by the agency for notice and comment"(Negotiated Rulemaking Act of 1996, §563(a)(7)). (See Appendix A for the U.S. EPA Fact Sheet on Negotiated Rulemaking.)

This convening assessment report is divided into sections on background, feasibility, categories of stakeholders, substantive issues by stakeholder group, key issues across stakeholder groups, procedural issues, participation, process design, protocols and procedures, and conclusion.

BACKGROUND

On January 11, 2002, the Small Business Liability Relief and Revitalization Act (Pub. L. No. 107-118), also known as the Brownfields Law, was enacted. The Brownfields Law, among other issues, pertains to the establishment of standards and practices for all appropriate inquiry (§101(35)(B) of CERCLA). The all appropriate inquiry standards and practices are relevant to:

- the innocent landowner defense to CERCLA liability (§101 (35));
- the contiguous property exemption to CERCLA liability (§107(q));
- the bona fide prospective purchaser exemption to CERCLA liability (§107 (r)(1) and 101(40)); and
- the brownfields site characterization and assessment grant programs (§104(k)(2)).

The Brownfields Law requires EPA to establish regulations setting forth "standards and practices" to carry out all appropriate inquiry by January 11, 2004, two years after enactment. In addition, the Brownfields Law establishes an interim standard for the conduct of all appropriate inquiry to be used until EPA promulgates federal standards. For properties purchased after May 31, 1997, Congress established the interim standard as the American Society for Testing Materials (ASTM) 1997 Phase I standard for assessment of properties. EPA is developing a direct final rule to allow for the use of the ASTM 2000 Phase 1 standard as an interim standard for all appropriate inquiry given consistent feedback from stakeholders that the 1997 standard is no longer current industry practice, nor is it readily available.

Susan Podziba of Susan Podziba & Associates, as convener, interviewed approximately sixty representatives of federal, state, county, local, and tribal government; for profit and not-for-profit developers, real estate and environmental attorneys, real estate brokers, bankers and lenders, environmental professionals, environmentalists, environmental justice communities, and insurance companies (See Appendix B for Listing of Interviewees). The purpose of the interviews was to determine the feasibility of a negotiated rulemaking process relative to criteria identified in the Negotiated Rulemaking Act and the U.S. EPA Fact Sheet on Negotiated Rulemaking including:

- the principal categories of stakeholders that will be affected by and are interested in the all appropriate inquiry standard;
- key issues and concerns of stakeholders relative to an all appropriate inquiry standard and the interdependence of interests among stakeholders;
- the likelihood of convening a balanced committee of representatives of stakeholders, who are willing and able to participate in good faith in the negotiation process;
- individuals and/or organizations that can best represent the views and perspectives of each stakeholder group for the negotiated rulemaking; and
- the likelihood of success of a negotiated rulemaking process to develop federal regulatory standards for implementation of all appropriate inquiry within the required timeframe.

FEASIBILITY

Susan Podziba finds that a negotiated rulemaking process to develop the all appropriate inquiry standard (the standard) has a reasonably good chance of resulting in consensus. Virtually every interviewee believed that a negotiated rulemaking would be successful. Only one person raised concerns about negotiated rulemakings, generally, but stated that given the clear scope of this effort, that is, defining all appropriate inquiry, it is an appropriate application for a negotiated rulemaking.

To be sure, there are differences of opinion on key aspects of the standard, but there is also a convergence of interests on many of its elements. There was a high degree of interest in participating among the interviewees and across all the identified stakeholder groups.

Overall, there is general agreement that the all appropriate inquiry standard should be clear and consistently applied, result in accurate information concerning the environmental conditions of assessed properties, and function to promote and not inhibit brownfields redevelopment.

An additional benefit of using a negotiated rulemaking process is that representatives of all stakeholder groups will have a thorough understanding of the new standard as well as the rationale for its elements. This will be useful as trade associations undertake their role of educating their memberships about the standard and about opportunities inherent in brownfields redevelopment.

> No matter how favorable the prospect for consensus, there is always uncertainty in prejudging outcomes of negotiation processes, particularly when potentially opposite points of view must be reconciled. The challenge for the negotiating committee will be to demonstrate commitment and flexibility to work together as a problem-solving team to develop the standard. The interviewees indicated a willingness to expend the effort necessary to achieve these objectives.

On balance, Susan Podziba, in her capacity as convener, finds that the application of a negotiated rulemaking process to develop the all appropriate inquiry standard has a reasonable likelihood of success, and if successful, will result in a high quality standard that balances the interests of the relevant stakeholders.

CATEGORIES OF STAKEHOLDERS

Susan Podziba identified nine categories of key stakeholders. She recommends that the U.S. Environmental Protection Agency invite representatives from each of the following categories[1] to participate in the negotiated rulemaking:

- Other Federal Agencies[2]

---

1. Some interviewees suggested that ASTM be included as a stakeholder. However, ASTM is an organization devoted to the creation of its own consensus industry standards. This convener recommends that ASTM not have its own negotiator. Individuals affiliated with the development of the ASTM standard are in key positions in their trade associations and highly knowledgeable of the elements of the standard. Therefore, it is highly likely that multiple individuals associated with ASTM will serve on the negotiating committee as representatives of their stakeholder groups.
2. Other federal agencies identified as federal stakeholders were the National Oceanic and Atmospheric Administration (NOAA), Department of Housing and Urban Development (HUD), and Department of Justice (DOJ). NOAA serves as a Trustee for Natural Resource Damages under CERCLA. NOAA will maintain contact with EPA throughout the negotiations, but will not require a separate negotiator. HUD and DOJ have each indicated a preference for participating in the negotiations, but will confer with EPA officials pending a decision to proceed with a negotiated rulemaking.

- State Government
- Local Government
- Tribal Government
- Developers: (residential, commercial, industrial, for profit, not-for-profit)
- Bankers and Lenders
- Environmentalists
- Environmental Justice Community
- Environmental Professionals

In addition, the following groups are interested parties with great depth of knowledge relevant to the implementation of the standard. These parties typically represent multiple stakeholders, for example, environmental attorneys and insurance companies include developers, environmental professionals, and state and local governments among their clients at any given time. Thus, it is suggested that the parties listed below serve as resource parties on the negotiating committee, given their ability to analyze the impacts of various options across multiple stakeholders.

- Environmental Attorneys
- Real Estate Brokers
- Environmental Insurance Professionals

SUBSTANTIVE ISSUES:

KEY CONCERNS IDENTIFIED BY EPA AND STAKEHOLDER GROUPS

U.S. Environmental Protection Agency

Congress mandated that EPA create an all appropriate inquiry standard to comply with CERCLA §101(35)(B), as amended by the Brownfields Law. The key interests of EPA relative to this standard, and generally reflected in its Brownfields Program, are to protect the environment and public health, support partnerships among brownfields stakeholders, encourage the private-sector marketplace for redevelopment of brownfields properties, and encourage sustainable reuse.

EPA will work to create a standard that satisfies the legal provisions of the statute regarding funding and liability, while promoting environmental protection, economic development, and community revitalization.

Other Federal Agencies

The Department of Housing and Urban Development (HUD) is engaged in activities to promote community revitalization. Among HUD's brownfields programs is its Brownfields Economic Development Initiative (BEDI), which makes grants to stimulate local government and private sector partnerships for the redevelopment of brownfields sites. Other HUD programs provide loan guarantees and mortgage insurance. HUD's key interests are to promote brownfields redevelopment as a strategy for community revitalization and to protect the public from environmental hazards. In addition, as a mortgage insurer, HUD is concerned about CERCLA liability on foreclosed properties.

The primary interest of the Department of Justice is the enforceability of the statute.

State Environmental Agencies

There is great disparity among states across the country with regard to brownfields programs. Some states include sophisticated site assessment standards within their voluntary cleanup programs whereas others have no programs at all. Some states will likely continue to require prospective purchasers and developers to conduct site assessments under their voluntary cleanup programs to obtain state-provided "no further action" letters. Other states will likely adopt the federal standard for their programs and want the standard to eliminate the need for their states to provide comfort letters or prospective purchaser agreements except under extraordinary conditions.

Some state programs require prospective purchasers to obtain specific information. The investigation must satisfy the state's informational requirements; time limits do not excuse prospective purchasers from meeting such requirements.

In addition, state programs typically require sampling when there is a likelihood of contamination based on past use. Interviewees suggested that there are some activities often undertaken within the context of phase I assessments that they deem unnecessary and other activities not undertaken which they require. For example, some state programs do not require previous owner interviews or a search for surplus sites within a three-mile radius, but do require a review of immediately adjacent properties. These states find that the clarity and certainty provided by their programs have given their states a comparative advantage in attracting developers to brownfields properties.

Returning brownfields properties to beneficial use is a key interest of states. However, states are also concerned about granting undeserved liability relief and then being unable to identify responsible parties to undertake cleanups when contamination is found. Some states have found a significant percentage of properties to be contaminated that were identified as clean properties in assessment reports.

Finally, as brownfields grantees receiving EPA assessment funds, states will have to conduct all appropriate inquiry assessments as required under the Brownfields Law.

Local Government

Local governments will be impacted by the standard in a variety of ways. First, there is great interest in the redevelopment of brownfields, which transform fallow properties into productive use thereby increasing tax rolls. Cites and towns have worked hard to attract developers to their brownfields sites. Local governments have viewed potential liability for new owners at brownfields sites as a barrier to increased redevelopment of brownfields sites and supported the Brownfields Law as a means to removing a barrier to redevelopment.

Local governments are concerned about contamination leaching into soils and groundwater and its potential for impacting human health. In addition, contaminated properties are potential liabilities, which can reduce municipal credit ratings.

As with states, local governments, as brownfields grantees, will be required to conduct all appropriate inquiries under the grant program. Municipalities often become new owners of contaminated properties through purchase, foreclosure for non-payment of taxes, and eminent domain. Thus, local governments are interested in the protection against CERCLA liability that the standard will provide.

Finally, local government interviewees raised the additional concern of their inability to gain access to properties subject to involuntary acquisition through eminent domain, condemnation, and/or non-payment of taxes. Thus, local governments are interested in an exemption from visual inspection and owner interviews for involuntary acquisitions when there is a recalcitrant owner.

Tribal Government

Tribal government will be impacted by the standard in a variety of ways. First, tribes want accurate assessments of contamination of their lands. For some tribes, brownfields programs are designed to de-contaminate and return land to open space. Tribal governments receive brownfields grants and so will be required to conduct all appropriate inquiry assessments under the grant program. Tribal brownfields projects often involve HUD and the Bureau of Indian Affairs, each of which have assessment requirements. Thus, tribal governments want the standard to be clear and well-defined so that it is easily melded with other federal agency requirements.

Tribal governments are concerned about the costs of assessments. Related to cost is a concern that too narrow a definition of environmental professional, that is, who can conduct assessments, could make it more difficult for tribes to access this work.

Developers

Developers want a standard that is clear, predictable, consistently enforced, reasonably inexpensive, and not too time consuming, and which, when complied with, will provide liability protection without reopeners. Clarity is crucial for developers, who fear that a lack of clarity could result in the loss of a credible liability defense.

Developers are motivated to learn about contamination on properties before purchase because if a property is more contaminated than expected, a developer may negotiate a reduced price or choose to invest in an alternative property. They do not see the standard as providing a "pass to existing owners, but rather immunizing new owners who are interested in putting property back into productive use."

The time necessary for an assessment is important to developers because an owner is usually not willing to keep a property off the market long and because a favorable financing package may become unavailable given fluctuating interest rates.

Many interviewees use the ASTM standard for their assessments. They stated that thousands of people know how to conduct these assessments, and are concerned that a changed assessment protocol will result in confusion within the industry. Thus, they want to be sure that any changes will result in significant environmental benefit.

Developers would like to reduce the discretion of environmental professionals and therefore, the need to negotiate assessment workscopes. They fear that rejecting a recommendation in a proposed workscope could leave them vulnerable to a loss of liability protection later. They would like to see a minimum standard for a phase I assessment with triggers for phase II assessments.

Additionally, some interviewees expressed the concern that it may be difficult for EPA to maintain a unified negotiation stance given the involvement of multiple offices within the agency.

Developers do not want the standard to supersede existing state statutory programs, which they point to as programs that have encouraged the cleanup and redevelopment of brownfield sites. Some expressed their satisfaction with rigorous state programs because of the certainty they provide and their use of creative means for dealing with contaminants.

Overall, developers want the standard to achieve the goal of promoting brownfields redevelopment, which will require that assessments not be too costly or time-consuming and that liability relief be sufficiently protective. They want to ensure that the standard is consistent with intent of the Brownfields Law, that is, to promote and not inhibit brownfields redevelopment.

Bankers/Lenders

Bankers and lenders are most interested in limiting risk when making loans. Lenders are protected from CERCLA liability by the secured creditor exemption, but on foreclosed properties they will use the all appropriate inquiry standard as an additional liability protection.

Banks require phase I assessments on properties in order to meet conditions set out by the secondary loan market and by rating agencies, even if their own requirements do not indicate the need for an assessment. As a result, the standard is expected to impact a great percentage of real estate transactions throughout the country.

To reduce risk, banks and lenders support a rigorous standard. However, it is also banks and lenders that typically drive the short time frames for obtaining information because fluctuating interest rates can impact the viability of a deal.

When a phase I assessment indicates a recognized environmental condition, most banks will require a phase II assessment and a resolution of the condition before approving the loan. Progressive banks and lenders have shown a willingness to make loans prior to cleanups, when cleanup plans, consistent with intended future uses, are in place through state programs. For these banks, a lack of willingness to clean a site indicates a negative character issue for the borrower, and the bank would not make the loan. Banks prefer good information on the site, but will also accept insurance policies to protect their loans when good information is not readily available.

Overall, the lending community wants a clear and rigorous standard that results in the information necessary to determine the environmental condition of a property at moderate cost and within a reasonable time frame. They see the challenge of developing the standard as one in which the negotiators identify the difference between necessary information and complexity for the sake of additional work.

Environmentalists

Environmental groups are primarily concerned that the standard require rigorous investigation of sites. They want historical searches to include title search, spills database, enforcement actions, prior investigations, and visible contaminated areas. They want the standard to trigger sampling when historical searches identify past contamination.

Environmentalists would like to include the possibility of reopeners as a means to motivate complete cleanups. They want to be sure that the standard is not written so broadly as to allow parties to escape from liability and also want some assurances regarding states' abilities to enforce federal standards.

Environmental groups are very supportive of brownfields redevelopment. They prefer brownfields redevelopment to fallow, contaminated properties but want to ensure proper cleanup of contaminated sites.

ENVIRONMENTAL JUSTICE COMMUNITY

The interests of the environmental justice community are similar to those of the environmental groups. However, as the communities where many brownfields sites are located, the environmental justice community raises an additional concern of public notification of contamination and proposed cleanup plans. They would like the standard to include a component defining when and how often the public should be notified of work on a brownfields site. As one interviewee stated, " it is frightening if you live across the street from a lot, and one day people show up in moon suits."

ENVIRONMENTAL PROFESSIONALS

The stakeholder group of environmental professionals is divided into two camps, primarily according to their preferred definition of an environmental professional. However, all expressed concerns about the possibility of inexperienced individuals characterizing contaminated sites as clean.

One camp believes strongly that an environmental professional should be defined as a licensed professional engineer, geologist, or hydrogeologist, which are regulated by state boards and require adherence to an ethical responsibility to protect human health and the environment. This camp believes that the standard should enable them to use their professional judgment to determine the necessary workscope required to accurately characterize the site. They state that engineers are familiar with industrial processes and therefore, know what chemicals to look for when an historical search yields information about a manufacturing facility and that geologists have a keen understanding of subsurface conditions. They are concerned that untrained individuals with little experience, who call themselves environmental professionals, will miss visible contaminants and will not know what to look for thereby identifying contaminated sites as free from environmental contamination. Members of this camp stated that assessments should performed by, or under the direction of, licensed professional engineers, geologists, or hydrogeologists.

The other camp wants to define an environmental professional more broadly and based on experience as opposed to a particular academic degree. This group is also concerned about inexperienced individuals potentially missing contamination. They raised the concern that some prospective purchasers simply want an environmental consultant with a liability insurance policy so that if contamination is found later, the purchaser can find recourse under the policy. However, some environmental consultants have begun to limit their own liability to the cost of the report. Some members of this camp want the standard to consist of a very clear step-by-step approach to assessments.

Finally, there is agreement between both camps of environmental professionals that a Phase II assessment requires the professional judgment of individuals with expertise related to the recognized environmental conditions identified in the Phase I assessment.

KEY ISSUES IDENTIFIED ACROSS STAKEHOLDER GROUPS

A primary focus of the all appropriate inquiry negotiations will be the statutory criteria listed in the Brownfields Law §223(2)(B)(iii), which amends CERCLA §101(35). In addition, interviewees across stakeholder categories raised other key issues, which are described below.

Brownfields Law §223(2)(B)(iii) Statutory Criteria:

In promulgating regulations that establish the standards and practices referred to in clause (ii), the Administrator shall include each of the following:

(I) The results of an inquiry by an environmental professional.

(II) Interviews with past and present owners, operators, and occupants of the facility for the purpose of gathering information regarding the potential for contamination at the facility.

(III) Reviews of historical sources, such as chain of title documents, aerial photographs, building department records, and land use records, to determine previous uses and occupancies of the real property since the property was first developed.

(IV) Searches for recorded environmental cleanup liens against the facility that are filed under Federal, State, or local law.

(V) Reviews of Federal, State, and local government records, waste disposal records, underground storage tank records, and hazardous waste handling, generation, treatment, disposal, and spill records, concerning contamination at or near the facility.

(VI) Visual inspections of the facility and of adjoining properties.

(VII) Specialized knowledge or experience on the part of the defendant.

(VIII) The relationship of the purchase price to the value of the property, if the property was not contaminated.

(IX) Commonly known or reasonably ascertainable information about the property.

(X) The degree of obviousness of the presence or likely presence of contamination at the property, and the ability to detect the contamination by appropriate investigation.

Legal Defense v. Proactive Requirement: The statute requires EPA to develop a standard for all appropriate inquiry, which is a legal defense against CERCLA liability for new owners. This would suggest a limited use for owners defending themselves against CERCLA liability in court. However, the standard will be used proactively as a standard of due diligence to avoid the risk of liability and is likely to be required by lenders for all property transactions where there is any risk of environmental contamination. As one interviewee stated, "Whatever EPA sets will become the de facto pre-market environmental assessment requirement."

General Fear of Change/Industry Disruption: Since the first ASTM standard was developed to "reduce legal uncertainty associated with analyzing and assessing real property and to provide lenders with objective information about a site to conduct proper risk analysis,"[3] it has become the industry standard for most private transactions. The stakeholder groups that use this standard are concerned about the potential for disruption of transactions as the industry moves from a known, to an as yet, unknown set of procedures.

Level of liability relief to be granted: There is not a clear sense among stakeholders of the level of liability relief to be granted under the standard. Some think liability relief will be

---

3. Crocker, Dianne, Editor, "Conflict-Compromise-Consensus: The Embroiled History of the ASTM ESA Standard," *Environmental Site Assessment Report*, Volume VII, Number 7, July 2002, page 1.

granted only for clean properties, that is, those determined to have no recognizable environmental conditions. Others assume the assessment will be used to determine recognized environmental conditions for which the new owner will not be liable. Still others expect that if a new owner conducts a cleanup for identified contaminants, the owner will not be liable for any additional past contamination found at the site.

Scope of the Standard: A key question raised by representatives of numerous stakeholder groups related to the scope of the standard is: Will the standard cover only the Phase I Assessment or provide direction for Phase I and Phase II assessments? Some interviewees supported the former and others the latter. In addition, some raised the question of whether or not the standard will include requirements for cleanup when contamination is found. Many interviewees suggested that the standard identify triggers for Phase II assessments. Those supporting a limited scope stated that historically, there has been little agreement on what a Phase II assessment should consist of given the unique aspects of each site.

Brownfields Site Assessments and All Appropriate Inquiry: The linking of these two caused concern for some interviewees who suggested two separate standards. However, the Brownfields Law states that Brownfields Site Assessments are to be performed in accordance with §101(35)(B), which is the regulatory citation for all appropriate inquiry.

Non-CERCLA Contaminants: Given that this regulation will be written to assess CERCLA liability, there are questions about the inclusion of petroleum products, which are specifically excluded under CERCLA as well as other contaminants such as radon, asbestos, lead, and mold. Many lenders require assessments that identify these contaminants as well. Interviewees referred to their use of "ASTM plus," whereby they use the ASTM standard as a starting point and then add a review of additional contaminants to the environmental assessment.

Starting Point for Development of the Standard: There are a number of ways to begin drafting the all appropriate inquiry standard. For example, one could begin with the statutory criteria listed in the Brownfields Law and work to further define each criterium. Other possibilities include beginning with either the ASTM standard or EPA or state documents that outline requirements of Phase I assessments and making revisions to meet the statutory requirements of the Brownfields Law. If the ASTM standard is used as a starting point, EPA will need to sort out copyright and licensing issues given that EPA will publish the eventual rule in the Federal Register, making it publicly available. Some interviewees involved in the development of the ASTM standard hope that it will be made available to be useful to EPA.

NationalTechnologyTransferandAdvancementAct(NTTA) Public Law 104-113: Interviewees had various interpretations of the requirements under NTTA, which encourages government use of existing voluntary consensus standards, relative to ASTM 1527. Some interviewees suggested that the Agency must use the ASTM standard if it meets statutory requirements. However, it was also indicated that the current version does not meet all statutory requirements and is currently under review. The process for revising ASTM 1527-97 was accomplished over a two-year period.

Searches for recorded environmental cleanup liens against the facility that are filed under Federal, State, or Local law: A question was raised regarding whether an assessment would require a search through federal, state, and local government agencies or only one of the above. There was some discussion about an administrative response such that EPA might create and maintain a database that lists all the relevant agencies to be contacted or to create a database of all the relevant information.

Informational criteria: Related to the stringency of the eventual standard, there are disagreements concerning the level of information that should be sought versus the level of information that is available. Some raised the idea of a performance-based standard such that if one got information from a source, one would not need to review all other sources. Others like the redundancy because it creates the possibility of finding additional issues.

Adjoining Properties: Some interviewees raised the question of when prospective purchasers should be required to include a visual inspection of adjoining properties.

Transaction Screen: ASTM developed a standard for a transaction screen, which is not done by an environmental professional. There are questions about whether or not this abbreviated screen will satisfy the requirements of all appropriate inquiry.

"Shelf Life" of an assessment: Questions were raised about how long an assessment would be considered useful in establishing the all appropriate inquiry liability defense. Some thought the shelf life of an assessment was 6 months, others one year, and still others, longer. This is especially relevant when a site has groundwater contamination and/or migrating plumes.

New Technologies Available: Many interviewees referred to the new, field-based technologies now available, which make sampling both cost effective and timely. Whereas in the past, samples were taken and sent to labs with results provided weeks later, technologies such as geoprobes provide immediate results. It is believed that such technologies provide better information about actual environmental conditions at reasonable cost.

Disclosure: Questions were raised about the disclosure of information obtained during due diligence research. What environmental information is a broker expected or required to disclose about a property to potential buyers? What, if any, information should be made available to the public?

Assessment Activities by Land Uses: Some interviewees suggested that the standard be constructed according to historic land uses. Each land use—residential, commercial, light industry, heavy industry—would require a different level of investigation.

Successive Purchasers: Many interviewees raised the question of the transferability of liability relief to a new purchaser.

PROCEDURAL ISSUES RELATED TO THE NEGOTIATED RULEMAKING PROCESS

There are three procedural issues to be considered if EPA decides to proceed with a negotiated rulemaking process to develop the all appropriate inquiry standard.

Schedule. The statute requires the final regulation be promulgated by January 11, 2004. This would suggest that a negotiated rulemaking process should be initiated by January 2003 to ensure enough time for the negotiations as well as the required comment period.

Representation. As required under the Negotiated Rulemaking Act and to ensure accurate representation at the negotiations, EPA is required to publish a Notice of Intent to Negotiate A Rule in the Federal Register, which would include a list of proposed members of the negotiating committee. During the comment period, additional parties may make nominations to the negotiating committee. EPA would decide if there were stakeholder groups that were not represented by the proposed committee members.

Starting Point: EPA will need to decide how to begin the drafting of the regulation. In other words, should the initial draft be a listing of the statutory criteria for all appropriate inquiry, the interim standard, or existing EPA guidance.

PARTICIPATION

Susan Podziba identified nine categories of stakeholders that she recommends the U.S. Environmental Protection Agency invite to participate in the negotiated rulemaking. In addition, there are three categories of resource parties that would provide technical expertise to the Committee.

Most of the interviewees were interested in participating in the negotiated rulemaking. Some had concerns and expertise regarding the actual elements of the standard, and some held broader concerns regarding its rigor, cost, and time requirements. Some simply wanted to participate in order to be able to educate their members and constituents for future transactions.

The actual negotiations will be best served by a negotiating committee that represents and can articulate the actual range of broad and specific interests that will need to be woven together to reach consensus on the all appropriate inquiry standard. Organizational members of the negotiating committee may consider selecting negotiators to create a committee that includes a combination and balance between individuals who will be directly affected by the standard and staff, who work with large numbers of people in the field and/or communities.

The resource parties have technical expertise that will be useful throughout the negotiations, but are not stakeholder parties in that they do not have a set of interests they will seek to satisfy during the negotiations. Resource parties may participate fully in the deliberations of the committee, but will not have the right to dissent on elements of the regulatory language.

In addition to the U.S. Environmental Protection Agency, it is recommended that the proposed negotiating committee include the following members:

Other Federal Agencies[4]	U.S. Department of Housing and Urban Development U.S. Department of Justice
State Government	Association of State and Territorial Solid Waste Management Officials to identify two negotiators National Association of Attorneys General
Local Government	US Conference of Mayors National Association of Local Government Environmental Professionals
Tribal Government	Gila Tribe, Department of Environmental Quality
Developers	
- Residential	National Association of Home Builders
- Commercial	Real Estate Roundtable
- Industrial	National Association of Industrial and Office Parks
- Not-for-profit	Trust for Public Land National Brownfields Association
Bankers/Lenders	Bank of America Freddie Mac

4. The U.S. Department of Housing and Urban Development and the U.S. Department of Justice have indicated preferences for participation on the negotiating committee, but will consult with EPA before a final decision is made.

	Mortgage Bankers Association
Environmentalists	Sierra Club Environmental Defense
Environmental Justice	Center for Public Environmental Oversight Partnership for Sustainable Brownfields Redevelopment
Environmental Professionals	Association of Soil and Foundation Engineers American Society of Civil Engineers National Ground Water Association Wasatch Environmental
Resource Parties	Environmental Attorneys (through the Section of Environment, Energy, and Resources of the American Bar Association) Real Estate Brokers Environmental Insurance Professionals

PROCESS DESIGN

To begin the negotiated rulemaking process, EPA will need to establish a formal advisory committee in accordance with the Federal Advisory Committee Act (FACA). As required under FACA, all meetings of the negotiating committee will be announced in the Federal Register and open to the public.

The negotiated rulemaking process will consist of a series of negotiating committee meetings and communications with and among negotiators between meetings. The process will be managed by a mediator.

Negotiations will begin with a preliminary meeting of all negotiators. The agenda for this meeting will be to prepare a set of organizational protocols, determine informational needs, define the negotiating agenda, determine the drafting method to be used, confirm a schedule of meetings, identify mechanisms for two-way feedback between negotiators and constituents, and articulate key concerns related to the negotiations.

The preliminary meeting will be followed by a series of 5 - 6 negotiating sessions of two - three days each. If the committee decides to make use of a drafting work group to develop proposals for the committee's review, part of these meetings may be set aside for such drafting.

After initial discussions of negotiators' key interests relative to the all appropriate inquiry standard, EPA will prepare a draft, including blank spaces for those areas which need more discussion before sections can be drafted. During the negotiating sessions, the committee will work its way through the agenda, which will encompass a review of the draft regulation. It is typical in a negotiated rulemaking for some sections of the rule to be more easily resolved than others. For the former, the committee will determine when it has reached "tentative agreements" indicating that the draft is satisfactory pending resolution of all other sections. Tentative agreements are sometimes reviewed after other decisions are made because of the impact of one section on another.

As the series of meetings proceeds, the agenda will consist of the remaining issues for which tentative agreements have not been reached and any tentative agreements, which a committee member asks to review, until all is resolved. The final draft will then be reviewed in total. After agreement is reached on all the regulatory language, EPA will draft the preamble to the proposed rule, which may then be subjected to negotiations until the committee reaches consensus on it.

PROTOCOLS AND PROCEDURES

At its preliminary meeting, the negotiating committee (Committee) will develop procedural ground rules that will govern its discussions and negotiations. The proposed ground rules will cover such matters as the following:

- mission of the negotiating Committee;
- obligations of and protections for Committee members;
- commitments that derive for members as a result of consensus agreements;

- composition of the Committee including its ability to add members, use alternates, have advisors, use workgroups to develop proposals, and caucuses;
- decision-making rule (definition of consensus);
- how to deal with media contacts;
- procedures to ensure the protection of confidential information;
- the recognition that meetings are open to the public;
- the manner in which a record of the sessions will be kept and distributed;
- schedule of meetings and planned completion date; and
- roles and responsibilities of the mediators.

CONCLUSION

Susan Podziba, as convener, finds that use of a negotiated rulemaking process to develop the all appropriate inquiry standard (§101(35)(B) of CERCLA), as required under the Small Business Liability Relief and Revitalization Act (Pub. L. No. 107-118), also known as the Brownfields Law, is feasible and appropriate, and that there is a reasonably good chance of successfully reaching a consensus agreement among stakeholders on this standard.

APPENDIX A:

U.S. ENVIRONMENTAL PROTECTION AGENCY NEGOTIATED RULEMAKING FACT SHEET

What Is a Rule?

A rule or regulation is the equivalent of an operating or implementation manual for a part of a statute or act of Congress. A rule gives those subject to its requirements more detailed instructions or prohibitions regarding activities that are addressed by the statute.

How Are Rules Usually Written?

Generally a federal agency's staff drafts the text of a proposed rule. After circulation and comment within the agency, the rule will be printed in the Federal Register as a proposed rule. The public is then invited to comment on the rule. After reading and analyzing the public's comment the agency may revise the rule to incorporate suggestions or eliminate problems identified as a result of the analysis. The rule is then published in final form in the Federal Register and becomes effective on the date listed in the notice. It is then incorporated into the government's Code of Federal Regulations, which lists all currently applicable regulations.

What Is Negotiated Rulemaking?

Negotiated rulemaking is a process, which brings together representatives of various interest groups and a federal agency to negotiate the text of a proposed rule. The goal of a negotiated rulemaking proceeding is for the committee to reach consensus on the text of a proposed rule.

How Is Negotiated Rulemaking Different?

In a negotiated rulemaking proceeding, a well-balanced group representing the regulated public, community and public interest groups, state and local governments, joins with a representative of the federal agency in a federally chartered advisory committee to negotiate the text or the outline or concept of a rule before it is published as a proposed rule in the Federal Register. If the committee reaches consensus on the rule then the federal agency can use this consensus as a basis for its proposed rule. The proposed rule is still subject to public comment. If consensus is not reached then the agency proceeds with its normal rulemaking activities.

What Are The Advantages of Negotiated Rulemaking?

Federal agencies that have used negotiated rulemaking have identified several advantages to developing a rule by negotiation before notice and comment. The regulatory negotiation process allows the interested, affected parties a more direct input into the drafting of the regulation, thus ensuring that the rule is more sensitive to the needs and limitations of both the parties and the agency. Rules drafted by negotiation have been found to be more pragmatic and more easily implemented at an earlier date, thus providing the public with the benefits of the rule while minimizing the negative impact of a poorly conceived or drafted regulation.

Because the negotiating committee includes representatives of the major groups affected by or interested in the rule, the number of public comments is reduced. The tenor of public comment is more moderate. Fewer substantive changes are required before the rule is made final. The committee can draw on the diverse experience and creative skills of the members to address problems encountered in writing a regulation. Often the group together can propose solutions to difficult problems that no one member could have thought of or believed would work.

How Are Rules Selected for Negotiated Rulemaking?

The Negotiated Rulemaking Act of 1996 suggests a number of criteria (see attachment) that a rule should meet to be a candidate for negotiated rulemaking. Generally, the federal agency conducts an internal assessment to determine its own interest in negotiating a rule. If it determines that a negotiation is a possibility, the agency retains a neutral third party facilitator/mediator to conduct a more rigorous assessment of the feasibility. This assessment involves interviews of agency management and staff and conversations with a wide range of organizations and individuals who might be affected by the rule. The facilitator will analyze the information gained about the issues and the parties and make recommendations to the agency regarding the feasibility of negotiating the rule and suggestions for designing the negotiation process. The agency considers the results of the feasibility study and makes a decision whether to proceed.

How Does The Process Work?

The federal agency establishes a formal advisory committee under the Federal Advisory Committee Act. A balanced mix of people representing the range of affected parties is invited by the agency to participate. Generally committees are composed of between 12 and 25 members representing both the public and private sectors. A neutral facilitator or mediator is used to manage its meetings and assist the parties in discussions and reaching an agreement.

Meetings are announced in the **Federal Register** (and sometimes in local or trade press) and are open to observation by members of the public. The number of meetings held depends on how complicated the rule is to draft, how much controversy there is amongst the committee members, and what the deadline is for the rule to be published and implemented.

Generally only the committee members speak during the meetings, although provisions are made for input by members of the audience. Caucuses can be called by committee members to speak with their constituency or with other members of the committee, caucuses may or may not be open to the public observers. Workgroups can be formed by committees to work on subsets of the issues posed by the rule.

Decisions are generally made by consensus, not by majority vote. The Committee discusses and decides upon their own definition of consensus prior to the start of its deliberations. Often the consensus is generally defined as an agreement by all parties that they can live with the provisions of the rule when taken as a whole package.

If consensus is reached, the agency will use it as a basis for their proposed rule. Committee members agree to support the rule as proposed if there are no substantive changes from the consensus agreement.

FOR ADDITIONAL INFORMATION ON REGULATORY NEGOTIATION:

Negotiated Rulemaking Sourcebook, 1995, Administrative Conference of the US; written and edited by David Pritzker and Deborah Dalton. Available from Deborah Dalton (dalton.deborah@epa.gov)

Selection Criteria for Negotiated Rulemaking

It is important to screen potential rulemakings to identify instances where negotiation of the rule has a high probability of success. The Negotiated Rulemaking Act of 1996 and past EPA experience suggest the following criteria to screen and select appropriate items. An item need not meet all of these criteria to be qualified as a candidate.

Criteria for the Item

- The proposal should require the resolution of a limited number of interdependent or related issues, none of which involve fundamental questions of value, or extremely controversial national policy.
- The policy implications of the issues to be resolved are more-or-less limited programmatically, i.e., the rulemaking will not establish binding precedents in program areas not encompassed by the negotiations.
- There must be a sufficiently well-developed factual base to permit meaningful discussion and resolution of the issues.
- There should be several ways in which the issues can be resolved.
- There should be a firm deadline imposed upon the negotiations by EPA due to some statutory, judicial or programmatic mechanism. The deadline should provide adequate time for negotiation of the issues.
- Any ongoing litigation does not inhibit the parties' willingness or ability to engage in genuine give-and-take.

Criteria for the Participants

- Those participants interested in or affected by the outcome of the development process should be readily identifiable and relatively few in number. Participants should be able to represent and reflect the interests of their constituencies.
- The parties should have some common goals. They should be in good faith about wanting to participate in negotiations. They should feel themselves as likely, if not more likely, to achieve their overall goals using negotiations as they would through traditional rulemaking.
- Some of the parties should have common positions on one or more of the issues to be resolved which might serve as a basis for agreement during the course of negotiations.

- The parties should view themselves as having an ongoing relationship with the Agency beyond the item under consideration.

APPENDIX B: LIST OF INTERVIEWEES

Mr. Paul Ackerman
Piper Rudnick, LLP
1200 19th Street, N.W.
Washington, DC 20036

All Appropriate Inquiry Workgroup
Patricia Overmeyer, Chair
U.S. Environmental Protection Agency
Ariel Rios Building
1200 Pennsylvania Avenue, N.W.
Washington, DC 20460

Ms. Bonnie Barnett
Drinker, Biddle and Reath, LLP
Eighteenth and Cherry Streets
Philadelphia, PA 19103

Ms. Kathy Blaha
Trust for Public Land
660 Pennsylvania Ave. S.E. Suite 401
Washington, DC 20003

Ms. Janet Bollman
Gela River Department of Environmental Quality
Phoenix, AZ

Mr. Karl Bourdeau
Beveridge and Diamond
1350 Eye Street N.W. – Suite 700
Washington, DC 20005
Ms. Carol Bowers
American Society of Civil Engineers
1015 15th Street N.W. – Suite 600
Washington, DC 20005

Mr. Chris Boyle
Drinker, Biddle and Reath, LLP
Eighteenth and Cherry Streets
Philadelphia, PA 19103

Mr. Kenneth Brown
National Association of Local Government Environmental Professionals (NALGEP)
1350 New York Ave. N.W. Suite 1100
Washington, DC 20005

Mr. Robert Colangelo
National Brownfields Association
5440 N. Cumberland Ave., Suite 238
Chicago, IL 60656-1452

Mr. Grant Cope
US Public Interest Research Group
218 D Street S.E.
Washington, DC 20003
Mr. Tom Crause
Illinois EPA
1021 N. Grand Avenue East
Springfield, IL 62702

Mr. Andy Darrell
Environmental Defense
New York, NY

Mr. Todd Davis
Hemisphere Corporation
25825 Science Park Drive, Suite 265
Cleveland, OH 44122

Mr. DeWitt
National Association of Industrial
and Office Parks
2201 Cooperative Way, 3rd Floor
Herndon, VA 20171

Ms. Dionne Farris
Partnership for Sustainable
Brownfields Redevelopment
Washington, DC

Mr. Jack Fersco
National Association of Industrial
and Office Parks
2201 Cooperative Way, 3rd Floor
Herndon, VA 20171

Mr. Rob Fox
Manko, Gold, Katcher, and Fox
401 City Avenue, Suite 500
Bala Cynwyd, PA 19004

Mr. Don Green
U.S. HUD
Washington, DC

Mr. John Hancock
Environmental Director
Pomo of Upper Lake
375 East Highway 20, Suite 1
Upper Lake, CA 95485

Mr. Rob Hazelton
Dominion Environmental
Virginia

Mr. Evan Henry
Bank of America
44820 Irvine Blvd.
Irvine, CA 92660

Mr. Steven Hirsch
U.S. Chamber of Commerce
1615 H Street N.W.
Washington, DC 20062-2000

Ms. Cathie Hutchins
National Association of
Attorneys General
750 First Street, N.E. Suite 1100
Washington, DC 20002

Mr. James Johnston
PMK Group
65 Jackson Drive
Cranford, NJ 07016

Mr. Karl Kalbacher
Maryland Department of
Environment
2500 Broening Highway
Baltimore, MD 21224

Ms. Julie Kilgore
Wasatch Environmental
2410 W. California Avenue
Salt Lake City, UT 84104
Mr. Ken Kloo
NJ Dept. of Environmental
Protection
P.O. Box 407
Trenton, NJ 08625-0407

Mr. David E. Lourie, P.E.
ASFE Codes & Standards
Lourie Consultants
3924 Haddon Street
Metairie, LA 70002-3011

Ms. Peggy Lynch
Solutions Realty
Richmond, VA

Ms. Mary Matta
National Oceanic and
Atmospheric Administration
Seattle, Washington

Mr. Kevin Matthews
AIG
1801 K Street N.W. Suite 404L
Washington, DC 20006

Ms. Deborah McKinnon
Mortgage Bankers Association
1919 Pennsylvania Ave., N.W.
Washington, DC 20006

Mr. Richard Meyer
Freddie Mac
8100 Jones Branch Drive (MS# 4BE)
McLean, VA 22102

Mr. Michael Mittelholzer
National Association of Homebuilders
1201 15th Street N.W.
Washington, DC 20005

Ms. Linda Morgan
OENJ Cherokee Corporation
251 Jersey Gardens Blvd. East
Elizabeth, NJ 07201

Mr. Tahir Naseem
Mortgage Bankers Association
1919 Pennsylvania Ave., N.W.
Washington, DC 20006

Ms. Mary O'Rourke
Fitch Ratings
New York, NY

Ms. Lindene Patton
Zurich North America
601 West 26th Street
New York, NY 10001

Mr. Michael Paulukiewicz
Urban Land Institute
Washington, DC

Mr. Ken Peters
Freddie Mac
8100 Jones Branch Drive (MS# 4BE)
McLean, VA 22102

Mr. Roger Platt
National Real Estate Roundtable
1420 New York Ave. N.W. – Suite 1100
Washington, DC 20005

Ms. Christine Reimer
National Ground Water Association
601 Dempsey Road
Westerville, OH 43081-8978

Mr. Joseph Schilling
International City/County Management Association
777 North Capitol Street, N.E.
Washington, DC 20002-4201

Ms. Judy Sheahan
U.S. Conference of Mayors
1620 Eye Street N.W.
Washington, DC 20006

Mr. Gene Smary
American Bar Association
740 15th Street, N.W.
Washington, DC 20005-1019

Mr. Jay Spector
National Association of Industrial and Office Parks
2201 Cooperative Way, 3rd Floor
Herndon, VA 20171

Ms. Samara Swanston
Mr. Daniel Smith
ASTM International
100 Barharbor Drive
West Conshohocken, PA 19428

Mr. Ed Stromberg
U.S. Department of Housing and Urban Development
451 Seventh Street, S.W. Rm 8134
Washington, DC 20410

Mr. Craig Thomas
Freddie Mac
8100 Jones Branch Drive (MS# 4BE)
McLean, VA 22102

Mr. Barry Trilling
National Association of Industrial and Office Parks
2201 Cooperative Way, 3rd Floor
Herndon, VA 20171

Ms. Danielle Miller Wagner
International City/County Management Association
777 North Capitol Street, N.E.
Washington, DC 20002-4201

Mr. Matthew Ward
NALGEP
Sierra Club
FDR Station
New York, NY 10150

1350 New York Ave. N.W. Suite 1100
Washington, DC 20005

Ms. Karen Wardzinski
U.S. Department of Justice
950 Pennsylvania Avenue, NW
Washington, DC 20530-0001

Ms. Sara Beth Watson
American Bar Association
740 15th Street, N.W.
Washington, DC 20005-1019

Mr. William Weissman
Piper Rudnick, LLP
1200 19th Street, N.W.
Washington, DC 20036

Mr. Marshall Williams
Marshall Williams, Inc.
Woodbury, TN

Ms. Julie Wolk
US Public Interest Research Group
218 D Street S.E.
Washington, DC 20003

Contacted but not interested in participating

Mr. Bill Allayaud
Sierra Club
1414 K Street
Sacramento, CA 95814

Ms. Kate Bicknell
Small Growth America
1100 17th Street N.W. – 10th Floor
Washington, DC 20036

Mr. Anthony Edwards
National Association of Real Estate Investment Trusts
1875 Eye Street, N.W.
Washington, DC 20006

Mr. Martin Harris
National Association of Counties
Washington, DC

Mr. Joel Hirshhorn
National Governors Association
444 North Capitol Street
Washington, DC 20001-1512

Mr. Robert Johnson
Wildlife Habitat Council
1010 Wayne Ave. Suite 920
Silver Spring, MD 20910

Ms. Carol Leftwich
ECOS
444 N Capitol St, NW
Suite 445
Washington, DC 20001

Final Convening Assessment Report for the Negotiated Rulemaking Process to Develop Minimum Standards for State-Issued Driver's Licenses and Personal Identification Cards as required under the 9/11 Commission Implementation Act of the Intelligence Reform and Terrorism Prevention Act of 2004 (Public Law No. 108-458)

Prepared for the U.S. Department of Transportation in consultation with the U.S. Department of Homeland Security

Submitted by
Susan L. Podziba
Alexis L. Gensberg
Susan Podziba & Associates

21 Orchard Road
Brookline, MA 02445
www.podziba.com

April 15, 2005
Order No.OTOS59-05-F-10048

Final Convening Assessment Report for the Negotiated Rulemaking Process to Develop Minimum Standards for State-Issued Driver's Licenses and Personal Identification Cards as required under the 9/11 Commission Implementation Act of the Intelligence Reform and Terrorism Prevention Act of 2004 (Public Law No. 108-458).

Table of Contents

Final Convening Assessment Report for the Negotiated Rulemaking Process to Develop Minimum Standards for State-Issued Driver's Licenses and Personal Identification Cards as required under the 9/11 Commission Implementation Act of the Intelligence Reform and Terrorism Prevention Act of 2004 (Public Law No. 108-458).

INTRODUCTION

In accordance with the 9/11 Commission Implementation Act of the Intelligence Reform and Terrorism Prevention Act of 2004 (Public Law No. 108-458), the U.S. Department of Transportation, in consultation with the U.S. Department of Homeland Security, is required to promulgate Minimum Standards for State-Issued Driver's Licenses and Personal Identification Cards, and to do so through a negotiated rulemaking process. This report describes the findings and recommendations of Susan Podziba of Susan Podziba & Associates, the Convener, regarding the negotiated rulemaking process that will be undertaken to develop minimum standards for driver's licenses and personal identification cards.

Negotiated rulemaking is a process whereby a committee composed of representatives of stakeholder groups that will be significantly affected by a proposed rule is charged with the goal of reaching consensus on the text of that proposed rule. The federal agency responsible for the regulation, "to the maximum extent possible consistent with the legal obligations of the agency, will use the consensus of the committee with respect to the proposed rule as the basis for the rule proposed by the agency for notice and comment"(Negotiated Rulemaking Act of 1996, § 563(a)(7)).

This convening assessment report is a compilation of information obtained through interviews with federal officials and representatives of potential stakeholders. It is divided into sections on background, categories of stakeholders, key issues across stakeholder groups, key issues by stakeholder group, dynamics affecting the negotiated rulemaking process, participation, process design, organizational protocols, and conclusion.

BACKGROUND

On December 17, 2004, the President signed into law the Intelligence Reform and Terrorism Prevention Act of 2004 (Public Law No. 108-458). Title VII of that Act is known as the 9/11 Commission Implementation Act of 2004 (the 9/11 Act). Subtitle B of the 9/11 Act addresses terrorist travel and effective screening and includes a mandate for the issuance of minimum standards for a variety of identity documents, including driver's licenses and personal identification cards (§ 7212).

This provision was enacted in response to the following recommendation in the 9/11 Commission report:

> Secure identification should begin in the United States. The federal government should set standards for the issuance of birth certificates and sources of identification, such as driver's licenses. Fraud in identification documents is no longer just a problem of theft. At many entry points to vulnerable facilities, including gates for boarding aircraft, sources of identification are the last opportunity to ensure that people are who they say they are and to check whether they are terrorists.

In making that recommendation, the Commission noted:

> All but one of the 9/11 hijackers acquired some form of U.S. identification document, some by fraud. Acquisition of these forms of identification would have assisted them in boarding commercial flights, renting cars, and other necessary activities.

For additional legislative detail on the statutory mandate for Minimum Standards for Driver's Licenses and Personal Identification Cards as required under the Intelligence Reform and Terrorism Prevention Act of 2004, Title VII, Subtitle B, § 7212, see Appendix A.

Susan Podziba (Convener) interviewed 57 representatives of the U.S. Department of Transportation, the U.S. Department of Homeland Security, state offices that issue driver's licenses and personal identification cards, state elected officials, organizations that represent applicants for and holder of driver's licenses—including consumer organizations and those that represent immigrants and non-citizens, privacy and civil liberties groups, law enforcement officials, the 9/11 Commission, and organizations with technological and operational expertise in document security. (See Appendix C: List of Interviewees). In accordance with the framework set out in the Negotiated Rulemaking Act[1], the purpose of the convening was to identify:

- the principal categories of stakeholders that will be affected by and are interested in the minimum standards;
- key issues and concerns of stakeholders relative to the minimum standards and the interdependence of interests among stakeholders;
- organizations that can best represent the views and perspectives of each category of relevant stakeholders for the negotiated rulemaking; and
- a balanced committee of representatives of stakeholders who are willing and able to participate in the negotiation process in good faith.

CATEGORIES OF STAKEHOLDERS

The 9/11 Act, § 7212(b)(4)(B), identified the following federal agencies and categories of stakeholders for representation on the Negotiated Rulemaking Advisory Committee on Minimum Standards for State-Issued Driver's Licenses and Personal Identification Cards (DL/ID Reg Neg Committee): U.S. Department of Transportation (DOT), U.S. Department of Homeland Security (DHS), state[2] offices that issue driver's licenses or personal identification cards; state elected officials; and other interested parties.

In its February 23, 2005 Federal Register Notice of intent to form a negotiated rulemaking advisory committee concerning Driver's Licenses and Personal Identification Cards (Appendix D), and in accordance with the relevant U.S. Senate Conference Report[3], DOT defined "other interested parties" as groups or organizations representing the interests of applicants for and

---

1. The convening assessment often includes a determination of the feasibility for application of a negotiated rulemaking process to the candidate rule. Since Congress mandated the use of a negotiated rulemaking process to develop the minimum standards, the Convener did not seek to determine feasibility.
2. For the purposes of this report, "state" refers to the 51 jurisdictions in the U.S. which issue driver's licenses and personal identification cards.
3. U.S. Senate Committee Colloquy on Driver's License and Personal Identification Card Provisions, Conference Report on the Intelligence Reform Bill, December 8, 2004

holders of driver's licenses and personal identification cards (DL/IDs) including consumers and non-citizens/immigrants, privacy and civil liberties groups, law enforcement officials, and organizations with technological and operational expertise in document security.

Based on the convening process, the Convener confirmed the following categories of stakeholders:

- Federal Government
    - Department of Transportation
    - Department of Homeland Security
- State offices that issue driver's licenses or personal identification cards
- Representatives of elected state officials
- Groups or organizations representing the interests of applicants for and holders of driver's licenses and personal identification cards
    - Consumers
    - Non-citizens/Immigrants
- Privacy and civil liberties groups
- Law enforcement officials
- Organizations with technological and operational expertise in document security.

KEY ISSUES ACROSS STAKEHOLDER GROUPS

Many key issues were identified by interviewees in multiple stakeholder categories. Below is a description of each of these issues.

Driver's License as De Facto ID: Many interviewees stated that first and foremost the driver's license is proof of ability to operate a motor vehicle. Others asserted that state driver's licenses function as de facto national identification because they serve as the "key to the kingdom," in that they are used to gain access to most commercial and government services. Most agree that the driver's license has evolved from what had in some states been simply a postcard, to a form of identification that today must be secure.

One license, one jurisdiction, one identity: For many stakeholders, a key goal of the minimum standards is to produce a system in which there is one license for one identity, linked to one jurisdiction. This would suggest an issuance process to determine the unique identity of each individual applying for or holding a DL/ID and would preclude applicants from having a DL/ID from more than one state in the nation. However, some interviewees think that it will be impossible to confirm that all applicants had rescinded their licenses in other states, and stated that a more reasonable goal might be to ensure that no individual had more than one license in a particular state.

Security requirements for the driver's license issuance programs: Interviewees identified the need to address security requirements of four distinct components of DL/ID issuance programs. They are:

- Documents accepted for proof of identity ("breeder documents") and the verifiability of those documents;
- Security of the actual driver's license document, including features that verify authenticity and resist tampering;
- Protection against corruption at processing locations; and
- Protection of materials and technology used to create the DL/ID documents.

Standardization vs. Flexibility: Some stakeholders support increased standardization and uniformity in the DL/ID issuance process and in design of the actual cards. In their view, greater adherence to best practices would produce more secure processes and credentials. Others emphasize the need for different approaches to issuance and card design. They are concerned that a uniform approach would be less secure because it would be more susceptible to counterfeiting and limit states' ability to innovate solutions as new problems arise and technologies emerge.

Breeder Documents: A key element of determining a unique identity for each DL/ID applicant is the validity of the documents used to prove identity in the issuance process, known as "breeder documents." Many interviewees stressed that the use of driver's licenses for proving cardholders' identity will only be as valid as the breeder documents used to issue them. Some interviewees support strategies for increased verifiability of documents such as birth certificates including the ability to scan them into databases for future verification. Others seek to maintain flexibility on allowable breeder documents to maintain access to DL/IDs for people with non-traditional documentation, such as refugees or the homeless. These interviewees supported strategies to determine reliability of these documents rather than verifiability. Interviewees identified various means used to verify documents presented by applicants to prove identity and residency. Some states currently verify social security cards through the Social Security Administration's on-line database and confirm immigration status through U.S. Citizen and Immigrations Service (USCIS) Systemic Alien Verification for Entitlements (SAVE).

Centralized v. De-centralized (State-level) Databases: Although many discussed a centralized (national) database of DL/ID card data, most interviewees believe such a database is currently technically impossible. Most prefer decentralized databases both for privacy and security reasons. Interviewees suggested that a centralized database would be more vulnerable to infiltration than decentralized databases and would create a single target for hackers and identity thieves. Interviewees discussed the value in linking state databases and the need to share data across states and with federal law enforcement. Interviewees acknowledge the paradox of security goals: the more uniform the database, the easier to share information about potential security threats, but also the more vulnerable the information.

Protection of Personal Data: Interviewees identified various issues related to protecting personal information collected for DL/ID purposes. They are:

- Personal data to be collected;
- Knowledge by person that data was collected;
- Ability to correct errors in data;
- Authorized access to data;
- Protections against unauthorized access;
- Protections against unauthorized release of data;
- Protections against use of data for purposes other than the purpose for which it was collected; and
- Protections against criminal invasion of data system (and punishment for criminal activity).

Reviews of Applicants: Currently, all states participate in the National Driver Register (NDR), which by federal statute, requires states to check an applicant against the NDR before issuing or renewing a driver's license. The NDR is a database of the names of individuals with suspended licenses or outstanding tickets. Many states also participate in the Driver's License Compact, which requires member states to determine whether new applicants are or were licensed in another member state. Additionally, some states check applicant names against the National Criminal Information Center (NCIC) database, and Terrorist Watch Lists.

Legal Presence Requirements: The 9/11 Act prohibits the minimum standards from infringing on a state's ability to set criteria concerning the categories of individuals eligible to obtain a DL/ID from that State (§ 7212(b)(3)(B)). The issue of legal presence is seen as an immigration issue by some and as a state's rights issue by others. Those that support legal presence to obtain a driver's license do not want to tacitly approve illegal immigration. The eleven states that do not require legal presence generally do so to increase driver safety and the number of insured drivers, as they expect that illegal immigrants will drive with or without a driver's license. In terms of security goals, some point to the difficulty of verifying foreign breeder documents, whereas others point to the value of having information about who is in the country.

Securing the Driver's License Document: There are numerous technologies available to create secure documents. Most states' DL/IDs include a layering of overt and covert security features to protect against counterfeiting. There is a sense that states must continuously upgrade their security features to stay ahead of sophisticated counterfeiters. Examples of security features include: coatings in lamination, micro-writing, 1-dimensional and 2-dimensional bar code, magnetic stripe, ultra-violet light, digital watermarking, biometric, photo, fingerprinting, digitized signature, optical variable device, hologram, and kinogram.

Standards for transliteration of names spelled with non-Roman alphabet letters: A related issue raised by multiple interviewees concerns the need to develop standardized transliteration rules for languages that have different alphabets, such as Chinese and Arabic.

KEY CONCERNS OF DOT, DHS AND STAKEHOLDER GROUPS

U.S. Department of Transportation (DOT)

Congress mandated that DOT create minimum standards for State-Issued Driver's Licenses and Personal Identification Cards under the Intelligence Reform and Terrorist Prevention Act, § 7212(b)(2) (The 9/11 Act).

DOT will ensure that the rulemaking effectively carries out the language of the statute and achieves the goals that Congress intended. DOT's focus is on ensuring that the negotiated rulemaking process allows stakeholders to work with the Federal government to establish minimum standards for drivers' licenses and identification cards.

U.S. Department of Homeland Security (DHS)

Congress mandated DOT consultation with DHS in the creation of the minimum standards for State-issued DL/IDs under the 9/11 Act.

The primary interest of DHS regarding this standard is to increase the security and reliability of the documents covered by § 7212. DHS seeks to ensure that the individual presenting a driver's license or personal identification card at a U.S. border, airport, or other federal facility, is who he or she claims to be and that the information on the document presented enables DHS personnel to identify terrorists.

Under the Homeland Security Act of 2002, DHS is statutorily prohibited from creating a national identification card (Title XV, Subtitle B, §1514. National Identification System Not Authorized). In addition, according to the Homeland Security Act of 2002, any federal agency creating a new database of personal information must provide to DHS a Privacy Impact Statement (§ 222).

DHS operates under a range of existing laws governing information sharing among local, state, tribal, and federal law authorities. DHS does not anticipate that the minimum standards will affect those laws and is not seeking to create additional authorities within the minimum standards for DL/IDs.

State Offices that Issue Driver's Licenses or Personal ID's

The key concern of state offices that issue DL/IDs is to ensure that their programs are sufficiently secure. Interviewees from these offices stated that the national security derived from secure driver's license processes is only as strong as its weakest link. No state wants to be that weak link, given evidence suggesting "forum shopping" by the 9/11 hijackers. State offices do not want a one-size fits all standard, but rather want flexibility to enable states to tailor programs to their unique needs and to sustain state innovation. On the other hand, they want programs that are easily understandable by their staff and that maintain conveniences for the driving public.

Interviewees identified a range of strategies used to develop secure programs, including specific breeder documentation requirements, document verification, security features of the DL/ID document, staff training to identify fraudulent documents, protections against staff fraud, and investigation and protection against the creation of fraudulent documents.

States accept a variety of breeder documents, and most require a combination of primary and secondary documents. Some states verify breeder documents through databases such as the Social Security Administration's on-line database or the U.S. Citizen and Immigrations Service (USCIS) Systemic Alien Verification for Entitlements (SAVE) database.

State offices that issue DL/ID's want clarity and ease in their programs to be better able to train their staff. They support a move to easily verifiable breeder and immigration documents to reduce the likelihood of employee error.

Cases involving personnel at state motor vehicles offices who illegally issued driver's licenses to individuals lacking proper documentation have led some states to employ internal management strategies to detect employee fraud. Examples include a two-stop process in which all new applicants see two clerks, random audits whereby computers freeze up and must be unlocked by a supervisor, and reviews of transactions by individual clerks. Some interviewees raised concerns about offices where transaction records are generated but not reviewed, analyzed, or acted upon.

In addition to security issues, states want to maintain conveniences for the public. Convenience is typically measured in time required to obtain or renew a DL/ID, which is affected by the need to verify documents, DL/ID validity periods, and opportunities to renew via internet. Some states provide DL/ID cards immediately, "over-the-counter," to applicants, while others prefer to use a centralized system in which the DL/ID is mailed to an applicant at the address on the document.

Validity periods for licenses range across states; the shortest validity period is four years. In Arizona, an original driver's license does not need to be replaced until the individual holding the driver's license reaches the age of 65, after which the license must be renewed every five years. Some states link the expiration dates of licenses issued to non-U.S. residents to the expiration dates of visas.

Representatives of Elected State officials

The key concerns of elected state officials are the costs of implementing the minimum standards, which they consider an unfunded mandate, and the timeframe required for compliance. In addition, states see themselves as best positioned to determine their driver's license processes and oppose a federal standard that would dictate one solution for all states.

State elected officials are concerned about the costs for developing and sustaining new DL/ID processes. They anticipate costs related to the design of a new issuance process; design and creation of secure DL/ID documents; technology needed to create, read, and upgrade the documents; technology to collect, store, and protect personal data; and technology to read covert security mechanisms such as bar codes, smart cards, or magnetic stripes.

State elected officials are also concerned about costs and time involved in verifying breeder documents. For example, interviewees pointed to the difficulties associated with verifying birth certificates, especially from small hospitals, which may not have electronic databases. Verification of immigration status also proves difficult. Interviewees suggested that on-line database checks through the SAVE program were successful in approximately 60% of cases. False positives require time consuming mailings to DHS, which has limited resources to research paper files. Given the high number of different visas and other documents that confirm legal presence, state officials believe the federal government should create a simple process to enable states to determine the validity of immigration documents rather than require states to assume this responsibility.

In addition, the phase-in time for compliance with the minimum standards is expected to greatly impact costs. For example, state elected officials are concerned that a requirement to re-issue licenses prior to current expiration dates will create a significant cost burden for states as they would need to add administrative capabilities to process the increased number of applicants or else cause significant inconvenience to the driving public. They also fear that if states are unable to comply with required time frames because resources are not made available by either federal grants or state legislatures, DL/ID holders from those states are at risk for being denied access to air travel and other federal facilities.

Elected state officials will look closely at projected costs for proposed elements of the minimum standards. Given their constituents' great concerns regarding identity theft, they hope that strategies selected will address both national security and identity theft, which may increase state funding opportunities.

Finally, state elected officials are looking to the federal minimum standards as a means to create a baseline, or minimum threshold, to ensure security without pre-empting state policy decisions or state innovation. For example, issues of eligibility for state-issued driver's licenses have been and are being fought out in state legislatures. Some states have large pools of uninsured motorists and have legislated eligibility requirements to increase the number of licensed and insured drivers in their states. States want flexibility to maintain state innovation and opportunities to benefit from technological advances. They see a diversity of strategies across states as contributing to security.

Interviewees prefer scattered state databases and oppose a centralized national database because of concerns about privacy and civil liberties. They are concerned that a centralized database would increase possibilities of law enforcement "fishing" for individuals. They are also concerned about identity theft. As one interviewee said, "Scattered data is protected data."

Organizations Representing the Interests of Applicants for and Holders of DL/IDs

Consumer organizations

The key concerns of consumer organizations are to ensure safety on the road and, secondly, consumer convenience. They are concerned that resources spent to implement the minimum standards may reduce safety and convenience. In short, consumer organizations view the issue of minimum standards as a question of how much security the public is willing to pay for.

Consumer organizations expressed concern about the cost burdens the minimum standards will place on state offices that issue DL/IDs. They fear additional resources will be diverted from road safety programs to improving security of the DL/ID processes and documents. In addition, they are concerned that if state legislatures do not allocate the necessary funding, some states may not implement the minimum standards, and consumers will be unable to access federal facilities and airports.

Consumer group interviewees, who have experience with state databases used to identify and remove dangerous drivers from the road, raised concerns about privacy issues of a federal database, but also are skeptical about successfully linking databases across states, given states' difficulties maintaining their own databases. Drivers convicted of operating under the influence have found ways to avoid detection through state databases. As a result, consumer groups have doubts about the success of linking databases to track individuals posing security threats.

Organization Representing Non-Citizens/Immigrants

The primary interests of organizations representing immigrants and non-citizens are to maintain access to and eligibility for DL/IDs for their constituents and to increase the security of DL/ID processes and documents. Interviewees representing immigrants are concerned about the special challenges for immigrants to prove identity and, where required, legal immigration status, in the DL/ID application process.

Immigrants and non-citizens prove identity and status using a wide array of documents, many of which are not in standard formats. Interviewees explained that in some cases, the only proof of legal immigration status might be a judge's decision or combination of documents in an applicant's file. Interviewees expressed the need for DL/ID issuance processes that account for this diversity of documentation to ensure that DL/IDs are not denied to eligible applicants.

Interviewees reject a two-tier system that provides an alternative DL/ID or "driving certificate" to applicants unable to provide certain identity or immigration documents. Their constituents with such certificates have complained of being treated with increased suspicion by law enforcement and of discrimination when they present their certificates. They have also faced higher car-insurance premiums and are fearful of the immigration consequences of having a certificate based on immigration status.

Organizations representing immigrants and non-citizens support the national security goals of the minimum standards. They support increased security in DL/ID processes and in features of the actual DL/ID cards. Interviewees favor a system in which as many immigrants as possible are included to assist the government in knowing who is in the country and to reduce the market for counterfeit documents.

Privacy and Civil Liberties Groups

Privacy and civil liberties groups are primarily concerned about what information is collected by government agencies, who has access to that information and for what purposes, and what will protect against illegal access and use. Interviewees questioned the actual security benefits arising from federal minimum standards for DL/IDs. All oppose a "national ID," which some defined as a nationally uniform card linked to a national database and others defined as any card meeting national standards.

Interviewees want limited information to be collected and stored on the card. They oppose features with large capacities for storage of data on the DL/ID because of concerns about future usage. They support such technologies as magnetic stripes or bar codes only to determine whether the visible information on the card is accurate and only with protections against misuse of the stored information. Interviewees related stories, for example, where bars have scanned information from DL/IDs and sold the information collected.

Privacy and civil liberties groups oppose a centralized national database. They prefer individual state databases. Although they support the concept of "one license—one identity—one jurisdiction," they point to difficulties within individual states to ensure one license per person within that state. If databases are to become linked, privacy and civil liberties representatives want established and enforceable protections against the use and sharing of data. Interviewees stated that individuals whose data is misused could be significantly harmed, despite future criminal prosecutions of those responsible for the misuse. Some interviewees expressed a preference for "1-to-1 matches" versus "1-to-many matches," given that the former provides merely a confirmation of the validity of identity information, while the latter makes it possible for those with access to the data to "fish" for individuals' personal data.

The worst case scenario for these groups is one in which individuals enjoy less privacy and less control over their personal data but get no significant increase in security.

Interviewees suggested ways to increase the security of DL/ID documents and issuance processes without increasing the release and sharing of individuals' personal data. They suggested internal management controls to protect against DMV clerk corruption, citing cases in which employees had been bribed to provide credentials to individuals without the necessary breeder documents. They support securing the machines, papers, inks, and other materials used to make the documents; creating tamper-proof cards; and training DMV employees to better identify fraudulent breeder documents.

Overall, privacy and civil liberties groups are concerned about the vulnerability of personal data stored on DL/IDs and in databases. Interviewees raised concerns about "mission creep," or the potential for data collected for one purpose to be used for another, citing the widespread use of Social Security Numbers for identification, despite its initial prohibition.

Law Enforcement Officials

The primary interest of law enforcement officials is to know and be able to verify that the person presenting a DL/ID is the person the document identifies them to be. They will look to the minimum standards to create sufficient safeguards to deter, to the greatest extent possible, individuals from tampering with or fraudulently obtaining a DL/ID, and as a means to facilitate verification by law enforcement officials.

Law enforcement officials support all means for securing the DL/ID issuance process and the document. They are dependent upon driver's licenses to identify individuals during traffic stops. If an officer has cause for reasonable suspicion, he or she may check the information on the driver's license through a state driver's license database, National Crime Information Center (NCIC) database, or Terrorist Watch Lists. Many arrests for violent crimes are made as a result of routine traffic stops in which the suspects were identified by their driver's license information. Law enforcement officials view DL/IDs as tools to identify individuals who may be suspected of criminal or terrorist activity.

Law enforcement does not expect to check a driver against a 50-state database, given the time it would take to do so. Some officers have laptop computers in their cars and/or can scan bar codes or magnetic stripes. Others need to call their central dispatchers to run checks for them. A traffic stop for a moving violation that nears 30 minutes would likely be considered an illegal detention by most courts.

Law enforcement officials support means to easily determine the integrity of DL/ID documents that are not likely to require costly equipment that must be added to their cars or on their belts. If an officer determines a DL/ID is fraudulent, officers in many states can arrest the individual for possessing the fraudulent document and can seize it as a "tool of the crime."

Organizations with Technological and Operational Expertise in Document Security

The primary interest for organizations with technological and operational expertise in document security is to ensure that the minimum standards are technically sound and functional and open to a wide variety of potential technical solutions. For example, DL/ID documents are best secured from tampering by layering different categories of overt, covert, substrate (e.g. papers and laminates), bio-metric-based, and machine-readable strategies. Combining particular features among these categories increases the security of the document.

In addition, these organizations have concerns about the proper management of databases, security of data, protections against unauthorized access, means for interoperability among different state databases, and creation of flexible infrastructures.

Finally, these organizations represent the vendors that produce and create various security products and do not want to limit innovation in security technologies, which will help government agencies keep ahead of counterfeiters.

DYNAMICS AFFECTING THE NEGOTIATED RULEMAKING PROCESS

There are six key dynamics that are expected to affect the negotiated rulemaking process to develop minimum standards for driver's licenses and personal identification cards: statutory mandate for negotiated rulemaking, statutory deadlines, schedule, technical expertise, issues to be negotiated and cost-benefit analysis, and active legislation. Each is described below.

Statutory Mandate for Negotiated Rulemaking: The Negotiated Rulemaking Process to Develop Minimum Standards for State-Issued Driver's Licenses and Personal Identification Cards is required under § 7212(b)(4) of the 9/11 Commission Act. As stated in its February 23, 2005 Federal Register Notice, DOT plans to provide adequate resources and administrative support for the process and will ensure the DL/ID Reg Neg Committee has the appropriate resources it requires to complete its work in a timely fashion. To the extent possible, consistent with its legal obligations, DOT plans to use any consensus arising from the Committee as the basis for the proposed minimum standards to be published as a Notice of Proposed Rulemaking (NPRM).

Given that this is a statutorily mandated negotiated rulemaking process, the Convener did not determine feasibility, as such determinations are used by government agencies to decide whether or not to proceed to the negotiation phase of voluntary negotiated rulemaking processes. DOT's current efforts to implement the negotiated rulemaking process are consistent with the experience of the Convener with regard to implementation of previous federal negotiated rulemaking processes.

Statutory Deadlines: The 9/11 Act requires that recommendations of the DL/ID Reg Neg Committee be submitted to the Secretary of Transportation no later than 9 months after the date of enactment, that is, by September 17, 2005.

The Secretary must issue a final rule establishing the standards no later than 18 months after the date of enactment, that is, by June 17, 2006.

Schedule: To meet the statutory deadlines, the negotiated rulemaking process will require a demanding schedule. The proposed schedule, as outlined in the March 29, 2005 Federal Register Notice, contemplates five meetings of three or three-and-a-half days, for a total of 17 meeting days. The first meeting is scheduled for April 19-21, 2005 and the last meeting is scheduled for July 12-15, 2005. DOT staff will have two months to prepare supporting documents for the Report to the Secretary based on the DL/ID Reg Neg Committee's recommendations.

Technical Expertise: The DL/ID Reg Neg Committee members have varying levels of expertise on document security features, driver's license processes, and privacy issues stemming from databases of personal information. To assist negotiators in their deliberations, panel presentations will be provided on technical subjects of interest to the committee. For example, the first meeting will include a presentation on document security and fraud to be provided by officials from the U.S. Secret Service, Forensic Services Division. Technical presentations will be assembled at the request of the DL/ID Reg Neg Committee. The presenters will be drawn from the memberships of the organizations represented on the committee as well as from the Document Security Alliance, a public-private partnership.

Issues to be Negotiated and Cost-Benefit Analysis: The DL/ID Reg Neg Committee will begin its discussions based on the issues outlined in § 7212 (B) of the 9/11 Act. This list includes a cost-benefit analysis of the committee's recommendations. DOT has an internal team that will prepare this analysis on behalf of and with input and feedback from the committee.

Active Legislation: H.R. 418: Real ID Act is currently under consideration by the U.S. Senate. If enacted and signed into law as passed by the U.S. House of Representatives, it would repeal §7212 of the 9/11 Act and thus terminate the negotiated rulemaking process. DOT, in consultation with DHS, is working to implement the negotiated rulemaking in accordance with current law, and the DL/ID Reg Neg Committee has been chartered under FACA for this purpose.

PARTICIPATION

Within the six non-federal categories of stakeholders, the Convener recommends that the Department of Transportation invite fourteen organizations to participate as members of the Negotiated Rulemaking Advisory Committee on Minimum Standards for State-Issued Driver's Licenses and Personal Identification Cards. Each organizational member has identified a principal negotiator and an alternate, who will participate in the absence of the principal negotiator.

In proposing organizational members of the DL/ID Reg Neg Committee, the Convener sought to create a balanced committee of relevant stakeholders, which includes a combination of organizations that represent individuals who will be directly affected by the minimum standards, individuals who will interact directly with the public in implementation of the minimum standards, and those who will work on various components of implementation of the minimum standards.

Efforts were made to propose state members that represented diversity among the states with regard to size, geographic region, rural/urban character, proximity to foreign borders, and over-the-counter/centralized system for delivering licenses.

Many individual companies sought membership on the DL/ID Reg Neg Committee within the stakeholder category of organizations with technological and operational expertise in document security. Rather than select from among companies, the Convener proposes participation by non-profit membership organizations that include among their members, most, if not all, of the individual companies that were nominated. It is expected that these non-profit organizations will assist in accessing the expertise of their members for panel presentations as requested by committee members.

In the category of applicants or holder of driver's licenses/ personal identification cards, some nominees identified interests related to highly specific elements of an issue, such as religious objections to photograph requirements or the need for flexibility for homeless people in providing breeder documents and proof of state residency requirements. For this category of stakeholders, the Convener recommended organizations with broader sets of interests, which include many of the specific elements identified by other nominees.

Based on the convening process and in accordance with § 7212(B) of the 9/11 Act, the Federal Advisory Committee Act, and the Negotiated Rulemaking Act, Susan Podziba, Convener, recommends the following organizational members:

Federal Agencies[4]
U.S. Department of Transportation
U.S. Department of Homeland Security

State Offices that Issue Driver's Licenses or Personal ID's
American Association of Motor Vehicle Administrators
New York State Department of Motor Vehicles
Alabama Department of Public Safety, Driver License Division

Representatives of Elected State Officials
National Governors Association
National Conference of State Legislators

Groups or Organizations Representing the Interests of Applicants for and Holders of Driver's Licenses and Personal Identification Cards
American Automobile Association
National Immigration Law Center

Privacy and Civil Liberties Groups
American Civil Liberties Union
Markle Foundation/Center For Democracy and Technology

Law Enforcement Officials
International Association of Chiefs of Police
Texas Department of Public Safety
Florida Department of Highway Safety and Motor Vehicles

Organizations with Technological and Operational Expertise in Document Security[5]

---

4. Other federal agencies with interests in the minimum standards will participate in an inter-agency federal partners workgroup. DOT and DHS will represent the concerns of other federal agencies during the negotiations.
5. The Document Security Alliance is a public/private partnership of government and private organizations and academics that focuses on how best to respond to the production and distribution of counterfeit documents. It is expected that DSA will assist the DL/ID Reg Neg Committee by providing panel presentations on specific security features, as requested.

Information Technology Association of America
Industry Advisory Board to AAMVA

See Appendix B for the individuals selected by these organizations to serve as their principal negotiators.

There are other means of participation for individuals and groups that identify themselves as having interests and expertise relevant to the development of the minimum standards, but who have not been appointed to the DL/ID Reg Neg Committee by the Secretary of Transportation. Individuals and organizations with specific technological and/or operational expertise may be called to serve on panels or work groups. Members of the public may address the DL/ID Reg Neg Committee during the public comment period that will be provided during each meeting as required under the Federal Advisory Committee Act. In addition, comments and written materials may be submitted to the Docket for distribution to committee members. To keep abreast of the negotiated rulemaking process, individuals may sign up for inclusion on a public e-mail list through which committee documents will be distributed.

PROCESS DESIGN

DOT has established the Negotiated Rulemaking Advisory Committee on Minimum Standards for State-Issued Driver's Licenses and Personal Identification Cards as a formal advisory committee, in accordance with the Federal Advisory Committee Act (FACA). As required under FACA, all meetings of the DL/ID Reg Neg Committee will be announced in the Federal Register and open to the public.

The negotiated rulemaking process will consist of a series of five negotiating sessions and communications with and among negotiators between meetings. A public policy mediator/facilitator will manage the process. If the DL/ID Reg Neg Committee decides to make use of a drafting work group to develop proposals for committee review, part of these meetings may be set aside for such drafting.

The first negotiating session will begin with discussion and decisions regarding preliminary issues including: organizational protocols or ground rules, informational needs, list of issues to be negotiated, schedule of future meetings, and overview of the negotiated rulemaking process.

The preliminary issues will be followed by discussion of the substantive issues under negotiation. Negotiators will identify their key interests relative to the minimum standards and then work toward agreements in concept for each issue. DOT will prepare draft regulatory text to reflect agreements in concept and options generated for unresolved issues. During the negotiating sessions, the DL/ID Reg Neg Committee will work through its list of issues to be negotiated, which will include all requirements of §7212 (b)(2) of the 9/11 Act. It is typical in a negotiated rulemaking for some sections of the rule to be more easily resolved than others. The Committee will determine when it has reached "tentative agreement" on a section, indicating that the draft is satisfactory pending resolution of all other sections. Tentative agreements may be reviewed when decisions concerning a particular section impact a prior tentative agreement.

As the series of negotiating sessions proceeds, the meeting agenda will consist of the remaining issues for which tentative agreements have not been reached and any tentative agreements that must be reviewed, until all is resolved. The final draft of the regulatory language will then be reviewed in total. For the five scheduled meetings, the DL/ID Reg Neg Committee will meet until agreement is reached on all regulatory language or it is determined that agreements on some issues cannot be reached.

To the maximum extent possible, consistent with its legal obligations, DOT will use the consensus of the DL/ID Reg Neg Committee as the basis for the NPRM to be published in the Federal Register for notice and comment. The DL/ID Reg Neg Committee may be reconvened to review and address the comments received on the NPRM prior to issuance of the final rule.

ORGANIZATIONAL PROTOCOLS

At its preliminary meeting, the DL/ID Reg Neg Committee will develop organizational protocols (ground rules) that will govern its discussions and negotiations. The ground rules will cover issues including:

- mission of the DL/ID Reg Neg Committee;

- participation, including composition of the committee and its ability to add members, use alternates, use workgroups to develop proposals, and hold caucuses;
- decision-making rule (definition of consensus);
- determination that agreements have been reached and meaning of those agreements;
- procedures to ensure the protection of confidential information;
- the recognition that meetings are open to the public;
- the manner in which a record of the sessions will be kept and distributed;
- roles and responsibilities of committee members; and
- roles and responsibilities of the mediators/facilitators.

CONCLUSION

As required under the 9/11 Commission Implementation Act of the Intelligence Reform and Terrorism Prevention Act of 2004 (Public Law No. 108-458), the U.S. Department of Transportation, in consultation with the U.S. Department of Homeland Security, will implement a negotiated rulemaking process to develop minimum standards for state-issued driver's licenses and personal identification cards.

The negotiated rulemaking process is being implemented in accordance with the framework established under the Negotiated Rulemaking Act of 1990, the Federal Advisory Committee Act, and pursuant to § 7212 of the 9/11 Act. DOT plans to provide adequate resources and administrative support for the process and will ensure the DL/ID Reg Neg Committee has the appropriate resources it requires to complete its work in a timely fashion. To the extent possible, consistent with its legal obligations, DOT plans to use any consensus arising from the negotiated rulemaking process as the basis for the proposed minimum standards to be published as a Notice of Proposed Rulemaking (NPRM).

This process will be implemented to ensure that the report and recommendations of the DL/ID Reg Neg Committee are submitted to the Secretary of Transportation in compliance with the statutory deadline of September 17, 2005.

APPENDIX A:

9/11 Commission Act of the Intelligence Reform and Terrorism Prevention Act of 2004 Title VII, Subtitle B, § 7212

Section 7212(b)(2) of the 9/11 Act requires that sta ndards to be established by the Secretary of Transportation include:

(A) standards for documentation required as proof of identity of an applicant for a driver's license or personal identification card;

(B) standards for the verifiability of documents used to obtain a driver's license or personal identification card;

(C) standards for the processing of applications for driver's licenses and personal identification cards to prevent fraud;

(D) standards for information to be included on each driver's license or personal identification card, including—

(i) the person's full legal name;

(ii) the person's date of birth;

(iii) the person's gender;

(iv) the person's driver's license or personal identification card number;

(v) a digital photograph of the person;

(vi) the person's address of principal residence; and

(vii) the person's signature;[6]

(E) standards for common machine-readable identity information to be included on each

---

6. Section 7214 of the Act prohibits no State or subdivision thereof may "display a social security account number issued by the Commissioner of Social Security (or any derivative of such number) on any driver's license, motor vehicle registration, or personal identification card (as defined in Section 7212(a)(2) of the 9/11 Commission Implementation Act of 2004), or include, on any such license, registration, or personal identification card, a magnetic stripe, bar code, or other means of communication which conveys such number (or derivative thereof)."

driver's license or personal identification card, including defined minimum data elements;

(F) security standards to ensure that driver's licenses and personal identification cards are—

(i) resistant to tampering, alteration, or counterfeiting; and

(ii) capable of accommodating and ensuring the security of a digital photograph or other unique identifier; and

(G) a requirement that a State confiscate a driver's license or personal identification card if any component or security feature of the license or identification card is compromised.

Section 7212(b)(3) requires further that the standards—

(A) shall facilitate communication between the chief driver licensing official of a State, an appropriate official of a Federal agency and other relevant officials, to verify the authenticity of documents, as appropriate, issued by such Federal agency or entity and presented to prove the identity of an individual;

(B) may not infringe on a State's power to set criteria concerning what categories of individuals are eligible to obtain a driver's license or personal identification card from that State;

(C) may not require a State to comply with any such regulation that conflicts with or otherwise interferes with the full enforcement of State criteria concerning the categories of individuals that are eligible to obtain a driver's license or personal identification card from that State;

(D) may not require a single design to which driver's licenses or personal identification cards issued by all States must conform; and

(E) shall include procedures and requirements to protect the privacy rights of individuals who apply for and hold driver's licenses and personal identification cards.

APPENDIX B:

Recommended Organizational Members of the Negotiated Rulemaking Advisory Committee on Minimum Standards for State-Issued Driver's Licenses and Personal Identification Cards (DL/ID Reg Neg Committee)

PRINCIPAL NEGOTIATORS

State offices that issue driver's licenses or personal ID's

American Association of Motor Vehicle Administrators
Linda Lewis-Pickett, President and CEO

New York State Department of Motor Vehicles
Raymond Martinez, Commissioner

Alabama Department of Public Safety, Driver License Division
Major Roscoe Howell, Division Chief

Representatives of elected State officials

National Governors Association
Matthew Dunlap, Secretary of State, State of Maine

National Conference of State Legislators
Michael Balboni, Senator, New York State Senate ***Alternate***:

Groups or organizations representing the interests of applicants for and holders of driver's licenses and personal identification cards

<u>Consumer organization</u>

American Automobile Association
Elizabeth Vermette, Director, State Government Relations

<u>Organization representing non-citizens/immigrants</u>

National Immigration Law Center
Joan Friedland, Immigration Policy Attorney

Privacy and civil liberties groups

American Civil Liberties Union
Barry Steinhardt, Director, Technology and Liberty Project

Markle Foundation and Center For Democracy and Technology
Ari Schwartz, Associate Director, Center for Democracy and Technology

Law enforcement officials

International Association of Chiefs of Police
  Colonel Mark V. Trostel, Chief, Colorado State Patrol

Texas Department of Public Safety
  Major Robert Burroughs, Texas Highway Patrol Division

Florida Department of Highway Safety and Motor Vehicles
  Lt. Colonel (Ret.) Billy Dickson

Organizations with technological and operational expertise in document security

Information Technology Association of America
  Brendan M. Peter, Co-Chair, ID Management Subcommittee of the Homeland Security Committee

Industry Advisory Board to AAMVA
  Barry Goleman, Chair of the Board

Federal Government

U.S. Department of Transportation
  Tyler Duvall, Acting Assistant Secretary for Transportation Policy

U.S. Department of Homeland Security
  Elaine Dezenski, Acting Assistant Secretary for Policy & Planning, Border & Transportation Security

APPENDIX C:
LIST OF INTERVIEWEES

Shirley André
Director
Motor Vehicle Division
Iowa Department of Transportation
800 Lincoln Way
Ames, IA 50010

Robert Ashby
Deputy Assistant General Counsel for Regulation and Enforcement
Office of the General Counsel
U.S. Department of Transportation
400 7th Street, SW
Washington, DC 20590

Richard Ashton
Grant/Technical Management Manager
International Association of Chiefs of Police
515 North Washington Street
Alexandria, VA 22314

Michael Balboni
Senator, New York State Senate
Room 803 Legislative Office Building
Albany, NY 12247

Michael Bates
Office for Civil Rights and Civil Liberties
U.S. Department of Homeland Security
Washington, DC 20258

Matthew Bettenhausen
Director, State and Territorial Coordination
Office of the Secretary
U.S. Department of Homeland Security
Washington, D.C. 20528
Major Robert Burroughs
Texas Highway Patrol Division
Texas Department of Public Safety
P O Box 4087
Austin, Texas 78773-0001

Mike Calvin
Senior Vice President
American Association of Motor Vehicle Administrators
4301 Wilson Blvd, Suite 400
Arlington, VA 22203

Cheye Calvo
Committee Director,
Transportation Standing Committee
National Conference of State Legislatures
444 North Capitol Street, NW, Suite 515
Washington, DC 20001

James Dempsey
Executive Director
Center for Democracy and Technology
1634 Eye Street NW, Suite 1100
Washington, DC 20006
Also representing: Markle Foundation

Lt. Colonel (Ret.) Billy Dickson
Florida Department of Highway Safety and Motor Vehicles
3228 Cranleigh Drive
Tallahassee, FL 32309

Diane Duff
Director, Economic Development and Commerce Committee
National Governors Association
444 North Capitol Street, Suite 267
Washington, DC 20001

Mathew Dunlap
Secretary of State
State of Maine
Office of the Secretary
148 State House Station
Augusta, Maine 04333

Tyler Duvall
Acting Assistant Secretary
Office of the Assistant Secretary for Transportation Policy
U.S. Department of Transportation
400 7th Street, SW
Washington, DC 20590

Maria Foscarinis
Executive Director
National Law Center on Homelessness & Poverty
1411 K Street, NW, Suite 1400
Washington, DC 20005

Emil Frankel
Former Assistant Secretary
Office of the Assistant Secretary for Transportation Policy
U.S. Department of Transportation
400 7th Street, SW
Washington, DC 20590

Jonathan Frenkel
Senior Policy Advisor
Border & Transportation Security Directorate
U.S. Department of Homeland Security
Washington, DC 20528

Joan Friedland
Immigration Policy Attorney
National Immigration Law Center
1101 14th Street NW, Suite 410
Washington, DC 20005

Barry Goleman
Chair of the Board
Industry Advisory Board to AAMVA
1057 47th Street
Sacramento, CA 95819

Jim Harper
Director of Information Policy Studies
Cato Institute
1000 Massachusetts Avenue, NW
Washington D.C. 20001-5403

John Hilliard
Deputy Commissioner of Operations
State of New York Department of Motor Vehicles
6 Empire State Plaza
Albany, NY 12228

Major Roscoe Howell
Division Chief
Driver License Division
Alabama Department of Public Safety
P.O. Box 1471
Montgomery, AL 36102-1471

Kim Johnson
Liaison to Border and Transportation Security
Office of the Secretary
U.S. Department of Homeland Security
Washington, DC 20258

Nolan Jones
Deputy Director, Office of Federal Relations
National Governors Association
444 North Capitol Street, Suite 267
Washington, DC 20001

David Kelly
Deputy Assistant Secretary
Office of the Assistant Secretary for Governmental Affairs
U.S. Department of Transportation
400 7th Street, SW
Washington, DC 20590

Janice Kephart
9/11 Public Discourse Project
One DuPont Circle, NW
Suite 700
Washington, DC 20036

Christopher Kojm
President
9/11 Public Discourse Project
One DuPont Circle, NW
Suite 700
Washington, DC 20036

Kathleen Kraninger
Advisor to the Secretary for Policy
Office of the Chief of Staff
U.S. Department of Homeland Security
Washington, D.C. 20528

Linda Lawson
Director
Office of Safety, Energy and Environment
Office of the Assistant Secretary for Transportation Policy
U.S. Department of Transportation
400 7th Street, SW
Washington, DC 20590

Linda Lewis-Pickett
President and CEO
American Association of Motor Vehicle Administrators
4301 Wilson Blvd, Suite 400
Arlington, VA 22203

Steve Lilienthal
Director, Center for Technology Policy
Free Congress Foundation
717 Second Street, NE
Washington, DC 20002

Joseph Maher
Attorney
Office for Civil Rights and Civil Liberties
U.S. Department of Homeland Security
Washington, D.C. 20528

Raymond Martinez
Commissioner
State of New York Department of Motor Vehicles
6 Empire State Plaza
Albany, NY 12228

Kathleen Marvaso
Managing Director, Government Relations/Traffic Safety Policy
American Automobile Association
607 14th Street NW, Suite 200
Washington, DC 20005

Brian McLaughlin
Senior Associate Administrator, Traffic Injury Control
National Highway Traffic Safety Administration
U.S. Department of Transportation
400 7th Street, SW
Washington, DC 20590

John Mercer
Document Security Alliance
Senior Associate
Kelly, Anderson & Associates
424 North Washington Street
Alexandria, VA 22314

Mary Moore
Office for Civil Rights and Civil Liberties
U.S. Department of Homeland Security
Washington, DC 20258

Kevin O'Brien
Director of Motor Carrier and Driver Safety Services
State of New York Department of Motor Vehicles
6 Empire State Plaza
Albany, NY 12228

Richard Outland
Assistant Chief, Forensic Services Division
U.S. Secret Service
245 Murray Drive, Building 410
Washington, DC 20223

William Paden
Associate Administrator
Federal Motor Carrier Safety Administration
U.S. Department of Transportation
400 7th Street, SW
Washington, DC 20590

Brendan Peter
Co-Chair, ID Management Subcommittee
Information Technology Association of America
1401 Wilson Boulevard
Suite 1100
Arlington, VA 22209

Jeff Rosen
General Counsel
Office of the General Counsel
U.S. Department of Transportation
400 7th Street, SW
Washington, DC 20590

Jeff Runge
Administrator
National Highway Traffic Safety Administration
U.S. Department of Transportation
400 7th Street, SW
Washington, DC 20590

Annette Sandberg
Administrator
Federal Motor Carrier Safety Administration
U.S. Department of Transportation
400 7th Street, SW
Washington, DC 20590

Ari Schwartz
Associate Director
Center for Democracy and Technology
1634 Eye Street NW, Suite 1100
Washington, DC 20006

Tim Sparapani
Legislative Counsel for Privacy Rights
American Civil Liberties Union
915 15th Street, NW, 6th Floor
Washington DC 20005

Helen Sramek
Director, Federal Relations
American Automobile Association
607 14th Street NW, Suite 200
Washington, DC 20005

Reed Stager
Document Security Alliance
Vice President for Public Policy

Digimarc
9405 SW Gemini Drive
Beaverton, OR 97008

Barry Steinhardt
Director, Technology and Liberty Project
American Civil Liberties Union
125 Broad Street
New York, NY 10004

Daniel Sutherland
Officer for Civil Rights and Civil Liberties
Office for Civil Rights and Civil Liberties
U.S. Department of Homeland Security
Washington, DC 20258

Elizabeth Vermette
Director, State Government Relations
American Automobile Association
607 14th Street NW, Suite 200
Washington, DC 20005

Gene Voegtlin
Legislative Counsel
International Association of Chiefs of Police
515 North Washington Street
Alexandria, VA 22314

Jeff Vining
Homeland Security and Law Enforcement Analyst
Gartner
8405 Greensboro Drive, 6th Floor
McLean, VA 22102

Laurel Weir
Policy Director
National Law Center on Homelessness & Poverty
1411 K Street, NW, Suite 1400
Washington, DC 20005

John V. Wells
Chief Economist
U.S. Department of Transportation
400 7th Street, SW
Washington, DC 20590

Elizabeth Withnell
Chief Counsel
Privacy Office
Department of Homeland Security
Washington, DC 20528

Steve Wood
Assistant Chief Counsel for Vehicle Safety Standards and Harmonization
Office of the Chief Counsel
National Highway Traffic Safety Administration
U.S. Department of Transportation
400 7th Street, SW
Washington, DC 20590

Declined to be interviewed
Electronic Privacy Information Center
National Immigration Forum

Unable to arrange interview within available timeframe
National Association of Attorneys General
Tohono O'odham Nation Police Department

Declined to be considered for membership on DL/ID Reg Neg Committee
Cato Institute
Free Congress Foundation
9/11 Public Discourse Project

INDEX

B

C

K

L

M

P

R

S

T

U

V

W

ACKNOWLEDGMENTS

This book is the culmination of more than twenty-five years of mediation practice and thought. Across those years, numerous people have contributed to my thinking and supported my endeavors, including teachers, colleagues, friends, family, and project participants.

Two teachers, in particular, made my mediation career possible. As an undergraduate at the University of Pennsylvania, I spent five semesters under the tutelage of Professor Phillip Rieff, who provided lessons that directly inform my work as a mediator. From him, I learned to draw multiple precise readings from the works of masters such as Nietzsche, Weber, and Kierkegaard. I rely on these skills to discern multiple interpretations of situations and to search for the precise words needed to satisfy nuanced interests and values of negotiating parties. In addition, the necessity to articulate, defend, and dispense with ideas that failed to withstand Prof. Reiff's critical review, made me increasingly aware that greater wisdom always lay beyond. This realization has allowed me to let go of sometimes treasured, but unworkable ideas to make space for more fitting ones to emerge.

Professor Lawrence Susskind, a founder of the field of public policy mediation, was my teacher and advisor during my graduate studies at the Massachusetts Institute of Technology. Larry not only provided a strong theoretical base, but offered practice opportunities including my first job as a policy mediator at Endispute, Inc. The MIT courses I taught with him, as well as my seminars with David Laws at the Program On Negotiation at Harvard Law School provided a platform for reflecting on my mediation and negotiation practice. This book builds on much of my early thinking in preparation for teaching those courses.

While a passion for philosophy was immediately evident to me, discovering how to apply it did not come easily. After hearing Larry Susskind speak at a conference, Scott Cassel told me with absolute conviction that I was meant to be a mediator. At Scott's insistence, I mediated a dispute at our local food coop and, in so doing, confirmed his instincts.

Almost 30 years later, my husband, Scott, along with our daughter, Sarah Cassel, my demanding partner in philosophical discourse, provided great support for writing this book, including talking through concepts and editing multiple drafts. During a most memorable marathon weekend review of the draft final manuscript, we reached final consensus on the entire text. Their love and support through all the years and at every turn has made my practice and this book possible. I also thank Satch, our loving dog, for joyful companionship.

In 1988, I began working with Howard Bellman in what would become my greatest professional partnership. Over the years, as you will note throughout the book, Howard has been my go-to mentor for sound advice at challenging moments. From his early trust in me as a "newbie" to a consistent alignment of our instincts as we co-mediate complex cases, I have been privileged to work with and learn from Howard. I also want to acknowledge his review of the manuscript and confirmation that the book describes "what we do."

I learn a great deal from each of my mediation cases, and especially from the participants. While there are too many parties to thank, I want to acknowledge key participants in the three cases described in this book.

Without the vision of Lewis "Harry" Spence, Chelsea's Receiver, and the political acumen of Stephen McGoldrick, his Chief of Staff, there would not have been a Chelsea Charter Consensus Process. There would be no consensus charter without the Charter Preparation Team of Carolyn P. Agostini, Vicente Avelloneda, Gwendolyn Robinson Coffer, Marilyn Contreas, Marlene Demko, Howard F. Dixon, John R. Hoadley, Jr., Asa J. Hubner, Joan E. Langsam, Charles L. MacFarlane, Bruce Mauch, Nadine H. Mironchuk, Paul R. Nowicki, Leticia Ortiz, Dominic Pegnato, Jr., Angel M. Rosa, Anthony "Chubby" Tiro, Sr., Helen L. Ularich, and Barbara E. Weston. These individuals poured their hearts into building a city charter that has sustained a new Chelsea. The residents of Chelsea would not have had the opportunity to express their opinions and have them integrated into the charter without the work of my colleague, Roberta Miller, and her team of facilitators. An additional special thanks goes to Steve McGoldrick and Asa Hubner for their reviews of the Chelsea and related chapters.

It was a great pleasure and privilege to work with the members of the Cranes and Derricks Negotiated Rulemaking Advisory Committee (C-DAC): Stephen Brown, Michael Brunet, Stephen P. Charman, Joe Collins, Noah Connell, Peter Juhren, Bernie McGrew, Larry Means, Frank Migliaccio, Brian Murphy, Chip Pocock, David Ritchie, Emmett Russell, Dale Shoemaker, Billy Smith, Craig Steele, Darlaine Taylor, Wally Vega, III, Doc Weaver, Rob Weiss, Doug Williams, Steve Wiltshire, and Chuck Yorio. In addition, others at the federal Occupational Safety and Health Administration provided great support to C-DAC, including Audrey Roller, Michael Buchet, Tressi Cordaro, Charles Gordon, David Grafton, Bruce Swanson, and Stacey Swanson, as did my Associate Mediator, Alexis Gensberg Roberts. I especially thank Rob Weiss, who clarified technical issues and brought to the draft C-DAC and related chapters the same masterful writing skills that he applied to the negotiations. I also thank Noah Connell for clarifying political issues and providing an honest appraisal of the chapter narrative. Finally, Emmet Russell's astute process observations, coupled with his support, enabled me to further reflect on key moments and dynamics of the negotiations described in the C-DAC and related chapters.

The abortion talks made for a life-changing experience for all participants, including my co-facilitator, Laura Chasin, and me. In their participation, the following women showed extraordinary passion, courage, and willingness to be intellectually and spiritually stretched:

Anne Fowler, Nicki Nichols Gamble, Frances X. Hogan, Melissa Kogut, Madeline McComish, and Barbara Thorp. My journey to understand our shared experience led me to write this book. I thank you all for your friendship and for the privilege of working with you. A special thank you to Barbara Thorp and Melissa Kogut for reviewing the abortion talks chapter.

Through the fits and starts of conceptualizing this book over the past ten years, Diana McLain Smith consistently and insistently supported the need for me to share my stories. My good friend and skype-mate, Amy Glass, connected me with ABA Publishing and supported and encouraged me throughout my year of writing.

This book is greatly improved because of the insights of my respected colleagues and trusted friends, Susan Carpenter and Howard Gadlin. Their section-by-section comments, detailed suggestions for revisions, and hours of focused conversation pushed my thinking well beyond the early manuscript.

A special thank you to Rachel Kremen, who provided invaluable editing support and to Rick Pazskiet of the ABA Publishing Co. and his team for their thoughtful attention in reviewing and producing the book.

Finally, much of this book was written at Café Fixe in Brookline, Massachusetts, and I'd be remiss if I failed to thank Maks for consistently perfect coffees, and the regulars for pleasant morning greetings and stimulating conversation.